How Ottawa Spends, 2(

THE SCHOOL OF PUBLIC POLICY AND ADMINISTRATION at Carleton University is a national center for the study of public policy and public management.

The School's Centre for Policy and Program Assessment provides research services and courses to interest groups, businesses, unions, and governments in the evaluation of public policies, programs and activities.

School of Public Policy and Administration
Carleton University
10th Floor Dunton Tower
1125 Colonel By Drive
Ottawa, ON
Canada K1S 5B6
www.carleton.ca/sppa

How Ottawa Spends, 2008–2009

A More Orderly Federalism?

Edited by

ALLAN M. MASLOVE

Published for
The School of Public Policy and Administration
Carleton University
by
McGill-Queen's University Press
Montreal & Kingston · London · Ithaca

© McGill-Queen's University Press 2008
ISBN 978-0-7735-3433-9

Legal deposit third quarter 2008
Bibliothèque nationale du Québec

Printed in Canada on acid-free paper that is 100 % ancient forest free
(100 % post-consumer recycled), processed chlorine free.

McGill-Queen's University Press acknowledges the support of the Canada Council for the Arts for our publishing program. We also acknowledge the financial support of the Government of Canada through the Book Publishing Industry Development Program (BPIDP) for our publishing activities.

Library and Archives Canada has catalogued this publication as follows:

How Ottawa spends.
1983–
Imprint varies.
Includes bibliographical references.
Continues: How Ottawa spends your tax dollars, ISSN 0711-4990.
ISSN 0822-6482
ISBN 978-0-7735-3283-0 (2008/2009 edition)

1. Canada – Appropriations and expenditures – Periodicals.
I. Carleton University. School of Public Policy and Administration

HJ7663.H69   354.710072'2   C84-030303-3

This book was typeset by Interscript in 10/12 Minion.

Contents

Preface vii

1 Introduction: A More Orderly Federalism? 3
   Allan M. Maslove

2 Vertical Imbalance in the Canadian Federation 15
   Stanley L. Winer and Walter Hettich

3 International Capital and Domestic Politics: Balancing Political and Economic Management 33
   Geoffrey Hale

4 Potential for a Regulatory Breakthrough? Regulatory Governance and Human Resource Initiatives 59
   Barry Stemshorn and Robert W. Slater

5 A Little Imagination Required: How Ottawa Funds Territorial and Northern Aboriginal Governments 82
   Frances Abele and Michael J. Prince

6 One Step Forward, Two Steps Back: Child Care Policy from Martin to Harper 110
   Cheryl Collier and Rianne Mahon

7 Telecommunications Policy: What a Difference a Minister Can Make 134
   Richard Schultz

8 How Ottawa Doesn't Spend: The Rapid Appearance and Disappearance – and Possible Reappearance – of the Federal Social Economy Initiative 163
Edward T. Jackson

9 Federal Higher Education Policies and the Vanishing Public University 179
Clara Morgan

Appendix A: Canadian Political Facts and Trends 201

Appendix B: Fiscal Facts and Trends 211

Contributors 229

Preface

This 29th edition of *How Ottawa Spends*, as always, is the result of our authors who are willing to contribute their analyses and insights to some of the leading issues currently on the public policy agenda[1].

Thanks also to Alin Charriere for his excellent research assistance in support of this volume and to Kimmie Huang of the School of Public Policy and Administration for her organizational and technical support. I also want to acknowledge Joan McGilvray and her team at McGill-Queen's University Press for their continued support.

Allan M. Maslove
Ottawa
January 2008

NOTE

1 The views and opinions expressed by the authors in this volume are their own and do not necessarily reflect the views of the editor or of the School of Public Policy and Administration at Carleton University.

How Ottawa Spends, 2008–2009

Introduction:
A More Orderly Federalism?

ALLAN M. MASLOVE

A particular focus of the 2008–09 edition of *How Ottawa Spends* is the changing nature of federal-provincial relations. The impacts of these changes are evident most directly in the financial arrangements between the two orders of government. But, they are also evident in other ways in areas of shared jurisdiction and even in purely federal areas of jurisdiction. At the same time, however, the developing patterns are complex and layered. They cannot simply be characterized as "decentralization" of the federation or as "disentanglement" between the two orders of government.

The renewed focus on the state of the federation is prompted by several underlying forces. In addition to these underlying factors, we have the coming to power of the Harper Conservative government (also known as Canada's "New Government" until the tagline finally became too embarrassing) with, initially at least, a distinctly different view of the role of Ottawa and of the federal system (characterized by Harper as "open federalism") from that held by the Chrétien or Martin Liberals.

In this introductory chapter, I briefly review the impacts of four current policy issues on the federal system. These issues partially define the context for the Harper approach to federal-provincial relations. I argue that each of these issues creates, in its own way, demands for a response by Ottawa and the Harper Conservatives in office find they are responding somewhat differently than what might have been expected from the Harper Conservatives on the campaign trail.

Before addressing these four policy questions, it is useful to set a bit of broader context. While the often-repeated rhetoric calling for more decentralization gives a different impression, Canada is already one of the most decentralized federal countries in the developed world. For example, in 1996 the Canadian federal government collected 48 per cent of total government (federal, provincial and local) revenues (before any intergovernmental transfers). The comparable proportions in other advanced federal countries were: Australia 69 per cent, the U.S. 66 per cent, Germany 65 per cent, and Switzerland 45 per cent. In the same year federal expenditures after transfers as a share of total (federal, provincial and local) government expenditures were 41 per cent in Canada, compared to 61 per cent in the U.S., 53 per cent in Australia, 41 per cent in Germany and 37 per cent in Switzerland.[1]

Further, there is no evidence that the Canadian federation is becoming more centralized in recent years. In fact, if there is any change it is in the opposite direction. For example, in 1984-85 Ottawa's program expenditures were 18.7 per cent of GDP; in 2005-06 the ratio was down to 12.5 per cent. When transfers to other governments are excluded the percentages were 14.6 and 9.8. Over the same years total provincial and territorial program expenditures went from 18.3 per cent to 15.7 per cent of GDP. Thus, Ottawa's spending relative to the economy declined substantially more than did the provinces. A similar pattern exists on the revenue side. Federal revenues over the same period went from 16.0 per cent of GDP to 16.2 per cent. Provincial and territorial own revenues grew from 13.8 per cent to 14.9 per cent, while revenues after transfers from Ottawa remained stable at 18.2 per cent. Federal transfers to the provinces and territories declined especially through to the late 1990s, and have been partially restored since then; nevertheless they constitute a smaller share of GDP in 2005-06 than they did two decades earlier, and thus while provincial own revenues grew, their total revenues remained the same (relative to GDP). While this may suggest a reason for provincial dissatisfaction with federal-provincial fiscal arrangements, it does not suggest any trend towards a more centralized federation.

The operation of federal systems is also impacted by the continuing global integration of markets in capital, goods and labour. The expanding geographical scope of markets creates differential constraints and opportunities for different orders of government. For example, much has been written about the importance of local infrastructure – physical, human, and cultural – in creating "world cities" as dynamic participants in the global economy.[2] That, in turn, creates demands on and opportunities for local governments. Much has also been written about the shifting relative importance and powers of federal and provincial governments. It has been argued that national governments will be more constrained by the evolution of global markets and international accords, and as a consequence sub-national governments (the provinces) will become relatively stronger; that is, federations, including Canada will become more decentralized. But it may be the case that power will shift both up and down – down to the local level and simultaneously up to the federal level as national governments are called upon more unilaterally or collectively to regulate global market forces. In that scenario, whether the federation becomes overall more or less decentralized is not clear, but there may be a shift from the provincial to the national level.

Finally, we should note the patterns of pressures and expectations that citizens direct to their governments. The most noteworthy recent example is health care. Though the provision of direct medical care services is clearly the responsibility of the provincial governments, health care was identified as the most important issue of concern among voters in the last several federal elections. Moreover, the issues on the table were not only the fiscal transfers from Ottawa to the provinces, but also specific concerns such as shortages of primary care physicians, and most especially wait times. Similarly, voters sometimes confuse or ignore jurisdictional assignments in other important policy fields such as environment and resource management. The point is that visions of Canadian federalism fitting neatly into federal and provincial boxes can run into political pressures that do not conform to these models.

FOUR CONTEXTUAL ISSUES

Now we turn to the four more immediate issues impacting current federal-provincial relations. The first of these is the rapid escalation of energy prices since 2006. The federal dimension of energy prices derives from two obvious, but important facts: 1) the provinces own their natural resources, and 2) petroleum and natural gas deposits are not evenly distributed across the provinces. The economies of the energy-endowed provinces (especially Alberta and Saskatchewan) are growing rapidly while those of the energy importing provinces (notably Ontario and Quebec) are losing manufacturing jobs and are relatively weaker (though still growing overall). By the same token, of course, the fiscal capacities of the energy-rich provinces are growing much more rapidly than the others (though in the case of Newfoundland and Labrador this may be relatively short-lived as currently known reserves pass their production peaks in coming years). The impact of high-priced resource exports on exchange rates further exacerbates these inter-provincial shifts in that the higher Canadian dollar erodes the ability of manufacturers (who are concentrated in central Canada) to compete in their traditional export markets.

The latter development has resulted in significant changes in the pattern and level of horizontal fiscal balances across the provinces. These real and major changes in economic activity and provincial fiscal capacities stand in sharp contrast to the largely non-existent vertical fiscal imbalance (VFI) that the provincial governments stridently demanded be corrected and which the campaign Conservatives promised to address. (See chapter 2 by Winer and Hettich for a full discussion of fiscal balance.)

Over the past half century, horizontal fiscal imbalance has been addressed most explicitly by the Fiscal Equalization Program, a purely federal regime of unconditional grants to the provinces. Equalization, which dates back to the 1950s, but which was written into the 1982 Constitution (Section 36) is explicitly intended to bring the fiscal capacity of provinces with below average capacity up to the average. Over the years the definition and calculation of "average" has been changed, mainly in response to relatively sudden and large spikes in resource prices that have dramatically increased the capacity of some provinces. In recent years the advent of petroleum revenues to the governments of Newfoundland and Labrador (NL) and Nova Scotia from off shore reserves has added a new complication to the mix. The nub of the problem, at least from the perspective of these provinces, was that the existing formula for calculating equalization payments would have resulted in them receiving much less in equalization grants from Ottawa, and potentially, nothing, depending on the price of oil.

One might argue that this result would be the correct one since the oil revenues simply increased the fiscal capacity of these provinces to the point where they were above the defined national average. Alternatively, one might take the position that there should be a special method of recognizing these revenues in the equalization formula because they are generated by non-renewable resources. The Martin Liberals took neither of these approaches; instead Mr Martin played "lets make a deal", striking one-off arrangements with NL and Nova Scotia that all but destroyed any remaining integrity of the equalization formula. Into this situation came the Harper Conservatives.

The provincial claim of vertical fiscal imbalance (and especially the Ontario variant of a fiscal gap) was distinct from the equalization issue, but the two became merged, and in the 2007 Budget the government proposed a new equalization formula, and largely through that manoeuvre (plus some increases in other transfers to ensure that Ontario and the non-equalization receiving provinces also gained), claimed to have fixed the vertical imbalance in the federation. We return to this below.

The second issue is the ongoing concern over productivity growth in Canada. As noted in the Fiscal Facts and Trends Appendix to this volume, Canadian productivity growth continues to lag that in the United States. This lag continues to be a preoccupation of many analysts in the business community and in government. The Harper government's response is a number of initiatives packaged under the title "Advantage Canada." The initiatives are a series of tax reductions, debt reduction (and in the long term, elimination), regulatory reform, human capital investment, and physical infrastructure investment. The government's tax policies are analysed in chapter 3 by Geoffrey Hale. The government's regulatory capacity is addressed by Barry Stemshorn and Robert Slater in chapter 4. The government's human capital policies impact, inter alia, on Canada's universities (which incidentally fall under provincial jurisdiction); this topic is taken up by Clara Morgan in chapter 9.

Investment in physical infrastructure is very much focused on municipalities. In 2005 the previous Liberal government concluded a series of agreements with all the provinces to provide grants to the municipalities (associated in name at least with federal gas tax revenues, but in reality simply a commitment from the government's consolidated revenue fund) for infrastructure renewal. The transfer amounted to $5 billion over five years, ending at a rate of $2 billion per year. In the 2007 Budget, the Harper government pledged to extend the program for an additional four years (2010/11 – 2013/14) at that $2 billion per annum level. Interestingly, even though this money was (ostensibly) earmarked for spending in an area clearly in provincial jurisdiction, all provinces readily signed on. Presumably the pressing need for municipal infrastructure renewal and the provinces' desire to get federal money trumped whatever concerns might have been expected to arise about Ottawa's meddling in provincial jurisdiction.

Market barriers within Canada have also been identified as impediments to improving our productivity growth. Renewed attention has been directed to the issue of inter-provincial trade barriers. The Agreement on Internal Trade (AIT), signed in 1995, was concluded only after a very long and difficult series of negotiations and only with the heavy prodding of Ottawa. Despite its existence, barriers remain as provinces continue to maintain regulatory provisions and procurement policies that protect local firms and workers. The AIT carves out numerous exceptions to accommodate regional interests and it lacks a binding dispute resolution process. A consequence of the continuing protectionist provincial policies is a negative effect on productivity advances in the primary and manufacturing sectors.

In 2006 the governments of British Columbia and Alberta reached agreement on a Trade, Investment and Labour Mobility Agreement (TILMA). TILMA quite explicitly addresses some of the limits of the AIT. It aims to provide a free trade structure between the two provinces especially with respect to labour mobility and resources, and provide for a binding dispute resolution process. TILMA is, in part, a statement of the limitations of the AIT which were addressed by two provinces with perhaps more common interests with each other than with some other provinces. At the same time, however, it is being viewed by other provinces as something of a model for a broader inter-provincial agreement; but the same incentives and protectionist sentiments that limited the AIT still exist and it seems unlikely that there can be much inter-provincial progress without the assistance of Ottawa.

A third contextual issue is the renewed (perhaps just continuing) popular concern over health care, especially with respect to wait times for access to services. Despite the First Ministers' Accords of 2003 (under Chrétien) and 2004 (Martin) and the significant infusion of federal cash that they entailed, public perception is largely that the problem is not getting better and perhaps even getting worse. While this perception may be lagging reality – many significant improvements are being recorded – it nonetheless puts pressure on both provincial governments and on Ottawa. The interesting point for our purposes is that while health care is recognized as being an area of provincial jurisdiction citizens continue to look to Ottawa for leadership on this issue, even though it might be argued that the 2003 and 2004 accords represent the federal contribution to the solution. Reducing wait times was one of the original five priorities of the Harper government, and arguably the one they were least successful in achieving.

Finally, there is the issue of the environment and climate change, which emerged quite suddenly on the public radar screen, catching the Harper government off guard. In this area public perceptions of responsibility do not necessarily correspond to the coordinated and overlapping federal and provincial jurisdictions. But clearly the pressure on the Harper government to address the climate change issue forced the government to change its course and replace the Minister responsible for the file.

The common refrains in these four areas – energy, productivity, health, and climate change – are that they involve both the federal and provincial orders of government, and that the demands for action by Ottawa do not always correspond to the formal allocation of responsibilities. In short, a more disentangled federalism where each order of government "sticks to its own knitting" is impractical.

THE UNFOLDING HARPER AGENDA

With the foregoing as background we now turn to the unfolding Harper conservative government agenda, focusing primarily on three major policy pronouncements over the last year: the Budget of 19 March 2007, the Throne Speech of 16 October and the Economic Statement of 30 October.

Two sets of initiatives in the Budget of March 2007 are of particular interest. First, there were measures intended to address and close the vertical fiscal imbalance (VFI) that the provinces claimed existed and the Harper government recognized. Foremost among these was a reformed and augmented Equalization program. Following the recommendations of the O'Brien Report (the Expert Panel on Equalization and Territorial Formula Financing established by the previous government in 2005), the 10-province standard was re-introduced, 50 per cent of provincial resource revenues were included in the equalization formula, and a cap was introduced to ensure that no equalization-receiving province reached a fiscal capacity level higher than any non-recipient province. The redesign of the Equalization formula, its modest enhancement along with increases in other transfers (primarily the Canada Social Transfer) led the government to claim that it had resolved VFI.

But, a complaint from provincial premiers that they "need" more money from Ottawa is not evidence that VFI exists. As Winer and Hettich argue in this volume, that VFI exists at all is questionable, and indeed the whole issue of fiscal balance in the federation is much more complex. Further, the government's "fix" was clearly not acceptable to several of the provinces, and in the ensuing months these provinces launched political and legal challenges to the new Equalization policy.

A second set of initiatives in the march Budget was directed towards strengthening the competitive position of the Canadian economy. In particular the government signalled its desire that there be a single securities regulatory system and a more effective regime to eliminate inter-provincial trade barriers. What is noteworthy about these proposals in relation to the foregoing discussion is that they would both be centralizing measures in the federation. While these measures may not enhance the powers of the federal government, both would constrain provincial policy discretion.

The Throne Speech inaugurated the new parliamentary session on October 16. The Speech established five new priorities for the government, succeeding those that the Conservatives campaigned on and which guided the government to that point. The five new priority areas were: strengthening Canada's sovereignty and place in the world; strengthening the federation; economic leadership; a crime and security agenda; and the environment. Unlike the first set of priorities which were limited to specific measures (e.g., the reduction in the GST, the Accountability Act), the new agenda is broader and more thematic, though specific initiatives are identified within each area.

The sovereignty priority largely focuses on the Arctic (see chapter 5 by Abele and Prince) and on investing in the military. A significant part of the economic agenda is a program of tax cuts, most of which were introduced in the economic statement later in October (see below). The crime and security file promised (yet again) to get tough on criminals. Perhaps the least specific of the five priorities identified in the Throne Speech is the environment; the need to address climate change was recognized but the commitments were vague.

The most intriguing passages in the Speech were those relating to the federation. The Conservative government stated its commitment to respecting "the constitutional jurisdiction of each order of government" and its continuing intent to focus on areas of exclusive federal responsibility such as trade, defence and security. To give weight to its commitment, the government pledged to introduce legislation to limit the federal spending power in areas of exclusive provincial jurisdiction, allowing provinces to opt out of a program with compensation if they offer comparable programs of their own.

What do these passages in the Throne Speech signal? Some observers have suggested (fretted) that this heralds a more decentralized federation, with Ottawa limiting itself to areas of purely federal jurisdiction, leaving the provinces to follow their own paths in major policy areas such as health and education without any federal presence, whether direct or indirect. Past statements made by Stephen Harper (and others from the Alliance wing of the Conservative Party) calling for a more decentralized federation lend some weight to this interpretation.

However, the wording in the Throne Speech on restraining the federal spending power does not really go beyond what is in the Social Union Framework Agreement (SUFA) signed by the Liberal government and all the provinces in 1999. From this perspective, all that appears to be on the table is a federal bill that would echo the SUFA in an act of Parliament, but not substantively change the current framework of federal-provincial relations. Moreover, other initiatives of the government suggest that even if Ottawa intends to be less active in terms of the federal spending power, it will continue to be active or become even more active in other ways. For example, the Throne Speech also states the government's intention to strengthen the economic union and signals its readiness to expand its use of federal trade and commerce powers finally to forge a meaningful free trade regime among provinces. Ottawa's clearly stated preference for a national securities regulator suggests another area in which it may be prepared to confront the provinces.

In general, whatever sentiment there might be for a "neater" federalism where each order of government is unconstrained by the other in its areas of jurisdiction must be tempered by the realities of a modern economy. For example, the federal responsibility for international trade impacts on the exploitation of resources which are under provincial ownership. International environmental treaties will have implications for provincial governments. Federal measures taken to avert or combat health threats originating abroad, such as SARS, will affect provincial health care systems. By the same token, provincial post-secondary education policies will affect national labour markets and national economic growth. The same is true of provincial policies towards their cities. In short, effective policy within one order's domain will often necessitate engagements with and/or encroachments into the others.

The third major policy event was the Economic Statement delivered by the Minister of Finance on October 30, 2007. The signature measure in this statement was the further reduction of the GST rate from 6 per cent to 5 per cent, effective 1 January 2008. At an initial annual cost of about $6 billion in forgone revenues, the GST reduction was clearly a popular move. As an economic measure however, its merits are much more dubious. A GST reduction may have an effect in terms of stimulating consumption spending, but most economists would argue that there would be much larger payoffs for the economy if the boost was given to investment instead, particularly to investments that would boost the rate of productivity growth. Moreover, because the GST cut is so expensive in terms of forgone revenue, it constrains the ability of the government to pursue other fiscal initiatives that would enhance productivity.

Tax reductions on personal and business income were more modest. On the personal income side the basic exemption was increased for 2007 and 2008 (above previously scheduled increases) and the tax rate for the lowest bracket was reduced to 15 per cent.[3] The rate reduction is estimated to cost about $1.3 billion per year in forgone revenue. On the business side the general business corporate tax rate was reduced (costing about $1.3 billion in 2008–09) and previously scheduled cuts in the small business rate were accelerated.

OVERVIEW OF THE CHAPTERS

The first three chapters following this introduction deal with macro themes: fiscal (im)balance in the federation, tax policy, and regulatory capacity. The remaining chapters discuss the Conservative government's policies and approaches in specific policy areas.

STANLEY WINER and WALTER HETTICH make the case that the concept of vertical fiscal imbalance (VFI) as commonly used in policy discussion is imprecise and misleading. It cannot be determined by looking at which governments are running deficits or seem to be under more fiscal pressures than others. The idea of balance, they argue, involves the efficient allocation of resources between the orders of government and between the public and private sectors. Accordingly, vertical and horizontal fiscal imbalances are inseparable. For example, in Canada, high oil prices have created pressures on Ottawa to augment its Equalization payments to recipient provinces. Further, the government's claim to have fixed the VFI problem is wrong because the increased transfers to the provinces do not address the public-private dimension of VFI. Winer and Hettich conclude that this would be addressed only by Ottawa lowering its tax take (as it did with the GST) and allowing the provinces to move in to that vacated room if higher provincial spending was warranted.

GEOFFREY HALE, in his chapter on tax policy, sees the government as grappling with five major challenges that affect its fiscal actions: a decade of surpluses has eroded the government's ability to maintain a regime of fiscal discipline; Harper's commitment to "open federalism"; the rapidly disappearing distinction between domestic and international capital markets; the increasing pace of corporate takeovers and reorganizations; and the short-term calculus that is part and parcel of a minority government. Hale argues that the Conservatives are navigating between their populist agenda on taxation (which gave rise to the GST cuts) and the business agenda (corporate taxation) which largely overlaps with the Liberals. In addition, the Conservatives have had to resolve some major tax issues (such as income trusts and foreign interest deductibility), which in part are indicators of the blurring of domestic and foreign capital markets.

BARRY STEMSHORN and ROBERT SLATER recognize in their chapter that government is becoming more conscious of the costs of regulation and of regulatory processes. Initiatives such as those undertaken under the rubric "Smart Regulation" attest to this recognition; the goal is to make the regulatory system more integrated and more streamlined across the range of Ottawa's concerns including areas such as natural resource development and financial market regulation which impinge on areas of provincial jurisdiction. In order to make this new regulatory approach and strategy work, Stemshorn and Slater point out the need for a human resource strategy to develop the public service to staff the agencies and operate the regulatory processes effectively and efficiently. They see some encouraging signs in this direction, but argue that much needs to be done to develop the capacity of the Canadian public service in the domain of regulation.

Canadian federalism is, of course, not only about Ottawa and the provinces but also about the Territorial and Aboriginal governments. The contribution of FRANCES ABELE and MICHAEL PRINCE provides an excellent insight into the challenges and objectives of the government's northern policies. Ottawa's policies are developing in the context of concern for Arctic sovereignty, the continuing evolution of responsible government in the Territories, and the challenges of Aboriginal self-government. So far, security and Arctic sovereignty concerns seem to be the main drivers of the Harper government's northern policy. Abele and Prince conclude that the economic, social and political development of the North needs expression as well and will require consistent and strong advocacy.

One of the initial five priority areas of the Harper government was in child care. CHERYL COLLIER and RIANNE MAHON trace the uneven history of early childhood education and care and argue that the initiatives adopted by the Harper government are a rejection of the model that is overwhelmingly favoured by the child care advocacy community. The government has returned to the traditional family-based (small-c) conservative model that coincides with the views of its core supporters. The government's initiatives, introduced in its first budget, were twofold: the introduction of a Universal Child Care Benefit of $100 per month (taxable) for each child under the age of six; and a plan to offer tax incentives to private forms that created new child care spaces in their workplaces. The costs of the Harper plan were to be paid for by the cancellation of the agreements on child care negotiated by the previous government with each of the provinces. The business incentives were, for the most part, not taken up, and in the 2007 Budget the funds earmarked for this were instead offered to the provinces (through the Canada Social Transfer) to create more childcare spaces; in this regard it was a very pale shadow of the previous Liberal program.

RICHARD SCHULTZ provides a fascinating insight into the relationship between the CRTC and the government, and particularly the impact of a

Minister (Maxime Bernier) with a clear vision of how he wished to see the telecommunications sector develop and who was not at all hesitant to inject his position into the CTRC decisions. Bernier became the first minister in a very long time successfully to exert his (and his government's) desired policy choices in this area of rapidly changing technology where traditionally the rulings of the CRTC had been largely unchallenged.

EDWARD JACKSON examines a policy area that was greatly affected by the change from the Liberal to Conservative governments. After a long and difficult effort by advocates, the Liberal government had adopted a modest Social Economy Initiative (SEI). When the Harper Conservatives came to office, this quickly disappeared (except for some elements that had already been locked into programming), partly for political reasons and partly because this initiative was more difficult to manage within the new environment of "hyper-accountability". Jackson argues that the SEI may not be dead, however. It may reappear because many communities continue to look for new responses to losses of manufacturing jobs, because a younger and more diverse group of workers are more open to non-traditional approaches, and because the sector itself will continue its advocacy work.

In the concluding chapter, CLARA MORGAN argues that federal funding of universities – both with respect to the areas of research supported and the methods of funding utilized – has created a form of "academic capitalism" that distorts the mission of our public universities. At the same time, while Ottawa and the provinces share many objectives in this area, such as the fostering of commercially useful research, the federal government has become deeply involved in a provincial jurisdictional domain. This began, of course under earlier Liberal governments but continues for the most part on the same trajectory under the Harper conservatives.

CONCLUDING COMMENTS

The areas analysed by the authors in this volume of *How Ottawa Spends* clearly demonstrate the unfolding agenda of the Conservative government. The GST cuts, early child care policy, Arctic sovereignty, and telecommunications policy are all cases in point. The government has also shown a determination to settle what it accepts as a vertical fiscal imbalance with the provinces as part of its pursuit of something it refers to as "open federalism". At the same time, however, the demands of governing and the nature of the policy issues require an active and engaged federal government in many areas that are under provincial jurisdiction as well, of course, as areas of joint jurisdiction. In short, while the Conservatives may engage with the provinces in different ways than their Liberal predecessors, they are not appreciably less active when a federal response to economic and social concerns is called for.

NOTES

1 Data from R. L. Watts, *Comparing Federal Systems* (Montreal and Kingston: McGill-Queens University Press, 1999).
2 The work of Richard Florida is particularly noteworthy on this subject. See, for example, *Cities and the Creative Class* (New York and Milton Park, UK: Routledge, 2004).
3 The Liberal government had reduced the lowest rate from 16 per cent to 15 per cent. In their first Budget the Conservatives had increased the rate back up to 15.5 per cent and the October reduction returned it to the level the Liberals had set.

2 Vertical Imbalance in the Canadian Federation

STANLEY L. WINER
AND WALTER HETTICH

INTRODUCTION

Vertical fiscal imbalance between the provinces and the federal government, usually referred to as VFI, is an issue that resembles the proverbial phoenix. It arises again and again out of the ashes of federal-provincial competition to reassert itself as a major concern in national debates. After playing a significant role in the deliberations by the historic Rowell-Sirois Royal Commission on Dominion-Provincial Relations[1], although not under this name, VFI was reborn four decades later as the main focus of influential studies by the Economic Council of Canada.[2] In the past few years the phoenix has arisen again in full force in current debates on intergovernmental relations.

The re-emergence of VFI as a central issue relates both to recent Canadian fiscal history and to current international and domestic economic conditions. After 1992, the federal government, faced with a recession and with the historically unprecedented peacetime buildup of public debt over the previous decade, made major cuts in fiscal transfers to the provinces as part of its broadly based policy of debt reduction.[3] As indicated in Figure 1, the cuts in grants were both dramatic and rapid. In the early 1960's, federal grants had accounted for around 3 per cent of GDP. By 1992 they had risen to approximately 4 per cent, only to be reduced in rapid succession to the lower level of the 1960's.

The comparison with grants to the states by the U.S. federal government, also shown in the figure, reinforces the view that something dramatic happened in Canada after the 1992 recession: By the measures shown, Canada and the U.S. federation show a very similar degree of decentralization after

Figure 1
Federal Grants to Lower Levels of Government as a Proportion of GDP, Canada and the United States 1929–2004

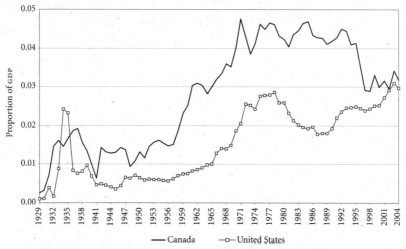

Source: Spread sheet accompanying Ferris and Winer (2007). At www.carleton.ca/~winers or at www.carleton.ca/~sferris. Abatements of tax points are not included.

that date, whereas in 1960, federal grants in Canada had exceeded those in the U.S. by as much as 2 percentage points of GDP. In the light of this recent history, provincial complaints that the federal government is not paying its proper share of the cost of important social services are hardly surprising.

A further reason for the current turmoil comes from a quite different direction. The rapid rise in international oil prices has led to fiscal pressures on the federal government because of the resulting obligations under the current Equalization program.[4] While this program is usually discussed in relation to horizontal equity rather than with regard to VFI, it has become linked to vertical imbalance because of the nature of the formula used in determining Equalization payments, a topic that will receive more attention in a later section of this paper. In addition, problems have become complicated further by the special treatment of resource revenues in the Atlantic Accord which was introduced by the previous Liberal government, and which partly sheltered resource revenues in the Atlantic provinces from the recapture aspect of the Equalization formula.

The renewed interest in vertical imbalance is reflected in several recent governmental publications, including the reports by the Advisory Panel on Fiscal Imbalance of the Council of the Federation, the Commission on Fiscal Imbalance of the government of Quebec (the Seguin Report), and the Expert

Panel on Equalization set up by the Department of Finance (the O'Brien Report).[5] In addition, the topic has led to a renewed debate among academic researchers, with contributions by prominent economists from different parts of the country and has been the subject of a chapter in a recent edition of *How Ottawa Spends*.[6]

A full and logical discussion of VFI requires a formal framework in which the terms "balance" and "imbalance" can be clearly defined. Many of the writings on the concept lack an adequate framework to accomplish this. Moreover, as we shall see, the fiscal aspects of imbalance are only one dimension of the problem. While our discussion will allude to a broader context, we shall nevertheless continue to make use of the adjective "fiscal" in referring to possible imbalances so as to keep the discussion in accord with the long history of the debate.

To come to grips with the essential nature of VFI, we need a framework that allows us to characterize the equilibrium allocation of taxing powers and public expenditures among levels of government in a federation. In addition, any model of vertical imbalance must consider the allocation of resources between the public and private sectors, an issue almost always omitted from the debates. Finally, we must devote attention to the questions of how the assignment of taxing powers and other fiscal (and nonfiscal) policy instruments occurs in a federation and to how it evolves over time.

In an earlier paper,[7] we proposed a simple framework to describe static equilibrium for fiscal balance and proposed a standard for judging under what circumstances VFI will occur. In this paper, we extend this framework in an informal manner to include the static mis-assignment and dynamic re-assignment of fiscal instruments among levels of government, noting that such re-assignment is a continuing fact of life in all federations.

A SIMPLE FRAMEWORK

The literature on VFI exhibits a lack of consensus on general underlying principles. This is reflected in widely differing assessments of how to characterize the concept. One view, often expressed in budget documents, is that persistent deficits at the federal level or at the provincial level of government indicate the existence of an imbalance in the structure of the federation. A test for distinguishing whether such deficits reflect a true imbalance in federal structure or whether they are caused by other influences on public budgets (such as the desire to avoid hard fiscal choices) is not provided.

A more useful definition of imbalance refers to a mismatch between revenue sources and expenditure responsibilities.[8] Boadway and Tremblay, working in this tradition, define VFI as a situation where the federal government does not provide the proper level of grants to bridge the *vertical gap* between revenue sources and expenditure responsibilities at the provincial and federal levels, a gap that arises because of the greater revenue-raising ability of the federal government.[9] VFI occurs when this gap is too large or too small relative to what would be efficient from a national point of view, as a result of coordination problems among the provinces and constraints on the federal government's ability to transfer resources between provinces. Their analysis includes the important assumption that the assignment of fiscal instruments is given.[10]

While Boadway and Tremblay keep the assignment of instruments fixed, it is less clear in the literature as a whole whether the imbalance identified is caused by an inappropriate use of given instruments, whether the assignment of instruments is itself faulty, or whether both possibilities play a role. Presumably, the Seguin Report is arguing that both aspects are involved when it states that one of the prime causes of VFI is the inappropriate use of federal spending power.[11]

One should note that the federal assignment as well as the mix and extent of use of each fiscal instrument employed at each level of government are determined in the course of electoral competition. This fact has led some observers, including for example McKenzie and Smart, to suggest that VFI is essentially political in nature, a view with which we have considerable sympathy.[12]

Key assumptions

We begin the presentation of our framework by listing several critical assumptions and by explaining how they depart from those commonly found in the existing literature.

1 There are three goods that must be part of any framework: federal goods (F), non-federal or provincial goods (NF) and private goods (P). Inclusion of private goods, which are usually omitted in the discussion, is essential in order to discuss the assignment of instruments and to assess the implications of VFI for the private sector and hence for economic well-being. Allocation of resources among all three types of goods is determined simultaneously.[13]

2 There is a market for policy instruments among levels of government with "rights", analogous to property rights, established by the constitution and defined and redefined by judicial interpretation. Although such a market is discussed by Breton and Scott, most analysts do not consider its existence or operation.[14] We follow Breton and Scott in assuming that the constitution helps to establish property rights in policy instruments, while electoral competition tends to force governments to trade instruments in order to exploit economies of scale, so that such instruments are efficiently allocated among them.

3 Competition among provinces is effective and drives "price" to "marginal cost" in the production and provision of provincial goods. To the extent

that taxes are perceived by voters as payments for desired goods and services, provinces are not at a disadvantage in raising revenues. In other words, mobility among provinces does not lead to "a race to the bottom" as has sometimes been argued. This key assumption is in accord with recent theoretical results in the literature, and finds informal empirical confirmation for Canada in a recent volume on this issue edited by Harrison.[15]

4 The assignment of policy instruments continually evolves in response to shocks. Although most observers treat the assignment as fixed, historical analysis of Canadian and Australian intergovernmental relations in works by Maslove and Winer and Winer, for example, shows that judicial reinterpretation together with the operation of the market for policy instruments leads to regular adjustment and redefinition of the constitutional assignment.[16] Similar responses have also been observed for the United States where the phenomenon has been referred to as "authority migration."[17]

5 To simplify the exposition in the paper, we add two further assumptions that are preliminary in nature and that will be relaxed in later sections of the paper.

There are no federal grants to provinces except those required to deal with interprovincial externalities. (Federal grants required to deal with interprovincial externalities are treated as part of F goods.) While we shall drop this assumption when focusing more specifically on the role of grants, it is initially useful in showing that VFI is not a problem arising from the grant system itself, or from the vertical gap between taxes collected by the federal government and spending by the provinces.

Governments do not engage in redistribution between regions. This removes, in the initial discussion, problems raised by Equalization and by conditional grants that are based in part on population, while being unrelated to income. The restriction will be relaxed when we consider how vertical and horizontal balance, two issues that are usually treated as separate in the literature, are intertwined in the Canadian context.

In summary, our framework depends on the following critical assumptions:

- There are three goods: F, NF and P.
- There is a well functioning market for policy instruments among levels of government.
- Competition among provinces drives "price" to "marginal cost" for provincial goods.
- The assignment of responsibilities among governments evolves over time.

These four assumptions are joined by the two additional ones mentioned above that are imposed initially, but that will be relaxed later. The set of assumptions provides the basis for a consistent and logical analysis of VFI and for a new and different understanding of the concept.

What is vertical balance in this framework?

In view of the preceding discussion, we may define a *balanced* situation from an economic perspective as one that involves an efficient allocation of resources (i) among levels of government and (ii) between the public and the private sectors. This must hold for any given assignment of policy instruments among levels of government. In the longer run, vertical balance must also include an efficient assignment of policy instruments among federal and provincial governments.

This means that the fundamental perspective in defining a balanced situation refers to economic efficiency from a national standpoint. However, in contrast to most discussions of VFI, we specifically include in the application of this definition the overall public-private balance and the federal assignment of policy instruments.

Competition among provinces that is effective enough to drive them to deliver desired public services at least cost for any given assignment of policy instruments is a prerequisite for the emergence of such an allocation. In addition, we must have conditions sufficient for an efficient allocation between F and P goods. This will occur if federal electoral competition is strong enough, so that winning political parties are forced to offer policy programs that allow no room for believable alternatives that will lead to further improvements in economic efficiency for voters.

Basic types of imbalance

Given this framework, we can identify three types of imbalances. In our approach, these imbalances are essentially political in origin:

TYPE 1 (STATIC VFI)
This type arises in the following circumstances. Although intergovernmental competition is strong at the provincial level, inappropriate or insufficient electoral competition at the national level, and/or impediments to the international mobility of labor, prevent achievement of an efficient trade-off between private (P) and federal public (F) goods.

Inappropriate political competition at the national level may be caused by the common pool problem, which tends to assert itself more forcefully at the federal than at the provincial level, where migration serves as an additional check.[18] Since legislators can draw on a nation-wide pool of taxable resources for financing decisions, while being responsible primarily to their more narrowly defined constituency to obtain votes, they may overspend on programs targeted to their constituents; and they may support each other by forming implicit or semi-formal coalitions to achieve such a result.[19]

A second factor affecting efficiency at the federal level is represented by international mobility of capital and labor resources. While it is very difficult for modern governments to impede the mobility of capital across international boundaries, they can and do limit the mobility of labor to some extent, although the possibility of outsourcing of blue- as well as of white-collar jobs limits the effectiveness of such attempts by serving as a partial substitute for the actual physical movement of labor. The lack of mobility for individuals makes the common pool problem worse at the national level and may permit political rents to persist.

VFI of type 1, first suggested by Wagner[20] and formalized by Hettich and Winer,[21] implies an imbalance among the relative size of F, NF and P, since the standard is defined in a general equilibrium setting. In particular, the federal sector is too large, while the private sector is too small. Note that such VFI exists even though by assumption the provincial sector is at an efficient level – there is no implication that the provinces should get more funds from the federal government as a remedy! While the provinces may be politically hungry for more funds (as they always tend to be), they are not "underfed" in relation to an efficient standard of reference. Furthermore, given the preliminary assumptions mentioned earlier, grants are *not* involved as a contributing factor and do not cause or affect such VFI.

TYPE 2 (VFI IN THE LONGER RUN DUE
TO MIS-ASSIGNMENT)

VFI may also arise if the market for intergovernmental instruments does not function efficiently. Imbalances of this kind may persist in static equilibrium as long as political processes fail to force the federal and provincial governments to reach efficient solutions in apportioning fiscal and service responsibilities and policy instruments.

TYPE 3 (DYNAMIC VFI)

VFI of this nature represents the dynamic counterpart to type 2. The ideal assignment of instruments and service responsibilities among levels of government evolves in response to significant changes of an economic, demographic or political nature. History demonstrates that the actual assignment, even though it may appear as constitutionally fixed, will also change, but it may not do so quickly or completely enough over time. In this case, maladjustment is related to a dynamic equilibrium, rather than to a static one and VFI becomes a dynamic concept.

The role of federal grants to the provinces

The greater elasticity of tax bases with regard to tax rates for the provinces than for the federal government is likely to lead to a situation where the federal government raises taxes on behalf of the federation to an extent beyond what is required for its own purposes. This phenomenon is driven by political competition at all levels to provide services to the electorate at least cost, with different orders of government exchanging functions in order to capitalize on efficiency gains.[22]

While VFI may occur in the absence of federal grants, their presence may add to the size of VFI. Federal grants to the provinces may be too large because of the common pool problem identified earlier, a problem that also applies to federal – provincial bargaining. Provinces, as political units, may act like citizens who want someone else to pay for benefits obtained. Elected representatives in Parliament will be complicit to some extent in this quest to shift tax burdens elsewhere. If there is an excess of federal grants over the efficient level, it may also increase the NF sector and/or alter the structure of NF goods, thereby adding another dimension to static imbalance.

The analysis of the role of grants bears on complaints by the provinces concerning the exercise of federal spending power. The Seguin Report appears to argue that almost any use of such power other than Equalization in areas of provincial responsibility creates an imbalance. This view is consistent with our analysis to the extent that federal grants are too large relative to the efficient level defined in the absence of the common pool problem.[23] One should note, however, that there are also other issues concerning provincial autonomy or sovereignty involved in the Seguin Report's analysis that go beyond a concern with VFI, and which lie beyond the scope of this chapter.

MEASUREMENT AND HISTORICAL RECORD

Measurement of the vertical imbalance arising because of the common pool problem or imperfect mobility at the national level has not been accomplished so far. Although it does not seem more difficult to measure such VFI than to deal with many other measurement problems that have been overcome successfully, we know of no relevant estimates for the Canadian federation as a whole, or of any studies quantifying the consequences of VFI for the economic well-being of citizens. This is a fruitful area for research.

In any event, the analysis suggests that one cannot take pronouncements at the provincial level at face value. As pointed out earlier, the provinces may be hungry for more resources, but they are not necessarily "underfed". In the framework we have outlined, complaints from the private sector about high taxes may be just as indicative of a possible imbalance in the federation as those by provincial officials.

While the magnitude of static VFI has not yet been estimated, it is possible to consider informally how mis-assignment and its dynamic counterpart have been kept in check over the decades by what appears to be efficient reassignments of policy instruments. Such an analysis imparts a positive view of the robustness of the Canadian federal system. In what follows we briefly consider three episodes in federal fiscal history dealing with (i) the allocation of the power of indirect taxation in the federation, (ii) the responsibility for and provision of unemployment insurance, and (iii) the Diefenbaker tax point transfer.

(i) *The allocation of sales taxation*: It is likely that provincial tax structure was inefficient before the courts effectively turned the *indirect* sales tax into a *direct* tax in a series of legal judgments during the 1930's and 1940's. The British North America Act of 1867 had granted to the provinces only the power of direct taxation. Thus it was difficult for them to take advantage of the growth of sales tax bases. Provincial sales taxes became constitutionally viable only when through a series of judicial interpretations retail merchants came to be viewed as agents levying taxes on behalf of the provinces on those supposed to bear the tax burden, thus satisfying the prevailing definition of a direct tax.[24]

In this example, the courts created a more efficient distribution of taxing powers in the federation after being faced repeatedly with the problems caused by a glaring mis-assignment of such powers. The reassignment left the provinces with a more efficient tax structure. It probably also led to an increase in the NF to F ratio and to an overall increase in the size of the public sector.

(ii) *Unemployment insurance*: Prior to a constitutional amendment in 1940 that made unemployment insurance a federal responsibility, the courts in the mid 1930s invented a provincial responsibility for such insurance. UI was not, and could not, be anticipated in the division of powers embodied in the BNA Act, and some such decision was required.[25] But the initial judicial assignment was surely inefficient, since it was likely to result in a level of insurance that was too small due to the difficulties of arranging interprovincial cooperation to provide portability and to deal with moral hazard issues.

Before the constitutional amendment assigning UI (now called Employment Insurance) to the federal government, VFI of the second type identified above evidently existed, and the assignment of policy instruments was not efficient.

(iii) *The Diefenbaker tax point transfer*: After the 1958 election in which John Diefenbaker assumed the office of Prime Minister with one of the largest majorities in Canadian history, his government increased abatement of tax points to the provinces from 10 per cent to 13 per cent.[26] This represented a substantial and rapidly implemented increase.

The re-assignment of income taxation represented a response by the federal system that kept the extent of dynamic imbalance in check. Key questions about this response that are prompted by our framework include the following: What were the shocks that lead to this reassignment? Was it the demands for provincially provided education, health and social welfare that were growing quickly in response to the baby boom? Was it new demands for autonomy in Quebec which could not be satisfied by asymmetric treatment of one province? How did the process unfold? And, finally, was the response of the federal system appropriate with regard to speed and structure?

VFI IN THE FUTURE

Before turning to the link between vertical and horizontal balance, it is interesting to speculate on how the federal assignment will develop in the future in response to significant changes in society. By so doing, it may be possible to predict where VFI and the consequent re-assignments may emerge in coming decades. Important developments that warrant attention include aging of the population, global warming, and the longer-run consequences of the Charter of Rights.

Care of the elderly may be increasingly provided for by higher provincial spending, by provincial and federal preferential tax treatment, or some combinations of these.[27] In view of the high costs of institutionalizing a growing proportion of elderly citizens, one may expect to see targeted reductions in private tax burdens so that individual families can deal with aging parents themselves to a much greater extent than in the past. If these reductions are entirely borne by the federal government, there will be a decrease in the relative size of the federal public sector. Tax reductions to support home-care and similar programs may, of course, also be implemented at the provincial level, making it unclear what may happen to the NF to F ratio. In any event, it is reasonable to suggest that aging will lead to an increase in the relative size of the private sector. The extent of VFI that may emerge will depend on how quickly the necessary adjustments occur.

Global warming is an externality par excellence where policy responsibility is best assigned to the federal government. A national carbon tax to deal with the matter, whether introduced by itself, or together with a trading and cap system of pollution permits, could provide substantial new resources to the federal government, some of which could be used to subsidize environmental innovation. Given the absence of any serious current policy to deal with carbon emissions and given the nature of the problem, one can argue that there is now a vertical imbalance, with the necessary adjustments requiring an increase in the ratio of F to NF sectors.

Finally, if U.S. experience with the Bill of Rights is any guide, it is likely that the Charter of Rights will exert a centralizing force in the coming decades in many areas where the public sector intersects with the private lives of Canadians. It will be a centralizing influence because the Charter places the federal government in an advantageous position to deliver public benefits in a non-discriminatory manner. The Charter may also lead to an increase in the relative size of the private sector because it gives more latitude to private action in areas, such as the provision of health services, where government action has been paramount.[28] Whether prolonged periods of imbalance in federal structure will occur as a consequence of these influences will depend on the responses of the public sectors at both the provincial and federal level.[29]

ALLOWING FOR INTERREGIONAL REDISTRIBUTION

To complete the analysis, we now drop the assumption that there is no coercive interregional redistribution. The analysis then leads to the conclusion that vertical and horizontal balance or imbalance are linked in the Canadian federation largely because of the existing constitutional assignment of policy instruments. As noted earlier, the literature on VFI has generally treated issues of vertical balance between federal and provincial public sectors as distinct from those dealing with horizontal balance among the provinces.[30]

Even if intergovernmental and political competition accomplish what they are supposed to do, the desire to redistribute interregionally will inevitably shift resources upwards. This re-assignment, one that we observe in most federal countries, limits the welfare costs of raising the taxes necessary to fund redistribution through the fiscal system, while bypassing the difficulties of arranging voluntary interprovincial arrangements.[31] It also leads to redistributive grants to lower levels of government. In Canada, it has lead both to formal Equalization payments and to equalization implicit in conditional grants, paid partly on the basis of the recipient provinces' population rather than on their per capita income. (While not formally labeled as such until 1957, redistributive grants have been in existence since Confederation.)

The current structure of the Canadian Equalization system is in all likelihood a source of VFI because of the particular nature of the present federal assignment. A central problem arises from section 36(1) of the Constitution Act of 1982 that requires Equalization, combined with section 192 that forbids the federal government from taxing provincial resource revenues flowing through the provincial public sector rather than into private hands (the Crown cannot tax the Crown).[32] Oil revenues entering the provincial treasury directly do not constitute federally taxable income. Similarly, implicit subsidies to citizens of Ontario and Quebec through the under-pricing of hydro power cannot be taxed by the federal government.[33]

In view of the current Equalization formula, this constitutional setup leads to a situation where a substantial increase in oil prices, which benefits oil-producing provinces, forces the federal government to raise national tax rates (including, but not limited to, tax rates in the oil-rich provinces) in order to finance Equalization payments to the relatively poorer provinces.[34] As a result, citizens in provinces that have no oil, such as Ontario, must pay higher taxes as well as higher oil prices. In this case, VFI results in a P that is too small because federal tax rates are too high, compared to a situation where all income sources are treated symmetrically and efficiently for the purpose of taxation, and where what one province gains, another directly loses. In addition, fairness in interregional distribution is put in question.

The imbalance and inefficiency of excessive federal tax rates created by the impact of oil prices since the OPEC oil embargo of 1973 have been reduced by a series of ad-hoc adjustments in the Equalization formula.[35] The federal government's responsibility for Equalization entitlements has been scaled back through changes of the formula. After 1973, the ten-province standard was reduced to a five-province standard that excluded oil-producing provinces. One can also see the National Energy Program and the oil export tax of the Trudeau era as a partial response and partial solution of the problem. While the federal budget of 2006 reintroduced the ten-province standard, only one-half of all resource revenues has been made subject to the revised formula. The latter feature keeps federal tax rates down, and limits the risk to the federal government of having to raise taxes in order to pay for Equalization if oil prices should increase further.

Usher has recently proposed a different and more consistent solution, one that may or may not be feasible given the current constitution.[36] He advocates the use of a 'macro' formula defining Equalization payments on the basis of provincial per-capita GDP, rather than on the current basis of the yield (relative to a national average) of a basket of provincial revenue sources. This would bring all resource revenues and implicit subsidies into the Equalization accounting framework. In addition, his proposed scheme involves Equalization "down-as-well-as-up", in contrast to the current system which equalizes "up-but-not-down", so that what the recipient provinces gain is financed at the expense of the oil-rich provinces.

Courchene has proposed another, related solution where oil-producing provinces in a series of strategic moves contribute a substantial portion of their oil revenues voluntarily to a fund jointly administered by the provinces.[37] Income in this fund would be passed back to the provinces in proportion to their populations, resulting in a transfer from the oil-rich provinces to those without oil without the intermediation of the federal fiscal system.

Exactly how either of these proposals could be implemented under the current constitution and in the current political situation is not clear, and is a matter for further debate. What is important in the present discussion is that these proposals both illustrate how the issues of vertical and horizontal balance are linked, and that the current assignment of fiscal instruments is not working well.

CONCLUSIONS

We complete the chapter by summarizing key points of the analysis and by offering some comments on the implications of some recent policy developments:

1. A set of general principles is required in order to discuss VFI. An analysis of government deficits does not result in an appropriate framework unless it can distinguish between structural deficits due to the federal assignment of policy instruments and deficits caused by the many other possible reasons for budget imbalances.
2. VFI can be analyzed both as a static and as a dynamic problem. In a dynamic framework, it is fruitful to place the emphasis on the inappropriate assignment or use of policy instruments among levels of government in long run equilibrium and in the transition from one equilibrium to the next. One should note that the concept of VFI does not inherently depend on intergovernmental grants and that VFI may exist in the absence of such grants.
3. Provincial arguments about imbalance are often invalid, while private sector complaints about the burden of taxation may point to the existence of an actual imbalance in a federation.
4. The need for reassignment of policy instruments is continuous, and VFI is a normal state of affairs. If one takes a negative view of this fact, one may perceive it as a chronic problem. On the other hand, if one looks at how VFI has been kept in check in the past, one is led to a more positive view of the robustness and responsiveness of the Canadian federal system.
5. We have no empirical assessments of the magnitude of VFI, or of its implications for economic well-being, especially when it relates to mis- or re-assignment of policy instruments. It may be possible to identify and measure the welfare consequences of mis-assignment in particular cases by creating an appropriate comparison of relevant benefits and costs.
6. It is interesting to predict how the federal assignment and VFI will evolve in the future, but it is difficult to do so successfully in practice. We may expect that big changes affecting society, such as the aging of the population, global warming and the introduction of the Charter of Rights will lead to VFI in the coming decades and require commensurate adjustments in federal structure.
7. VFI includes what is often treated as a separate problem, namely horizontal balance. Because of the mis-assignment of instruments under the current constitution, the federal government must pay Equalization without having adequate access to all resource revenues and implicit subsidies, a situation that has only partially been dealt with by excluding half of oil revenues from the Equalization formula. Thus it is most likely that we currently experience VFI in Canada related to the pursuit of horizontal balance.

The federal government recently claimed in its Budget of March 19, 2007 that it eliminated VFI by adjusting the Equalization formula and by transferring funds to the provinces while also adjusting the basis for the Canada Social Transfer grants to a per-capita basis. Our analysis suggests to the contrary that Equalization continues to be a source of interprovincial inequities, and that it remains a reason for the existence of VFI. The problems in this regard call for bolder steps than those so far adopted. As concerns intergovernmental transfers to the provinces, such payments do not remove the underlying basic issues connected to the relative size of the private and public sectors. Nor will they deal with structural changes occurring over time, such as the aging of the population or global warming, that may require substantial changes in the way policy instruments at different levels are used.

Concerning the public-private aspect of imbalance, a more helpful policy would be to cut federal taxes, thus allowing the provinces to raise additional funds directly from their own revenue bases (thereby reducing the size of the private sector) if they think these tax increases will be supported by the their electorates. Recent federal cuts in the GST and in income taxes may thus represent a more effective response and may have resulted in a reduction of VFI. Ultimately, it is electoral competition that must drive the federal system to an efficient allocation of resources among federal, provincial and private sectors. In the absence of work on the measurement of vertical imbalance, it is difficult to determine whether such competition has served its role in a sufficiently effective way and whether recent policy changes have made a significant and substantial contribution to the resolution of the problems associated with imbalance in the structure of the fiscal system.

ACKNOWLEDGEMENTS

Allan Maslove and Susan Phillips provided helpful comments, and Haizhen Mou provided research assistance. This chapter benefitted from a panel discussion with Paul Boothe and Nicolas Marceau at Carleton University in the fall of 2007.

NOTES

1 See Royal Commission on Dominion-Provincial Relations (1940) – the Rowell-Sirois Commission. Canadian Library Series.
2 Economic Council of Canada, *Financing Confederation* (Ottawa: Queen's Printers, 1982).
3 On the history of this retrenchment, see Stephen J. Ferris and Stanley L. Winer, "Just How Much Bigger Is Government in Canada: A Comparison of the Size and Structure of the Public Sectors in Canada and the United States," *Canadian Public Policy* 33, no.2 (2007): 173–206.

4 We follow the convention of capitalizing the term equalization when it refers to the relevant federal program in Canada.
5 See Council of the Federation, Advisory Panel on Fiscal Imbalance, *Reconciling the Irreconcilable* (Ottawa: Council of the Federation, 2006); Commission on Fiscal Imbalance, *A New Division of Canada's Financial Resources* (Montreal: Bibliothèque nationale du Québec, 2002). (The Seguin Report); Expert Panel on Equalization and Territorial Formula Financing, *Achieving a National Purpose: Putting Equalization Back on Track* (Ottawa: Department of Finance, 2006). (The O'Brien Report).
6 See Andrew Teliszewsky and Christopher Stoney, "Addressing the Fiscal Imbalance Through Asymmetrical Federalism: Dangerous Times for the Harper Government and for Canada," in Bruce Doern, ed., *How Ottawa Spends 2007–2008: The Harper Conservatives – Climate of Change* (Montreal & Kingston: McGill-Queen's University Press, 2007). See also Gilles Paquet, "Fiscal Imbalance as Government Failure," in Bruce Doern, ed., *Innovation, Science, and Environment 2007–2008: Canadian Policies and Performance*. (Montreal & Kingston: McGill-Queen's University Press), in addition to the contributions cited in the text.
7 See Walter Hettich and Stanley L. Winer, "Vertical Imbalance in the Fiscal Systems of Federal States." *Canadian Journal of Economics* 19 (1986): 745–65.
8 For reviews of the literature, see Richard M. Bird, "Fiscal Flows, Fiscal Balance and Fiscal Sustainability," Working Paper 03–02, Andrew Young School of Policy Studies, Georgia State University, 2003; Harvey Lazar, France St. Hilaire and Jean-François Tremblay, "Vertical Fiscal Imbalance: Myth or Reality?" In H. Lazar and F. St. Hilaire, eds., *Money, Politics and Health Care* (Montreal: Institute for Research on Public Policy, 2004); and C.K. Sharma, "Vertical Fiscal Imbalance and Vertical Fiscal Gap: A Study in Sorting the Semantics," Munich Personal RePec Archive, MPRA Paper 237, October 2006. At mpra.ub.uni-muenchen.de.
9 Robin Boadway and Jean-François Tremblay, "A Theory of Fiscal Imbalance," *FinanzArchiv* 62 (2006): 1–27.
10 See Bev Dahlby and L.S. Wilson, "Fiscal Capacity, Tax Effort, and Optimal Equalization Grants," *Canadian Journal of Economics* 27, no. 3 (1994): 657–72. These authors also take the assignment of instruments as fixed and define VFI as a situation where the marginal cost of funds is not equalized across jurisdictions. In their view, this situation may be created by differences in the ability of taxpayers to migrate from local as opposed to national jurisdictions and by federal grants that are not properly structured to compensate for this.
11 Commission on Fiscal Imbalance, *A New Division of Canada's Financial Resources*, (The Seguin Report), 25.
12 See Kenneth J. McKenzie, "Reflections on the Political Economy of Fiscal Federalism in Canada," C.D. Howe Institute Working Paper, September 2005; Michael Smart, "Federal Transfers: Principles, Practice, and Prospects," C.D. Howe Institute Working Paper, September 2005.
13 Hettich and Winer, "Vertical Imbalance in the Fiscal Systems of Federal States."

14 Albert Breton and Anthony Scott, *The Economic Constitution of Federal States* (Toronto: University of Toronto Press, 1982); Albert Breton, *Competitive Governments: An Economic Theory of Politics and Public Finance* (New York: Cambridge University Press, 1996).

15 See Kathryn Harrison, ed., *Racing to the Bottom? Provincial Interdependence in the Canadian Federation* (Vancouver: UBC Press, 2005). Theoretical contributions casting doubt on the "race to the bottom" include Breton, *Competitive Governments: An Economic Theory of Politics and Public Finance*; Dennis Mueller, "Constitutional Constraints on Governments in a Global Economy," *Constitutional Political Economy* 19, (1998): 171–86; David E. Wildasin, "Global Competition for Mobile Resources: Implications for Equity, Efficiency and Political Economy," *CESifo Economic Studies* 52, no. 1 (2006): 61–110; and Amrita Dhillon, Myrna Wooders and Ben Zissimos, "Tax Competition Reconsidered," *Journal of Public Economic Theory* 9, no.3 (2007): 391–423. See also Ian Parry, "How Large Are the Welfare Costs of Tax Competition?" *Journal of Urban Economics* 54, no.1, (2003): 39–60. Here, Parry has made an interesting attempt to calculate the welfare cost of interregional tax competition in the United States, and finds it to be quite small. To the best of our knowledge, no such calculations have been made in Canada.

16 Allan M. Maslove and Stanley L. Winer, "Fiscal Federalism in Canada and Australia: A Brief Comparison of Constitutional Frameworks, Structural Features of Existing Fiscal Systems and Fiscal Institutions," in Paul Boothe, ed., *Reforming Fiscal Federalism for Global Competition: A Canada-Australia Comparison*. Western Studies in Economic Policy. (The University of Alberta Press, 1996), 45–85; Stanley L. Winer, "On the Reassignment of Fiscal Powers in a Federal State," in G. Galeotti, P. Salmon and R. Wintrobe, eds., *Competition and Structure: The Political Economy of Collective Decisions: Essays in Honour of Albert Breton* (New York: Cambridge University Press, 2000), 150–73.

17 Jonathan Rodden, ed., Symposium on the Migration of Fiscal Sovereignty. *Political Science and Politics* July (2004) 427–31.

18 On the common pool problem in a federation see, for example, Robert Inman and Daniel Rubinfeld, "Rethinking Federalism," *Journal of Economic Perspectives* 11, no. 4 (1997): 43–64; Reza Baqir, "Districting and Government Overspending," *Journal of Political Economy* 110, no. 6 (2002): 1318–54; and Jean-Luc Migué, "The Political Economy of Overlapping Jurisdictions and the French/Dutch Rejection of the EU Constitution," *Economic Affairs* 26, no. 1 (2006): 61–4. Inman and Rubinfeld, Migué and others have suggested that decentralization in a federation may in fact be a way of bounding the size of the common pool problem by limiting the scope of spending at the national level where the problem is likely to be most intense.

19 From an analytical perspective, this common pool problem in politics has a lot in common with the analysis of overfishing. The matter is more complicated here, however, because we are dealing with citizens who vote rather than with fish, and with the working of political institutions rather than with regulation of the fishing industry.

20 Richard E. Wagner, *The Fiscal Organization of American Federalism.* (Chicago: Markham Publishing, 1971).
21 Hettich, and Winer, "Vertical Imbalance in the Fiscal Systems of Federal States."
22 Costs are defined in this context to include the welfare loss from taxation. For further analysis of this process, see Breton and Scott, *The Economic Constitution of Federal States.*
23 The possibility that elected members of Parliament may be complicit in exploiting the common pool problem to arrange for federal grants to their own constituents at the expense of the average taxpayer in the federation tempers the force of any such criticism.
24 See G.V. LaForest, *The Allocation of Taxing Power Under the Canadian Constitution* Canadian Tax Paper No. 65, 2nd edition (Toronto: Canadian Tax Foundation, 1981); and for the history of the adoption of provincial sales taxes in the federation, Winer, "On the Reassignment of Fiscal Powers in a Federal State"
25 Dan Usher, *Political Economy* (Blackwell Publishers, 2003), 394.
26 See Hettich and Winer, "Vertical Imbalance in the Fiscal Systems of Federal States." As shown by Figure 1, grants to the provinces also began to increase quickly relative to GDP in the late 1950's.
27 On aging and federalism see, for example, David K. Foot, "The Demographic Future of Fiscal Federalism in Canada," Canadian Public Policy 10, no. 4 (1984): 406–14; and Helmut Seitz and Gerhard Kempkes, "Fiscal Federalism and Demography," *Public Finance Review* 35, no. 3 (2007): 385–413.
28 The Chaoulli decision of the Supreme Court (2005), opening the door to private insurance in Quebec for medically necessary services, may represent a case in point, though the decision was made on the basis of the Quebec charter of rights so that its impact on the country as a whole is not (yet) clear.
29 We are aware that introducing Charter issues into the discussion raises questions of equity in addition to those concerning efficiency.
30 In contrast, these issues are effectively linked in normative discussions of intergovernmental competition, where it is often argued that the onus is on the federal government to redistribute interregionally in order to offset the adverse economic consequences of horizontal competition among the provinces.
31 One may also note here that in a recent contribution bearing on our key assumption that intergovernmental competition does what it is supposed to, (see Albert Breton and Angela Fraschini, "Competitive Governments, Globalization, and Equalization Grants," *Public Finance Review* 35, no.4 (2007): 463–79.) Breton and Fraschini argue that equalization enhances such competition by maintaining the financial viability of the smaller provinces in the face of globalization.
32 Dan Usher, "The Reform of Equalization Payments," *Canadian Public Policy* 33, no. 3 (2007): 337–66.
33 It would be interesting to measure the size of these implicit subsidies.
34 The current Equalization formula is, in Usher's useful terminology (see "The Reform of Equalization Payments"), one that equalizes "up-but-not-down," so that equalization is financed by the federal government using taxation levied on all Canadians in

the same way in all provinces in order to reduce tax rates in recipient provinces to a national average. This is in contrast to what he refers to as Equalization "down-as-well-as-up"; in that sort of scheme, what one province gains, another loses, so that an overall increase in federal taxation is not required when oil prices increase.

35 For a recent discussion of the history of Equalization and its relationship to natural resources, see Thomas J. Courchene, "Energy Prices, Equalization and Canadian Federalism: Comparing Canada's Energy Price Shocks," *Queen's Law Journal* 31, (2006): 644–96.
36 Usher, "The Reform of Equalization Payments."
37 Courchene, "Energy Prices, Equalization and Canadian Federalism: Comparing Canada's Energy Price Shocks."

3 International Capital and Domestic Politics: Balancing Political and Economic Management

GEOFFREY HALE

INTRODUCTION

The evolution of the Harper government's fiscal and tax priorities during its first two years in office provides an instructive example of both policy learning and tactical skill in managing the constraints imposed by minority parliaments. Its adaptation to changing political and economic circumstances appears to reflect its growing political confidence, especially in what appears to be a calculated decision to combine a semi-populist approach to personal taxation with a more strategic approach to business taxation sharply at odds with the policy signals of its first eighteen months in office.

This chapter examines the political and economic challenges facing the Harper government during its first two years in office – and their implications for its fiscal and tax policies. It relates these challenges to prevailing theories of taxation. It considers the effects of electoral politics on the evolution of Canada's personal tax system – and the mix of different tax sources that provide the federal revenue stream. It reviews major changes in the structure of the Canadian economy that have blurred distinctions between corporate and investment income, as well as those between domestic and international business operations. It assesses the effects of these trends in the context of case studies on two controversial measures: the taxation of income trusts, and the tax treatment of interest on funds borrowed to finance the international operations of Canadian businesses. Finally, it considers the implications of these issues for the Harper government as it navigates the shoals of a minority Parliament and attempts to develop more coherent, longer-term economic policies that can contribute to its pursuit of a majority at the next election – particularly the tax changes introduced in Finance Minister Jim Flaherty's economic statement of October 2007.

THE POLITICAL AND ECONOMIC ENVIRONMENT FOR FEDERAL FISCAL AND TAX POLICIES

The federal Conservatives inherited five major challenges in the fields of fiscal and tax policies when taking office in January 2006. First, chronic federal surpluses had eroded public support for the kinds of fiscal discipline that had underpinned Canada's remarkable fiscal turnaround during the previous decade – creating a fertile political climate for a return to distributive politics, including the use of the tax system as a tool for conferring benefits on particular societal interests.

Secondly, the Harper government found itself caught between competing commitments to "open federalism" – respect for provincial jurisdictions in the design of federal-provincial fiscal transfers – and commitments to resource-producing provinces that Ottawa would not include their non renewable resource revenues in planned revisions to the federal equalization formula. These issues were addressed in part by changes to equalization and other fiscal transfers in its first two budgets – and in part by side-deals with individual provinces of the sort they had criticized while in opposition.

Third, structural economic changes have blurred traditional distinctions between domestic and international business activity, and between personal and corporate income tax systems – creating fertile opportunities for tax arbitrage by investors, businesses and their professional advisors. Fourth, these changes, reinforced by persistently low interest rates, increasingly assertive institutional investors, and the growing activity of pension funds and other tax-deferred investment vehicles seeking higher returns, have contributed to an increasingly dynamic market for corporate reorganizations, mergers and acquisitions largely outside the direct control of governments. As a result, the effectiveness of Canadian tax policies – especially in balancing the financing of government expenditures with the promotion of economic growth and competitiveness – requires policy makers to take into account both the policies of Canada's major trading partners and the creative anarchy of Canadian and international capital markets.

Finally, the complexity of the tax system and the electoral calculations of political parties, especially in a minority government, lend themselves to short-term political calculations, rather than more comprehensive approaches to managing the trade-offs among competing policy goals.

The 2007 federal budget, in attempting to straddle these issues, further increased spending pressures, seemingly reinforcing Ottawa's need to maintain revenues in the face of a potential economic downturn and a politically inconvenient return to deficit spending. By contrast, Finance Minister Jim Flaherty's economic statement of October 2007 appears to signal a return to modest spending discipline, incremental personal tax reductions, and an evolving strategy to position Canada's corporate tax rates as the most competitive among G-7 industrial nations.

THEORIES OF TAXATION AND TAX REFORM

The tax system has two broad purposes: to raise revenues for public purposes, and do so in ways that optimize the balance between economic efficiency and equity. The principle of promoting efficiency has several dimensions. Historically, it has reflected the principle of tax neutrality: the idea that the tax system should avoid measures that encourage rational individuals (or businesses) to make economic decisions based primarily on tax considerations. Contemporary economic theories also emphasize the promotion of micro-economic efficiency: the use of labour and capital to maximize levels of output for each unit of input. Related economic analyses have shown that certain taxes may impose more (or fewer) impediments to economic growth than others.

The principle of equity holds that individuals in comparable situations should pay comparable levels of tax, while accommodating differences among people in substantially different situations, including but not limited to the ability to pay ("vertical equity").[1] In reality, all governments pay lip service to equity and efficiency while often using the tax system to pursue a variety of micro-economic, distributive and other political goals.

The appetite for government spending typically exceeds the revenue generating capacity of any single tax source without creating significant disincentives to economic growth – or to competitive tax avoidance strategies. Consequently, governments typically depend on multiple revenue sources.

Personal income taxes (PITs) have been much the largest source of federal revenues in recent decades – rising from 42.7 per cent in 1988–89, following Michael Wilson's tax reform budget, to 48.2 per cent in 1999–2000 and 46.8 per cent in 2006–07, despite significant tax cuts since 2000. The much maligned Goods and Services Tax (GST) accounts for about 70 per cent of federal consumption tax revenues – the next largest set of revenue sources at 19.2 per cent in 2006–07.[2] Corporate income tax (CIT) revenues, which reflect the variability of corporate profits over the business cycle, have been the fastest growing source of federal revenues in recent years, growing from a cyclical low of 5.7 per cent in 1992–93 to 16.0 per cent in 2006–07 – the highest level since 1980.[3] Table 1 summarizes the evolution of the federal tax mix since Canada's last major set of tax reforms in the late 1980s.

Table 1
Major Federal Revenue Sources, Budget Balances as percentage of GDP: 1988–2007

Fiscal year ending Mar. 31	1988	1991	1994	1997	2000	2003	2006	2007
Personal Income Tax	7.6	8.3	7.6	8.1	8.7	7.8	7.6	7.6
Corporate Income Tax	1.9	1.7	1.3	1.9	2.3	1.9	2.3	2.6
Consumption Taxes	4.3	3.5	3.7	3.5	3.5	3.6	3.4	3.1
(Un)Employment Insurance	1.9	1.6	2.7	2.4	1.9	1.5	1.2	1.2
Total Revenues	7.4	17.6	17.0	17.9	18.0	16.5	16.2	16.3
Surplus / (Deficit)	(4.4)	(5.0)	(4.6)	(1.0)	1.1	0.8	0.5	1.0

Source: Department of Finance, *Fiscal Reference Tables* (Ottawa: Department of Finance September 2007).

Economic analysts have long suggested that the concepts of equity and efficiency can reinforce one another, rather than conflicting, by broadening tax bases – that is, reducing the number of exceptions and exemptions from a particular tax – and lowering rates so individuals and businesses have greater incentives to maximize their incomes rather than investing time and money in efforts to avoid high tax rates. More recent analyses have identified significant differences between the efficiency (or productivity) effects of raising or lowering different *types* of taxes. For example, a 2005 Finance department study suggests that the greatest stimulus to economic growth come from reducing overall taxes on personal investment income, including dividends and capital gains, followed by taxes on corporate income, and personal income. Such tax shifts – by encouraging capital investments that contribute to greater productivity – are also seen to foster greater competitiveness, economic growth and higher living standards. Reductions in consumption taxes were seen to have the smallest effects on efficiency and growth.[4]

However, political realities tend to work at cross-purposes with idealized visions of tax systems in which the lions of efficiency and lambs of equity lie down together in perfect harmony. It is often more effective to target tax benefits to particular groups to promote particular social or economic goals than to distribute small tax reductions to large numbers of people on a more-or-less non-discriminatory basis. Governments' use of the tax system to pursue multiple policy goals has entrenched a wide range of measures within the tax system, each of which with its own constituency which, over time, tends to view its benefits as entitlements conducive to the public good.

However, these measures can often function at cross-purposes with one another, as well as eroding the tax base, leading government officials periodically to look for ways to rationalize existing benefits, with lower overall rates, to promote greater overall economic efficiency and growth.

Allan Maslove, writing about episodic tax reforms between the 1960s and 1980s, described this process as the "tax reform cycle." Governments attempt to rationalize the provisions of the income or consumption tax systems to bring it closer to theoretical ideals of "tax reform." Over time, political and economic pressures (and vote seeking by politicians) lead to the proliferation of exceptions and exemptions which reduce both revenues, efficiency and at least some perspectives of equity. Other costs include growing complexity and compliance costs to taxpayers, reduced predictability of revenues to governments, and occasionally, political embarrassment from evidence of large scale or high profile tax avoidance – often calling into question the fairness of the tax system.[5]

In practice, the politics of tax reduction are far easier to package than the politics of tax reform. Organized minorities facing significant tax increases have much stronger incentives to fight base broadening measures than a dispersed majority of citizens have to support them. Politically successful tax reforms are usually carefully structured to provide net benefits to both a significant majority of citizens and members of major stakeholder groups.[6] Although tax economists stress the relative benefits to economic efficiency and growth of reductions in taxes on capital and investment income, political realities usually dictate that tax reductions be distributed in ways that will provide visible benefits to the majority of citizens. As a result, personal tax reductions of one sort or another are usually prior to and a precondition for lower taxes on business.

The politics of taxation are further complicated by the realities of Canada's aging society. Demographic trends suggest that the costs of providing health and other benefits to the steadily growing proportion of pensioners will have to be financed by a static and ultimately declining number of working-age Canadians. As a result, *any* form of tax reduction is likely to be contingent on continued debt reduction. These assumptions are embedded in Finance Minister Jim Flaherty's "tax back guarantee," which links promises of future personal tax reductions to federal interest savings resulting from regular debt repayments from annual budget surpluses. After modest tax reductions associated with federal income tax reforms in 1987–88 and the introduction of the GST in 1989–90, personal and corporate income tax rates crept upwards during the 1990s as successive governments sought to bring their chronic deficits under control.

During the mid-1990s, the federal government commissioned a major review of business taxation, chaired by University of Toronto economist Jack Mintz – later President of the C.D. Howe Institute. Although the 1998 report of the "Technical Committee"[7] informed a series of incremental changes to business taxes over the next several years, near-record corporate profits after 2001 have generated enough CIT revenues to compensate for most of these changes.

With an election looming in 2000, the Chrétien-Martin government anticipated its political opponents by reducing taxes – phased-in over several years – for both individual and businesses. However, it preserved most of the salient features of the tax system inherited from the Mulroney government. It gradually broadened and extended the system of refundable tax benefits introduced to replace the old Family Allowance and transfers to parents through the National Child Benefit. To "enhance access to post-secondary education" – and offset rising tuition costs – it expanded education tax credits over several years and made their application more flexible. In 2000, it restored inflation indexing for tax brackets and most allowances. To "replace" the GST, it had bribed three provinces to join the federal government in a "Harmonized" federal-provincial sales tax during the 1990s. To prevent a repeat of the tax competition of the late 1980s, in which both Ottawa and provincial governments shifted the costs of their own policy choices to the other, Ottawa also negotiated a revised tax collection agreement with the provinces to allow provinces to set their own tax rates, rather than setting them as a percentage of the applicable federal PIT rate.[8]

Persistent budget surpluses and growing opposition pressures, especially after the 2004 election returned a minority government, led the Liberals to ramp up spending substantially during their last three years in office. As a result, the Conservative government elected in January 2006 inherited a fiscal environment oriented towards distributive politics – along with a disposition to use the surplus to maximize its own political leverage in the pursuit of a majority government.

ELECTORAL POLITICS AND THE PERSONAL INCOME TAX SYSTEM

Persistent economic growth, combined with Ottawa's strong finances, meant that economic issues played a relatively marginal role in the 2006 federal election that brought the Harper Conservatives to power. Rather than reflecting the preoccupations of tax economists and business-oriented think tanks with issues of productivity and international competitiveness,[9] much of the Conservative platform was carefully targeted towards domestic political constituencies. In particular, most personal tax measures were targeted towards groups of swing voters capable of providing them an electoral plurality without providing major targets to opposition parties – although business tax measures reflected a combination of populist elements and measures calculated to enhance both efficiency and competitiveness. (See below.)

Although both the Liberals and Conservatives offered voters tax cuts spread over several years, the Conservatives decided to challenge received economic wisdom in making reductions to the GST the centrepiece of their fiscal platform. Several measures were targeted to middle-class families, viewed as the most vital group of swing voters. A universal $1,200 per child benefit for children under age 6 would replace the Liberals' long-deferred measures beginning to implement a national child care plan.[10] Parents would also receive tax credits for childrens' "fitness" programs. Pensioners and disabled persons were also promised targeted tax reductions. Urban commuters would receive tax credits for purchasing public transit passes. These measures were implemented in Finance Minister Jim Flaherty's first budget in May 2006.[11] To pay for these targeted tax reductions, he rolled back a previous Liberal cut in the lowest PIT rate from 15.5 to 15 per cent.

Flaherty also borrowed several measures from the Liberal agenda, increasing the basic personal exemption, eliminating the corporate capital tax earlier than planned,[12] increasing tax benefits for apprentices and post-secondary students, and promising to reduce general corporate taxes towards the end of the decade. He also began to implement the Liberals' planned changes to dividend taxation in an effort to stem the flood of corporate conversions to income trust status which had become a major issue during the previous year.[13]

Several elements of Flaherty's second budget, in March 2007, followed the pattern of narrowly targeted tax measures set in his first budget. Responding to the government's political vulnerability on environmental issues, it introduced a new system of tax rebates and penalties on new car and truck sales based on relative gas consumption (and by extension, greenhouse gas emissions). It later emerged that one beneficiary of the measures was a large "flex-fuel" car made in Flaherty's Ottawa-Whitby constituency, which would have been a major symbol of green innovation except for Canada's almost total absence of gas stations selling E-85 fuels.[14] Flaherty also introduced a new $2,000 universal child tax credit – in addition to the previous year's measure, equalized the spousal tax credit with the basic personal exemption, and increased the lifetime capital gains exemption for farmers and small business owners from $500,000 to $750,000, restoring much of the measure's value lost to inflation since 1985.[15]

To offset increased taxes on income trusts, a measure discussed later in this chapter that disproportionately affected middle class investors and pensioners, Flaherty had previously introduced several major tax changes to assist seniors, substantially increasing the existing age credit (from $1,000 to $5,666), allowing for pension income splitting among seniors.[16] In the 2007 budget, he increased the maximum age for converting RRSPs into annuities from 69 to 71, and introduced measures to permit phased retirement by older workers.

However, some elements in Flaherty's budget reflected more traditional tax policy analyses, including a Working Income Tax Credit of up to $500 for lower-income Canadians earning less than $12,833 for single individuals and up to $1,000 for single parents and families earning less than $21,167.[17] Table 2 outlines the value of these tax reductions in fiscal year 2007–08.

Table 2
Tax reductions in 2007 Federal Budget (Fiscal Year 2007–08) (in $ billion)

Child tax credit	$1.4
"Tax fairness" measures incl. age credit; pension income splitting	1.0
Working Income tax benefit	0.6
EI premium reductions	0.4
Equalizing spousal, basic personal amounts	0.3
Other measures	0.4
Total PIT, EI reductions	$4.1

Source: Department of Finance, *Aspire ... The Budget Plan: 2007*, 33, 157.

Although the Harper government was clearly "revving its engines" in preparation for a possible election, its package of transfers to the provinces[18] – largely based on the report of an expert Task Force appointed by its Liberal predecessors – was sufficient to secure Parliamentary passage of the budget with PQ support and thus, its survival.

The populist orientation of the first two Conservative budgets, reminiscent of the distributive politics of the 1970s, generally received tepid reviews from economic observers, particularly from business-oriented think tanks such as the Conference Board of Canada and the C.D. Howe Institute. Noting Canada's anemic productivity growth, particularly when compared with the United States, these groups tended to advocate a mix of broadly-based tax reductions, similar to those belatedly proposed by the Martin government, that provide benefits to a broad cross-section of taxpayers while supporting individual and business activities conducive to sustained growth in productivity, competitiveness and living standards.[19] One exception was Flaherty's decision to remove the preferred tax status of income trusts – discussed later in the chapter.

However, the Harper Conservatives had few political incentives to follow such expert advice – reflecting both electoral imperatives and the political business cycle. As a minority government, the Conservatives required the support of marginal voters – particularly in major urban regions such as Toronto and Vancouver – to secure the additional 30 to 40 seats necessary to elect a majority government, failing a collapse of the Bloc Quebecois vote in Quebec.

Previous changes to the tax system have taken steadily larger proportions of tax filers off the income tax rolls. In recent years, about 30 per cent of Canadians filing tax returns – mainly people earning less than $20,000 a year – pay no income tax whatsoever.[20] As noted in Table 3, the 50.2 per cent of actual taxpayers who earned less than $35,000, the threshold for the second income tax bracket – generated only 13 per cent of federal PIT receipts in 2004. As a result, it becomes increasingly difficult to "buy" political support

Table 3
Distribution of Tax Returns, Personal Income, Taxes Paid, and Average Rates by Income Class – 2004 (%)

2004 tax year	0–$35,000	$35,000–$70,000	$70,000–$100,000	Over $100,000
Total returns	55.4	25.0	6.0	3.6
Taxable returns	50.2	36.0	8.6	5.2
Taxable income[a]	28.7	36.4	14.1	20.8
Federal PIT paid	13.1	35.1	17.3	34.5
Provincial PIT paid	10.1	32.5	17.8	39.6
Total PIT paid	12.3	34.4	17.4	35.9
Avg. fed. PIT rate	5.9	12.6	16.0	21.6
Avg. prov. PIT rate	1.8	4.5	6.3	9.5
Avg. total PIT rate	(7.7)	(17.0)	(22.3)	(31.1)

[a] Taxable returns only.
Source: Canada Revenue Agency, Income Statistics 2006: 2004 Tax Year, Table 2, author's calculations
Available at: http://www.cra-arc.gc.ca/agency/stats/gb04/pst/interim/pdf/table2-e.pdf

through PIT cuts to lower income earners – most of whom pay a significantly larger share of their incomes in payroll and sales taxes, together with clawbacks in refundable tax credits targeted towards lower and middle income earners. Reductions in the GST provide a proportionately greater benefit to lower- and middle-income earners – particularly those who pay little or no federal income tax.

Secondly, prolonged economic growth and fiscal surpluses have undermined public support for the fiscal austerity that underpinned the recovery of federal and most provincial finances during the 1990s and early 2000s. Generalized prosperity and buoyant public sector revenues tend to increase public expectations of higher spending – particularly on services and transfers directed towards the broader middle class. This trend has been reflected in the fiscal performance of most Canadian governments – particularly in the larger provinces in which federal elections are usually decided.

However, these political pressures have been partially offset by the growing impact of longer-term economic trends on politically important segments of the Canadian economy. In particular, Ontario's manufacturing sector, damaged by major shifts in Canada-US exchange rates and rapidly growing imports from China and other emerging economies, has suffered significant layoffs during the past two years, even though overall unemployment levels in most of Canada remained at or near 30 year lows throughout 2006 and 2007.

These pressures are seen to be harbingers of the structural changes noted in the introduction that are challenging the Harper government to address longer-term issues of capital formation and competitiveness in the corporate tax system. Media headlines have tended to focus on the symptoms of these challenges – the rapid growth in income trust conversions (until October 2006) and growing numbers of foreign takeovers of Canadian-based firms – rather than their underlying causes.

Flaherty's November 2006 economic statement, *Advantage Canada*, reflected a partial restatement of Finance department officials' assessment of Canada's long-term economic challenges, including Canada's relatively high income tax rates – especially for upper-income earners and major businesses, the need for higher rates of business investment, growing competition from emerging economies, and the long-term effects of population aging on economic growth, labour shortages, and fiscal constraints.[21] Flaherty promised to use interest savings from ongoing debt repayment to reduce income taxes for all Canadians and, over the longer-term, to "achieve the lowest tax rate on new business investment in G7 countries."[22]

Flaherty's decision to speed up corporate tax reductions in his October 2007 economic statement, and to announce longer-term CIT reductions suggest a two-tier strategy. On one hand, he has borrowed parts of the federal Liberals' agenda for incremental, broadly-based PIT reductions, subject to overall fiscal performance. On the other, he has adopted a more assertive strategy to reduce and restructure business taxes over several years.

STRUCTURAL ECONOMIC CHANGES AND THE POLITICS OF BUSINESS TAXATION

Discussions of business taxation have focused on four major issues in recent years: overall tax rates on capital income relative to other countries, efforts to increase the relative efficiency and equity of existing business taxes – both federal and provincial, and changing provisions of investment income taxes on individuals and businesses that create major incentives for both domestic and international tax shifting and avoidance. For the most part, these discussions suggest that both think tanks and business groups recognize that political realities and constraints, as well as the demands of other elements of an evolving "competitiveness agenda," require an incremental approach rather than sweeping changes to tax policies.

The 1998 report of the Technical Committee on Business Taxation noted that the corporate income tax serves three main purposes: "helping to insure that income is subject to current taxation ... ensur(ing) that foreign investors pay a Canadian tax on corporate income earned ... and ensur(ing) that corporations pay for the benefits derived by them from services provided by governments."[23]

It has been a relatively fixed principle of Canadian business tax policies since the 1970s that marginal CIT rates on Canadian manufacturers should be competitive with those in the United States to reduce incentives for firms to service North American markets from U.S. rather than Canadian facilities, all other factors being equal. As a result, Canadian governments attempting to reduce deficits and provide more stable revenue sources imposed or increased a variety of other taxes affecting businesses during the 1980s and 1990s.

Some of these taxes – including property, social insurance, gasoline taxes and provincial resource royalties – recognize benefits and services provided to businesses. Others, such as federal and provincial capital taxes, were based directly on capital invested rather than levels of profitability. The Technical Committee report noted that federal and provincial CITs accounted for only 22 per cent of overall taxes paid by corporations in 1995 – although that figure has undoubtedly grown given increases in overall levels of profitability during the past decade.[24] As noted in Table 1, rising corporate profits have enabled governments to increase their CIT revenues significantly.

After 2000, as noted earlier, the Liberals reduced cumulative business tax rates from their peaks of the late 1990s, broadly paralleling some European and Asian countries. Chen and Mintz note that marginal effective tax rates for Canadian corporations – the combined effect of general tax rates and particular tax preferences on each additional dollar of profit – dropped an average of 17 per cent from 44.3 per cent in 1997 to 36.6 per cent in 2006. Subsequent tax reductions would have reduced this figure to 33.5 per cent by 2010. However, despite these measures, effective Canadian rates on capital remained relatively high by international standards.[25]

Even so, the contemporary economic literature emphasizes that taxation is only one of several factors affecting productivity, competitiveness, and economic growth. Others include issues of governance and regulatory efficiency, infrastructure, education and related issues of labour productivity, and openness to trade and investment.[26] These ideas are reflected in the 2007 budget's extension of the previous government's policies of direct and transfer-based support for infrastructure – projected at between $4.5 and $5.6 billion annually over the next seven years, along with selection investment partnerships with the private sector. They are also reflected in Finance Minister Flaherty's ongoing efforts to develop a national framework for securities regulation and enforcement as part of a broader capital markets policy framework contained in the budget.[27]

These initiatives speak not only to current issues of delivering government services or a stable environment for economic activity, but also the challenges facing both businesses and governments in adapting to the changing dynamics of domestic and international markets resulting from Canada's growing integration within the North American and global economies. Both the rapid increases in foreign investment, incoming *and* outgoing, and the emergence of income trusts as a major component of Canada's business sector in recent years, have demonstrated the ways in which markets often function independently of government policies – and often in ways not anticipated by policy-makers.

The fiscal policies of both federal Liberal and Conservative governments in recent years have suggested that Finance Department officials accept many of the economic arguments for business tax reforms – if as a secondary priority subordinated to short-term political pressures and longer-term commitments to debt reduction and fiscal sustainability. The 2000 tax reduction budget began the twin processes of reducing overall CIT rates and lowering the general CIT rate to the lower level historically reserved for manufacturers – albeit over four years. Similar, "over-the-horizon" tax reductions were promised by Liberal Finance Minister Ralph Goodale before the Martin government's defeat in January 2006 – and subsequently by the Harper Conservatives.

Issues of efficiency were addressed by the promised elimination of the federal corporate capital tax which, as a tax that applies without regard to profitability, was a major priority of academic tax economists. Although this tax was finally removed by Flaherty's 2006 budget, his 2007 budget went a step further by offering to refund to provinces any additional revenues received by Ottawa as a result of provinces eliminating *their* capital taxes, most of which are deductible against federal income taxes. While several provinces had already initiated this process, by the end of the 2007 budget season, all provinces had committed to eliminate their capital taxes (at least on non-financial corporations) by 2012.[28]

In another piece of unfinished business from the GST reforms of the early 1990s, Flaherty also appealed to provinces to eliminate their sales taxes on business inputs – possibly by harmonizing their sales tax systems with those of the federal government: a measure already taken by Quebec and three Atlantic provinces.[29] If implemented, this proposal would complement federal business tax proposals by eliminating provincial sales taxes on business purchases – a savings equivalent to an average 6.2 percentage point reduction in METRs on business investment.

Media reports suggest that Ottawa is contemplating the creation of a $5 billion reserve to "compensate" the five provinces that currently levy retail sales taxes (Ontario, British Columbia, Saskatchewan, Manitoba, and PEI) for harmonizing their sales taxes with the GST. However, as this sum only covers two-thirds of prospective provincial revenue losses, while requiring provinces to impose new sales taxes on a wide range of services currently taxed by Ottawa and GST-compliant provinces, political progress towards this goal is likely to be slow.[30] These realities may well explain Flaherty's decision to announce the second phase of his promised GST cut – to 5 per cent – in his October 2007 economist statement, rather than making it contingent upon the outcome of protracted negotiations with the provinces.

However, two other sets of issues have proven rather more controversial and difficult to resolve: the proliferation of income trusts as vehicles for Canadian companies to reduce their financing and tax costs, primarily for domestically-based firms, and the financing of foreign affiliates of Canadian-based multinationals.

As noted in previous editions of *How Ottawa Spends*, Ottawa's benign neglect turned the taxation of income trusts into the hottest potato of Canadian public finance during the Liberals' last two years in power.[31] The rapid growth of Canadian MNCs during the 1990s also raised growing concerns over perverse incentives to engage in tax arbitrage by organizing business activities across several countries to allocate costs to relatively high tax jurisdictions, including Canada, while reporting profits in lower-tax countries whose tax treaties with Canada reduced the likelihood of double taxation.

These activities reflect several major trends in Canadian corporate organization and finance. A combination of regulatory reforms, beginning in the late 1980s, falling inflation and interest rates prompted unprecedented levels of financial market innovation and a flood of capital from passive savings into equity markets in Canada, as in other industrial countries. For example, the value of Canadian-based mutual funds increased from $25 billion in 1990 to $419 billion in 2000, and $660 billion in 2006 – despite a major stock market correction in 2001–03.[32]

These trends spurred increased assertiveness from money managers and institutional investors seeking higher returns, often by challenging the performance of corporate executives and encouraging corporate takeovers or reorganizations in pursuit of greater shareholder value. Mergers and acquisitions reached record levels at the peak of the stock market boom between 1998 and 2000 and again between 2004 and mid-2007, resulting in the restructuring of several major industries – especially the North American steel industry and much of Canada's mining sector. Changes in the governance of several major public sector pension funds including the Canada Pension Plan, Quebec's Caisse de Dépôt, and the Ontario Teachers Pension Plan – with mandates to maximize returns for current and future pensioners – reinforced these trends, changing the face of Canadian corporate *and* public finance. Federal studies have suggested that about one-third of Canadian corporate assets are now controlled by pension funds and other tax-sheltered investment funds.

At the same time, Canada's growing integration within the North American and global economies led to the rapid growth of Canadian investments abroad – both *direct* investment involving controlling ownership of foreign subsidiaries or affiliates and *portfolio* investment involving smaller, non-controlling equity or debt investments. These trends were reinforced by a gradual relaxation of the limits on the share of pension and retirement savings funds that could be invested outside Canada.[33] By 1997, the total value of Canadian direct investments abroad exceeded the value of foreign direct investment (FDI) in Canada for the first time. Between 2000 and 2006, the total value of annual Canadian investment flows abroad exceeded the value of foreign investments in Canada – despite a record number of corporate takeovers by foreign firms in Canada towards the end of the cycle.[34]

These trends had several major effects on Canadian economic, regulatory and tax policies. The interests of middle-class savers and investors became increasingly central to government policy calculations, sometimes complementing the interests of corporate executives seeking to maximize profits and shareholder returns, sometime challenging those interests by forcing corporate boards to give priority to shareholder interests when considering takeover bids – whether friendly or hostile. Similarly, when regulating foreign investment or takeovers, Canadian governments had to consider the implications of their policies for Canadian firms seeking to expand in foreign markets – or to compete with foreign-based MNCs in those markets.

The rapid growth of the income trust sector – from an estimated $18 billion in 2000 to more than $170 billion by mid-2005 – was driven by two major factors: the substantially lower tax rates paid by trusts' "unitholders" compared with corporations and their shareholders, and the promise that trusts would use their "tax efficient" status to increase the share of their income paid directly to unitholders. When Liberal Finance Minister Ralph Goodale attempted to limit income trust holdings by pension funds and other retirement savings vehicles in his 2004 budget, the backlash from the financial community forced a prompt retreat. Goodale's November 2005 effort to fix the income trust problem by promising lower taxes on corporate dividends and a longer-term cut to CIT rates temporarily slowed the rate of conversions – but not financial market pressures on major firms to explore the possibility of restructuring themselves into income trusts to boost their share prices.[35]

The government faced a similar challenge in regulating major Canadian multinationals. Corporate tax rules in Europe, the United States, and other industrial countries generally accommodated the use of low-tax offshore financial centres, subject to bilateral tax treaties and financial disclosure rules to reduce the likelihood of (illegal) tax evasion. These rules generally allowed Canadian and other MNCs to write-off interest costs from money borrowed to finance the operations of foreign affiliates. At the same time, most dividends paid by foreign affiliates to Canadian firms could be repatriated tax-free to avoid double taxation of corporate income. These favourable rules reduced corporate borrowing costs, allowing Canadian MNCs to compete on more equal terms both in their foreign operations and in the growing market for corporate reorganizations and takeovers.[36]

These trends – which blurred traditional policy distinctions between personal and corporate income, domestic and foreign business operations, and between traditional and unconventional business structures – outpaced the capacity of domestic regulators and tax authorities to adapt to the new market realities. Although Flaherty respected Liberal commitments on income trusts in his first budget, he gave no signal of his intentions as both the income trust and foreign takeover booms gained momentum during the fall of 2006.

TRICK OR TREAT? INCOME TRUSTS AND FLAHERTY'S HALLOWE'EN SURPRISE

Before taking office in January 2006, the federal Conservatives had deftly exploited debates over the future of income trusts to position themselves as defenders of the small investor – particularly seniors dependent on income trusts for much of their retirement incomes. However, when some of Canada's largest corporations including Telus and BCE announced plans to convert to income trusts valued at $22 and 27 billion, respectively, Finance Minister Flaherty acted decisively. After markets closed on October 31, 2006, he announced legislation to halt future income trust conversions and begin the process of phasing-out most trusts' preferred tax status over four years.[37] In partial compensation to older investors, he also announced the introduction of pension splitting for seniors and other "tax fairness" measures noted earlier in this chapter. The result was panic selling in stock markets as trusts lost $26 billion, or an average of 13 per cent of their market value, within two weeks – although the effects on individual companies varied widely.[38]

Flaherty's announcement – which stressed the protection of federal revenues against growing leakage from income trusts – received mixed reviews. Most independent economists, newspaper editorials, and many corporate executives responded positively, arguing that many income trust conversions owned more to tax considerations and pressures for higher after-tax returns from institutional shareholders than sound business principles – and that Flaherty deserved credit for taking a tough political decision, despite its impact on major Conservative-leaning constituencies.[39] Existing restrictions on income-trust like vehicles in other countries gave Flaherty the freedom to apply his new rules to most sectors – real estate excepted – without affecting Canada's international competitiveness.[40]

But many small investors and income trusts executives responded with fury at the government's betrayal of its election promises. The newly formed Canadian Association of Income Trust Investors took out a series of sharply worded full-page newspaper ads to mobilize public opposition against the measure. Seeking to exploit this political opportunity, the federal Liberals proposed a slower phase-out for income trusts, possibly including exemptions for energy firms, which had made extensive use of the trust structure.[41] However, although the Commons' Finance Committee held hearings on the measure that allowed the industry to challenge federal Finance department projections of revenue losses, estimated at $600 million annually, the Conservatives headed off the Liberal challenge with support from other opposition parties.

By late-2007, the income trust sector had regained much of its market value lost after Flaherty's coup. A CIBC World Markets study indicated that average price of business trusts (outside the real estate, energy and utilities sectors) actually increased by 9.3 per cent between October 2006 and September 2007 despite the initial effects of policy changes.[42] Ironically, many of these gains resulted from takeovers by Canadian or foreign firms, financed by borrowed funds. Moreover, BCE's aborted conversion to an income trust triggered a successful $51 billion takeover bid led by the Ontario Teachers' Pension Plan – suggesting that Flaherty had plugged one form of revenue leakage, only to open the door to others.[43]

The income trust incident demonstrated the rapid adaptability of capital markets to changing regulatory and tax rules – and the growing challenges facing Canadian governments in sustaining current levels of corporate tax collection in the face of the growing mobility of capital and record levels of corporate takeovers.

TRICK OR TRUMP? PLAYING FOR TIME ON INTEREST DEDUCTIBILITY

The 1998 report of the Technical Committee on Business Taxation noted that "as corporate tax rates are pushed above international norms, multinational businesses will have an increasing incentive to structure operations so that income is assigned to other countries and costs are assigned to Canada. This would appear to be particularly true with respect to interest costs. High rates thus have the potential to erode the tax base and there is evidence that the Canadian corporate income tax base has experienced such erosion during the last decade."[44] These observations would appear to be reinforced by international investment statistics indicating that four of the ten largest destinations for foreign investment by Canadian firms since 2000 have been Barbados, Bermuda, the Cayman Islands and the Bahamas.[45] The Technical Committee recommended several steps to facilitate lower corporate tax rates including the elimination of tax preferences providing disproportionate benefits to particular sectors to "encourag(e) businesses to maximize economic opportunities rather than minimize taxes."[46]

Among other things, it noted the desirability in theory of both "capital export neutrality" and "capital import neutrality" – so that firms operating both in Canada and abroad could pay the same levels of taxation on equivalent amounts of income. It suggested the elimination of withholding taxes on investment income earned by foreign firms and investors as an incentive for higher levels of foreign investment in Canada. However, it also noted that applying these principles could reduce the competitiveness of Canadian businesses operating abroad particularly "when foreign taxes are less than Canadian tax on income earned from abroad" and well as reducing the benefits to Canadians from the activities of such firms.[47] Statistics Canada estimated the total sales of Canadian firms' foreign affiliates at $385 billion in 2005.[48] Even so, the Technical Committee concluded that the deductibility of interest for larger firms should be restricted to the proportion of a company's assets located in Canada, despite significant administrative challenges and the potential for large-scale tax avoidance.[49]

Following his attack on income trusts, Finance Minister Jim Flaherty announced plans to take action against the use of foreign tax havens.[50] His March 2007 budget included significant restrictions on the deductibility of interest used to finance offshore investments, to be phased in over three years, along with plans to toughen information sharing rules in future tax treaties with other countries.[51] Flaherty defended the measures on the grounds of tax fairness – arguing that firms operating abroad should not be allowed to "double dip" by claiming interest deductions both in Canada and in low-tax foreign countries. The budget also provided for the phasing out of withholding taxes on foreign investment income.

However, the measures triggered a storm of outrage from business executives, who argued that interest deductibility was a vital factor in allowing them to compete in the international takeover market, as well as from leading tax policy experts. Len Farber, a former senior tax policy official now in private practice, argued that the measures were totally inconsistent with broader policies intended to promote international competitiveness – particularly during a period of record foreign takeovers of Canadian firms. Former Technical Committee Chair Jack Mintz noted that the budget had overlooked its proposal to provide a long transition period to limit possible effects on existing business activity.[52]

Following a series of contradictory explanations and "clarifications," Flaherty backtracked in mid-May, 2007 by referring the measures to a committee of outside experts – suggesting that the new "Anti-Tax Haven Initiative" would be implemented by 2012.[53] Although it is doubtful that much of the Canadian public followed this debate over arcane matters of corporate finance and tax policy, the flap over interest deductibility seriously eroded Flaherty's credibility in business and financial circles. Draft legislation released in October 2007, which confirmed the government's intention to eliminate existing "double dip" arrangements by 2011, were sharply criticized by business groups as likely to result of higher taxes of $1–2 billion annually. Ironically, the greater value of the Canadian tax deduction – due to Canada's higher marginal tax rates – may well result in foreign governments taking advantage of much of this windfall.[54]

The policy trade-offs and conflicts associated with both the interest deductibility issue and Flaherty's broader agenda of encouraging Canada's growing competitiveness and integration in global capital markets are unlikely to go away. Flaherty's approach to international tax policies appears to draw on OECD initiatives to limit individual and corporate tax avoidance through a combination of cooperative action among industrial countries and more restrictive tax treaties. His approach to capital market harmonization appears to involve the negotiation of mutual recognition agreements with the EU and US, while moving towards the creation of a pan-Canadian system of capital markets regulation more reminiscent of British than American regulatory models – although recent writings by SEC officials suggest that this could be a more complicated process than previously anticipated.[55] Finally, a task force appointed by Flaherty in July 2007 to review Canadian policies governing foreign investments, large-scale foreign takeovers, and related issues of competition policy will face major challenges in balancing the interests of internationally competitive Canadian businesses, Canadian business interests fearful of foreign takeovers, and financial sector firms and investors – who play *both* sides of the street for fun and profit.

THE OCTOBER 2007 ECONOMIC STATEMENT: A TAX CUT IN HAND IS WORTH TWO IN THE BUSH

By the middle of 2007, the Harper government had largely implemented the major policy commitments from its 2006 election campaign. However, it had not yet spelled out a clear, forward-looking agenda that could justify an appeal to the electorate for a majority government, or provide a politically viable program for governing under the constraints of a minority government.

However, with the federal Liberals in disarray following by-election losses in Quebec, persistent internal sniping at the leadership of Stéphane Dion, and poll results suggesting the possibility of a Conservative majority should the government be defeated in Parliament, Harper deftly exploited these divisions to drive several pieces of legislation through the Commons, including a late-October economic statement containing substantial, broadly based tax cuts. Ironically, the new Conservative tax plan not only included previous commitments to reduce the GST by an additional percentage point to 5 per cent, but several parts of the Liberals' emerging tax plan.

Dion and his Finance critic, former bank economist John MacCallum, echoing the concerns of major business groups, had embraced the conventional economic critique of Flaherty's promised GST cuts. (Indeed, *The Globe and Mail* commissioned a survey of 20 business, labour and academic economists shortly after the Throne Speech, which was highly critical of the plan.) Dion's response to the fall Throne Speech also committed the Liberals to expand corporate tax reductions already promised by the Conservatives.[56]

However, high levels of employment, personal and corporate tax revenues boosted federal surpluses sufficiently – to $13.6 billion in 2006–07 and a projected $11.8 billion in 2007–08 – for Flaherty to trump the Liberal proposals in his economic statement of late October 2007 while committing $23 billion to debt repayment over the two years. (See Table 4.)

Table 4
Cutting up the Cash: October 2007 (in billions of dollars)

	2006–07	2007–08[b]	2008–09[b]
March 2007 Underlying Surplus	9.2	3.3	3.0
Impact of projected revenue changes	3.7	12.1	1.6
Impact of projected spending changes	0.7	1.3	–0.8
Public debt charges	0.2	–0.2	
Revised surplus	13.8[a]	16.4	13.8
Measures announced in Econ. Statement	–	–4.8	–9.4
Planned Debt Reduction		–10.0	–3.0
Planning surplus		1.6	1.4

[a] Allocated to debt reduction.
[b] Projected.
Source: Department of Finance, *Economic Statement: 2007* (30 October), 43.

In essence, Flaherty's tax measures turned both Liberal flanks. A mixture of broadly based tax reductions – the GST cut, a reversion of the lowest personal tax rate from 15.5 to 15 per cent, and a one-year acceleration of promised increases of the basic personal exemption (the income threshold for PIT payments) – targeted the bulk of tax benefits to lower and middle-income earners. The PIT cuts, valued at $4.8 billion in 2007–08, were applied retroactively – providing a small benefit to most taxpayers almost immediately, along with the prospect of a bigger tax rebate in the spring of 2008. The GST cut accounted for about three-quarters of the $7.9 billion in personal tax reductions scheduled for 2008–09.[57]

However, while flaunting his "broadly based" tax cuts, Flaherty has maintained the value of GST credits and rebates by continuing to base their calculation on values equivalent to a 7 per cent GST rate. The result is a cumulative annual tax transfer to low-income earners of $1.1 billion, to new home buyers of $290 million, and to broader public sector entities such as schools, universities, and hospitals of $165 million.

Flaherty also accelerated planned reduction of corporate income taxes – cutting both the general corporate rate and the small business rate by 1 per cent to 19.5 per cent and 11 per cent respectively in 2008, and ultimately to 15 per cent in 2012. (See Table 5.) These measures were valued at $1.5 billion in 2008–09. Fiscal projections estimated a 4.1 per cent average annual spending growth during the coming five years – although such projections are notoriously unreliable and subject to both economic and political shifts. Technical documents tabled with the minister's statement indicated that the

Table 5
Corporate Income Tax Rate Reductions

	2007	2008	2009	2010	2011	2012
Existing CIT rates	22.12	20.5	20.0	19.0	18.5	18.5
Proposed CIT rates	22.12	19.5	19.0	18.5	16.5	15.0

Source: Department of Finance. *Economic Statement 2007*, 75.

Table 6
Repositioning Canadian Business Taxes in the Global Economy Projected METRs on New Business Investment on Selected Country Groups, 2012 (%)

United States (current and projected)	34.4
Canada prior to 2006 budget	33.3
Canada prior to Oct. 2007 Economic Statement	27.7
Lowest in G-7 prior to Economic Statement	27.1 (Italy)
Including Measures in Economic Statement	25.5
Canada – if fed-prov CIT rates reduced to 25%	23.7
OECD average	21.8
Small Developed Countries Average[a]	20.8
Provincial Retail Sales Tax Harmonization + Fed-Prov CIT rate of 25%	16.4

[a] Includes Australia, Austria, Denmark, Finland, Greece, Hong Kong, Iceland, Ireland, Luxembourg, the Netherlands, New Zealand, Norway, S. Korea, Spain, Sweden and Switzerland.
Source: Department of Finance. *Economic Statement 2007*, 80.

private sector economic projections on which these figures are based vary widely – and are subject to considerable uncertainties.

Flaherty emphasized the government's commitment to a package of tax changes – several previously announced – that would lower METRs on Canadian businesses to the lowest level in the G-7 – a projected 25.5 per cent in 2012, even without further provincial actions. (See Table 6.)

Faced with the competing demands for the disposition of high and growing projected surpluses in the months leading up to its next budget, the federal government deftly preempted the debate by introducing its enabling legislation to allocate most of its projected surplus to debt and tax reduction. While not fully addressing business concerns over the deductibility of offshore interest payments, the Harper government's agenda has sought to reposition Canada from being a relatively high-tax jurisdiction to a relatively low-tax one capable of competing with other advanced industrial countries for foreign investment. However, the deferral of the largest business tax cuts until 2011 and 2012 allows the government to suggest that individuals will benefit from 75 per cent of the value of tax cuts over the next five years, with about 25 per cent going to businesses.

CONCLUSION

The initial tax policies of the Harper government were widely portrayed as a triumph of politics over economics. Its quasi-populist approach to targeted tax cuts, GST reduction, and subsequent attempts to trumpet its policy reversals on income trusts and the deductibility of offshore interest payments as part of a broader commitment to "tax fairness" not only confronted the received wisdom of most business and tax economists, but put it at cross-purposes with many of its upper-middle income supporters and significant elements of the business community.

However, during the past year, the government has deftly repositioned itself across the broad centre of the political spectrum – with considerable assistance from its Liberal opponents and the continuing flood of revenues generated by Canada's service and resource sectors. Personal tax policies continue to be driven largely by considerations of distributive politics: whether in the form of broadly-based PIT cuts targeted at middle-income earners, income splitting for pensioners, GST reductions, or the maintenance of refundable GST credits at levels higher than would be warranted by a "neutral" policy. These changes suggest that the progressivity of Canada's personal income tax system will continue to increase – with the top 20 per cent of income earners generating an even larger share of federal tax revenues.

At the same time, the Harperites have largely co-opted the tax reduction agenda of business-oriented think tanks such as the C.D. Howe Institute and the Conference Board of Canada – partially if not fully offsetting the effects of its 2007 budget changes to the taxation of international investment income. However, its decision to cut the GST before negotiating any further sales tax harmonization with provinces deprives it of a useful bargaining chip: the possibility that a tax transfer could help provinces offset potential revenue losses. As a result, any progress on this file is likely to be incremental, at best. The government's discussion paper on foreign investment and competition policies,[58] released on the same day as the economic statement, suggests a strongly market-oriented response to the challenges of international competition – while stretching out consultations on these issues long enough to maintain control of debate on the issue.

The politics of fiscal and tax policies dictate, above all, that the federal government be able to retain as much discretion as possible given the vagaries of a minority government, the economic effects of an overvalued currency, and multiple sources of economic uncertainty. The government's priorities on personal income taxes have been dictated primarily by domestic political factors. However, its actions on corporate and investment tax issues seem to owe more to its determination to control the allocation of whatever tax reductions can be built into future budgets (and the political credit that goes with them), rather than contracting the job out to private sector tax professionals, financial markets, or the political whims of provincial governments.

Although tax experts constantly remind those willing to listen that personal and corporate tax systems are deeply intertwined, creating potential opportunities for large-scale tax avoidance, the government appears to have regained control over the public agenda, while taking advantage of a fragmented opposition through skilful political triangulation. It has shown considerable creativity in providing incentives to provincial governments to cooperate with federal changes to the tax system – particularly in phasing out growth-hindering capital taxes on business.

By defying conventional wisdom, both political and economic, the Harper government has succeeded both in defining itself, adapting to changing circumstances, and securing enough political manoevering room to govern effectively – despite the constraints imposed by a minority parliament. It continues to face the challenges it has inherited from the Liberals on taking office – magnified by the unpredictable effects of the U.S. dollar's unprecedented collapse. However, for the moment, it appears to be managing those challenges with a combination of luck and skill, rather than merely reacting to them or drifting with events.

NOTES

1 For example, see David Laidler, ed., *Approaches to Economic Well-Being* (Toronto: University of Toronto Press, 1986); Allan M. Maslove, *Tax Reform in Canada: The Process and Impact*, (Montreal: Institute for Research on Public Policy, 1989), 12–15; Geoffrey Hale, *The Politics of Taxation in Canada* (Peterborough, ON: Broadview Press, 2001), 37–61.
2 In 2005–06, before GST reductions announced in the 2006 budget, the federal government collected $46.2 billion in consumption taxes, or 20.8 per cent of its total revenues: 71.7 per cent from the GST, 10.9 per cent from energy taxes, 6.7 per cent from customs duties, and the balance from other excise taxes and duties, including air travel security charges. Canada, *Annual Financial Report of the Government of Canada* (Ottawa: Department of Finance, September 2006).
3 Department of Finance, *Fiscal Reference Tables* (Ottawa: Department of Finance, September 2006), Table 5.
4 Maximilian Baylor, "Ranking Tax Distortions in Dynamic General Equilibrium Models: A Survey," Working Paper 2005–06. (Ottawa: Department of Finance, 2005).
5 Maslove, *Tax Reform in Canada*, 16–20.

6 The Mulroney government purchased business support for its modest income tax reforms of 1987–88, financed by net increases in effective corporate tax rates, by promises of sales tax reform. The latter, while economically successful (and unavoidable), prompted a massive political backlash. Hale, *Politics of Taxation in Canada*, 207–22.
7 Canada. *Report of the Technical Committee on Business Taxation* (Ottawa: Department of Finance, 1998).
8 Geoffrey E. Hale, "The Tax on Income and the Growing Decentralization of Canada's Personal Income Tax System," in Harvey Lazar, ed., *State of the Federation: 2000–01 – Towards a New Mandate for Fiscal Federalism* (Montreal and Kingston, McGill-Queen's University Press, 2000), 263–92.
9 For example, see Baylor, "Ranking Tax Distortions"; Jack M. Mintz, *The 2006 Tax Competitiveness Report*, Commentary # 239 (Toronto: C.D. Howe Institute, September 2006); Conference Board of Canada, *How Canada Performs: A Report Card on Canada* (Ottawa: Conference Board of Canada, 2007), 40–50.
10 Canada had been one of the few advanced industrial countries to eliminate universal family benefits *and* tax preferences in favour of a more targeted regime in the early 1990s.
11 Department of Finance, *The Budget Plan 2006: Focusing on Priorities* (Ottawa: Department of Finance, 2 May 2006), 12–15.
12 Flaherty also promised to eliminate the corporate income surtax, most recently introduced in 1989 as a "deficit reduction" measure, by January 2008.
13 Geoffrey E. Hale, "Trading Up or Treading Water: Federal Fiscal and Budgetary Policies in Search of a New Mandate," in G. Bruce Doern, ed., *How Ottawa Spends: 2006–07* (Montreal and Kingston: McGill-Queen's University Press), 27–49.
14 Bill Curry, "Finance added cars eligible for green incentives," *The Globe and Mail*, 24 March 2006.
15 Department of Finance, *The Budget Plan 2007: Aspire to a Stronger, Safer, Better Canada* (Ottawa: Department of Finance, 19 March 2007), 25.
16 Department of Finance, "Canada's New Government introduces tax fairness plan," Release # 2006–061 (Ottawa: Department of Finance, 31 October 2006). Available at http://www.fin.gc.ca/news06/06-061e.html; accessed 26 January 2008.
17 Department of Finance, *The Budget Plan 2007*, 78–82.
18 Department of Finance, *The Budget Plan 2007*, 104–16.
19 Mintz, *Tax Competitiveness Report: 2006*; Conference Board of Canada, *How Canada Performs*; Duanjie Chen, Jack Mintz and Andrey Tarasov, "Federal and Provincial Tax Reforms: Let's Get Back on Track," *Backgrounder # 102* (Toronto: C.D. Howe Institute, July 2007).
20 Persons earning less than $20,000 accounted for 96.6 per cent of non-taxable returns in 2004. Canada Revenue Agency, *Income Statistics: 2006 – 2004 Tax Year* (Ottawa: Canada Revenue Agency, 2006), Table 2.
21 Department of Finance, *Advantage Canada: Building a Strong Economy for Canadians* (Ottawa: Department of Finance, November 2006), 19–21.
22 Department of Finance, *Advantage Canada*, 33.

23 Technical Committee on Business Taxation, 4:1
24 Technical Committee on Business Taxation, 2:19. No comparable breakdown of business taxation has been published since 1998. However, in 2004, federal and provincial CITs totaled $45.7 billion – compared with $18 billion in 1995, social insurance taxes (CPP, WCB, and EI) $36.7 billion, customs and excise taxes about $15.2 billion, resource royalties $5.5 billion, and corporate capital taxes $3.3 billion. Statistics Canada, *National Income and Expenditure Accounts* Cat. # 13–001 (Ottawa: Statistics Canada, 2007); Statistics Canada, *Financial and Taxation Statistics for Enterprises*, Cat. # 61–219 (Ottawa: Statistics Canada, February 2007), 20. These figures do not include data on two other major categories – business property taxes and provincial retail sales taxes on capital inputs. See also Janet McFarland, "Commodities boom feeds tax bonanza," *The Globe and Mail*, 12 November 2007, B1.
25 Jack M. Mintz *The Tax Competitiveness Report 2006*, 10; Duanjie Chen and Jack M. Mintz, "Federal-provincial combined marginal effective tax rates on capital: 1997–2006, 2010," (Toronto: C.D. Howe Institute, 20 June 2006).
26 For extensive discussions of these issues, see the World Economic Forum's annual *Global Competitiveness Reports* (http://www.weforum.org/en/initiatives/gcp/index.htm) and the analyses of Ontario's Institute for Competitiveness and Prosperity. (www.competeprosper.ca)
27 Department of Finance, *The Budget Plan: 2007*, 161–71; Department of Finance, *Creating a Canadian Advantage in Global Capital Markets* (Ottawa: Department of Finance, 19 March 2007); available at: http://www.budget.gc.ca/2007/pdf/bkcmae.pdf; accessed 26 January 2008.
28 The budget measures made an exception for capital taxes on financial institutions, subject to their conversion to a new "minimum tax" meeting certain federal specifications. Department of Finance, *The Budget Plan: 2007*, 440–41; Chen, Mintz and Tarasov, "Federal and provincial tax reforms."
29 Department of Finance, *Advantage Canada*, 75–8.
30 John Ivison, "One sales tax on table," *National Post*, 19 October 2007, A1; Paul Vieira, "Next budget may harmonize sales taxes," *Financial Post*, 1 November 2007, FP6.
31 Hale "Trading up or treading water," 27–49.
32 Investment Funds Institute of Canada (www.ific.ca)
33 The Martin government eliminated these restrictions in 2005. As a result, offshore investments by pension and mutual funds averaged about one-third of their portfolios by 2007 – about the level forecast by industry observers.
34 Michael Hart, *Canadian Engagement in the Global Economy* (Montreal: Institute for Research in Public Policy, September 2007), 186; Geoffrey Hale, "The Dog That Hasn't Barked: Contemporary Debates on Canadian Foreign Investment Policies," April, mimeo, April 2007.
35 Geoffrey Hale, "Income Trusts: what will Ottawa do?" (Lethbridge, AB: www.policy.ca, September 2005); Hale "Trading Up or Treading Water?"
36 Robert D. Brown and Finn Poschmann, *On Taxes and Foreign Investment, Flaherty's Aim is Off* (Toronto: C.D. Howe Institute, 7 May 2007). The Technical Committee

report noted that the details of foreign tax rules vary widely, with some countries, including Australia and the Netherlands, having reduced or eliminated deductibility for interest borrowed to finance foreign affiliates. Technical Committee on Business Taxation 6:11.

37 www.canada.com, "Transcript on Jim Flaherty on coming changes to how the government handles income trusts," 31 October 2006; Steven Chase, "Flaherty drops bomb on income trusts," *The Globe and Mail*, 1 November 2006, A1; Sean Silcoff, "BCE put gun to Ottawa's head," *Financial Post*, 2 November 2006, FP1. Other news reports suggested that energy giant EnCana Corporation was seriously considering an income trust conversation for some or all of its assets – valued at more than $40 billion. Sinclair Stewart, Andrew Willis and David Ebner (2006), "EnCana's trust plans triggered crackdown," *The Globe and Mail*, 4 November 2006, A1.

38 Jack Bernstein, "Income trusts for sale," *Canadian Tax Highlights* 15, no. 5 (June 2007). This figure is significantly lower than the $35 billion estimate used by the Canadian Association of Income Trust Investors in its advertisements.

39 *The Toronto Star*, "Flaherty correct to close loophole," Editorial, 2 November 2006; Finn Poschmann and William Robson, "Twice bitten," *Financial Post*, 3 November 2006, FP17; Richard Blackwell, "Anger, relief over tax move," *The Globe and Mail*, 27 November 2006, B1; Derek deCloet, "Flaherty will get you nowhere," *Report on Business Magazine*, 31 August 2007, 36–43.

40 Peter Morton, "Canada alone in tolerating trusts," *Financial Post*, 2 November 2006, FP4.

41 Canadian Association of Income Trust Investors, "Lie, conceal, fabricate: Stephen Harper's $35 billion income trust scandal," 2007. Available at http://caiti-online-media.blogspot.com; accessed 26 January 2008. George Kesteven, "Trust fiasco helps hollow out Canada," *Financial Post*, 12 April 2007, FP15; John McCallum, "Dear Jim Flaherty ...," *National Post*, 3 January 2007, A10; Derek DeCloet, "'Half-baked' trust plan won't do it for Grits," *The Globe and Mail*, 31 May 2007, B2; Steven Chase and Norval Scott, "Liberals float lifting moratorium on trusts," *The Globe and Mail*, 5 September 2007, B1.

42 Carrie Tait, "Was it a trick or a treat," *Financial Post*, 27 October 2007, FP3.

43 Steven Chase, "Trust tax under fire as drain on revenue," *The Globe and Mail*, 9 April 2007; Paul Vieira, "Flaherty's tax conundrum," *Financial Post*, 18 April 2007, FP3; Heather Scoffield, "Trusts going for a premium," *The Globe and Mail*, 1 May 2007, B3; Sean Silcoff, "Teachers VP says trust decision set up Bell deal," *Financial Post*, 3 July 2007, FP8.

44 Technical Committee on Business Taxation, 3:28.

45 Francois Lavoie, *Canadian Direct Investment in Offshore Financial Centres*, Cat. # 11–621, # 021 (Ottawa: Statistics Canada, March 2003), 2.

46 Technical Committee on Business Taxation, 4:1.

47 Technical Committee on Business Taxation, 6:2–3..

48 Statistics Canada, "Foreign Affiliate Trade Statistics: 2005," *The Daily*, 7 June, 2007.

49 Technical Committee on Business Taxation, 6:11–18.

50 Eric Beauchesne, "Now Flaherty clamps down on offshore tax havens," *Financial Post*, 10 November 2007, FP1.
51 Department of Finance, *The Budget Plan: 2007*, 239–44; 419ff.
52 Steven Chase, "Business warns new tax will cost billions, not millions," *The Globe and Mail*, 13 April 2007, B1; Steven Chase, "KPMG sees 'exodus' over killed tax break," *The Globe and Mail*, 23 April 2007, B5; Janet McFarland and Steven Chase, "Flaherty chided on business tax, hints at change," *The Globe and Mail*, 25 April 2007, B1.
53 Steven Chase, "'Besieged' Flaherty to rework plan to cut tax break," *The Globe and Mail*, 7 May 2007, B1; Paul Vieira, "Flaherty flip sparks confusion," *Financial Post*, 15 May 2007, FP4; Terence Corcoran, "Flaherty's double dip," *Financial Post*, 17 May 2007, FP19.
54 Steven Chase, "Revamped tax plan angers business," *The Globe and Mail*, 11 October 2007.
55 Ethiopis Tafara, Robert J. Peterson, "A Blueprint for Cross-Border Access to U.S. Investors: A New International Framework," 48 Harvard International Law Journal 31 (2007); online at: http://www.harvardilj.org/ online/90; James C. Baillie and Edward J. Waitzer, "Opening borders," *Financial Post*, 11 September 2007, FP15.
56 Paul Vieira, "Dion would wield tax axe to spur growth," *National Post*, 11 September 2007, FP1; Perrin Beatty, "All taxes aren't created equal," *Financial Post*, 3 October, FP19; Tavia Grant, "Tories rebuked on GST," *The Globe and Mail*, 25 October, B1; Andrew Coyne, "Stéphane Dion, tax cutter," *National Post*, 17 October, A18.
57 Department of Finance, *Economic Statement: 2007* (Ottawa: Department of Finance, 30 October 2007), 45.
58 Competition Policy Review Panel, *Sharpening Canada's Competitive Edge* (Ottawa: Industry Canada, 30 October 2007).

4 Potential for a Regulatory Breakthrough? Regulatory Governance and Human Resource Initiatives

BARRY STEMSHORN
AND ROBERT W. SLATER

INTRODUCTION

Over the past year regulatory issues have drawn significant public and political attention in areas as diverse as nuclear safety, telecommunications, securities regulation and the safety of imported toys and foods. Yet in a comprehensive review of Canada's regulatory system Doern observed that regulations are rarely subject to the systematic priority setting and high level analysis, debate and scrutiny that are applied to taxation and spending.[1] Indeed regulatory matters are frequently managed as technical issues rather than as political priorities deserving of sustained attention in spite of the fact that an efficient and effective regulatory system can be an important comparative advantage to nation states in an ever more competitive world.

In this chapter we look at the factors that have shaped the context within which the current Canadian government has taken some potentially significant regulatory initiatives and report on the status of those initiatives. We then describe the cadre of officials that run the Government of Canada's regulatory system, some key challenges they face and the steps that are being taken to equip them to deal with the growing demands that are being placed upon them. We argue that development of a broad array of expert and managerial skills is needed in order to achieve sustained improvements in the administration of the regulatory system and to support the essential engagement of senior officials and parliamentarians.

THE CONTEXT

Over the past 25 years, numerous proposals have been made for change to the federal regulatory system.[2] These include the Nielsen Taskforce reviews circa 1984–86, the introduction of Regulatory Impact Assessments, the 2005 report of the External Advisory Committee on Smart Regulations[3] and the most recent suite of reform initiatives set out in Budget 2007,[4] including the new cabinet Directive on Streamlining Regulations.[5]

The Smart Regulation[6] report provides the most comprehensive and recent diagnosis of the issues. This report was commissioned by the Chrétien government, received by the Martin government and provides the conceptual, if unacknowledged, framework for actions taken by the Harper government. It takes the view that "regulation in its broadest sense is equated with governing. It is a principle, rule or condition that governs the behaviour of citizens or enterprises ... [it] is used by government, in combination with other measures such as taxation, program delivery and services to achieve policies to protect the health safety and socio-economic well being of Canadians and the natural environment. Regulation encompasses statutes, subordinate legislation (regulations), ministerial orders, standards, guidelines, codes, education and information campaigns."

Most importantly the Smart Regulation report provides a current context for effective regulatory reform by recognizing three key drivers of change:

- The speed of modern society – new technologies, flow of commerce and instant access to information
- Increased complexity and new products, services or ideas that do not fit conveniently into traditional pigeon holes
- Increasing demands on government to offer freedom of choice, increased regulation, transparency and accountability.

The report argued cogently for improvements in seven main areas:

- Putting the national house in order by substantially increasing cooperation and coordination between and within federal, provincial, territorial and municipal governments
- A strategic approach to international aspects – health, environment and security matters are ever more frequently determined in international settings. Canada needs the reputation and the ability to advance the national interest whether it is a matter of ensuring food safety or challenging an inappropriate condition attached to trade with a major trading partner
- Listening to and understanding the many voices of Canadians who have particular interests at stake

- Increasing system efficiency in terms of reduced transaction time, costs and energy
- Increasing the focus on results through monitoring and reporting and using that to improve regulatory performance
- Continuous improvement of an evidence based system that provides better performance and accountability measurement and offers recourse to an independent party when normal processes fail
- Changing cultures – an area on which we will focus later in this paper.

The Smart Regulation report concluded that implementation of these changes would enable Canada to achieve its social, economic and environmental priorities; support a transition to sustainable development; improve the confidence of business and civil society in the regulatory system; and ultimately position Canada as an attractive place to do business.

One motivation for regulatory reform is concern about the increasing number, complexity and intrusiveness of regulations as governments respond to threats to public health, security, ecological integrity and financial propriety.[7] Doern has argued[8] that the scale, scope and import of regulation is such that the federal government should prepare a transparent annual regulatory agenda so that priorities and resource needs can be announced, debated and agreed upon. It is illustrative that there is no undisputed estimate of both the costs and the benefits of regulation other than that they are both very large. We identify in Table 1 the areas of regulation addressed by a number of federal Departments and Agencies; while no doubt incomplete it illustrates the broad scope, impact and the complexity of the regulatory work of the federal government. An annual regulatory agenda and coordinated reports on progress would support informed debate and research of the type that accompanies federal budgets and the resulting programs.

We believe, based on our extensive experience with regulatory Departments, that the general public has a generally positive view of the value of regulations and typically gives higher approval ratings to legal action than to alternative non legislated approaches especially when health and environment issues are concerned. Canadians also expect regulatory agencies to act prudently for the public good although they are often critical of implementation practices and have a less sanguine view of the merits of voluntary approaches conducted by the private sector itself.[9] The public can be unforgiving in the event of regulatory failures – witness the angry attacks on industry and regulatory officials involved with the contaminated blood tragedy even after the Ontario Superior Court ruled that allegations of criminal conduct were not only unsupported by the evidence, but that they were disproved.[10]

Many Canadians would be worried by the suggestion of Fels,[11] citing the work of Grabosky and Brathwaite[12] in Australia, that the most common

Table 1
Departments and their principal areas of regulation

Department/agency	Area of regulation	Acts Administered
AGRICULTURE AND AGRIFOOD PORTFOLIO		
Agriculture and Agri-Food Canada	Livestock breeds and commodity marketing	Animal pedigree Act Agricultural Products marketing Act
Canadian Dairy Commission	commodity marketing	Canadian Dairy Commission Act
Canadian Food Inspection Agency	Meat, Fish, Dairy, Other Foods, Feeds, Fertilizers, Plant and Animal Health, Plants with novel traits, Veterinary biologics,	Meat Inspection Act Health of Animals Act Plant Protection Act Fertilizers Act Feeds Act Seeds Act Canada Agricultural Products Act Fish Inspection Act Food and Drugs Act Consumer Packaging and Labeling Act Plant Breeders Rights Act Agriculture and Agri-Food Administrative Monetary Penalties Act Appropriation Acts CFIA Act
Canadian Grain Commission		Canada Grain Act
Canadian Wheat Board		Canadian Wheat Board Act
National Farm Products Council		Farm Products Marketing Agencies Act
ENVIRONMENT PORTFOLIO		
Environment Canada	Prevention and control of pollution, protection of species at risk, protection of water and migratory birds	Canadian Environmental Protection Act (CEPA) Species at Risk Act International Boundary Waters Treaty Act International River Improvements Act Canada Waters Act Fisheries Act Canada Wildlife Act Migratory Birds Convention Act
Canadian Environmental Assessment Agency	Environmental Assessments	Canadian Environmental Assessment Act

Table 1
Departments and their principal areas of regulation (*Continued*)

Department/agency	Area of regulation	Acts Administered
Parks Canada	National Parks and Historic Sites	Canada National Parks Act Canada National Marine Conservation Areas Act Heritage Railway Stations Protection Act Historic Sites and Monuments Act Species at Risk Act
FINANCE PORTFOLIO		
Finance Canada	Taxes	Income Tax Act Excise Tax Act Federal Budgets
Office of the Superintendent of Financial Institutions	Financial Institutions and Pension Plans	Bank Act Trust and Loan Companies Act Cooperative Credit Associations Act Insurance Companies Act Pension Benefits Standards Act
HEALTH PORTFOLIO		
Health Canada	Drugs Food Veterinary Drugs Medical Devices Cosmetics Natural Health Products Etc	Assisted Human Reproduction Act Canada Health Act CEPA Controlled Drugs and Substances Act Food & Drugs Act Hazardous Materials Information Review Act Hazardous Products Act Patent Act Pesticide Residue Compensation Act Quarantine Act Radiation Emitting Devices Act Tobacco Act
Pest Management Regulatory Agency	Pesticides	Pest Control Products Act
INDUSTRY PORTFOLIO		
Industry Canada	Intellectual Property Bankruptcy Technical Standards	Bankruptcy and Insolvency Act Copyrights Act Industrial Design Act Integrated Circuit Topography Act Patent Act Trade Marks Act

Table 1
Departments and their principal areas of regulation (*Continued*)

Department/agency	Area of regulation	Acts Administered
Canadian Radio and Telecommunications Commission (Industry Canada?)	Telecommunications and broadcasting	Telecommunications Act Radio Communications Act Broadcasting Act CRTC Act
Competition Bureau (Industry Canada)	Promotes and maintains fair competition	Competition Act Consumer Packaging and Labeling Act Textile Labeling Act Precious Metals Marketing Act
Corporations Canada (Industry Canada)	Federal corporations	Business Canada Corporation Act
Measurement Canada	Weights and Measures	Weights and Measures Act Electricity and Gas Inspection Act
Standards Council of Canada	Voluntary standards (alternatives or complementary to regulation)	Standards Council of Canada Act
Statistics Canada	Census and national statistics	Statistics Act
NATURAL RESOURCES PORTFOLIO		
Natural Resources Canada	Explosives	Explosives Act
Canadian Nuclear Safety Commission	Use of nuclear energy and materials	Nuclear Safety and Control Act
National Energy Board	International and inter-provincial aspects of the oil, gas and electric utility industries	National Energy Board Act
PUBLIC SAFETY PORTFOLIO		
Public Safety Canada	Firearms control	Firearms Act
Canadian Border Services Agency	Cross-border movement of people and products	Acts and regulations of Agriculture and Agri-Food Canada, Canadian Food Inspection Agency, Customs and Immigration Canada, Health Canada, Environment Canada and others

Table 1
Departments and their principal areas of regulation (*Continued*)

Department/agency	Area of regulation	Acts Administered
TRANSPORT PORTFOLIO		
Transport Canada	Aviation, marine, rail, road, and transport of dangerous goods	Aeronautics Act Air Canada Public Participation Act Arctic Waters Pollution Prevention Act Canada Marine Act Canada Shipping Act Canada Transportation Act Canadian Air Transport Security Authority Act Carriage by Air Act Civil Air Navigation Services Commercialization Act Coasting Trade Act Department of Transport Act Government Property Traffic Act International Bridges and Tunnels Act International Interests in Mobile Equipment (aircraft equipment) Act Marine Liability Act Marine Transportation Security Act Motor Vehicle Safety Act Motor Vehicle Transport Act Navigable Waters Protection Act Northumberland Strait Crossing Act Pilotage Act Railway Safety Act Safe Containers Convention Act Shipping Conferences exemption Act Transportation Appeal Tribunal of Canada Act Transportation of Dangerous Goods Act
Transportation Safety Board of Canada	Accident investigations	Canadian Transportation Accident Investigation and Safety Board Act
OTHER DEPARTMENTS AND AGENCIES		
Canadian Revenue Agency	Collect taxes	Income Tax Act Excise Tax Act
Citizenship and Immigration Canada	Immigration, citizenship and refugee programs	Citizenship Act Immigration and Refugee Act

Table 1
Departments and their principal areas of regulation (*Continued*)

Department/agency	Area of regulation	Acts Administered
Fisheries and Oceans Canada (including the Canadian Coast Guard)	Fish harvest, habitat and marketing; aquatic organisms Marine safety	Fisheries Act Canada Shipping Act Coastal Fisheries Protection Act Fishing and Recreational Harbours Act Freshwater Fish Marketing Act Great Lakes Fisheries Convention Act Oceans Act Species at Risk Act
Foreign Affairs and International Trade	Export Controls	Export and Import Permits Act
Heritage Canada	Official Languages Broadcasting Publishing Trade in Cultural Property Archives	Broadcasting Act CRTC Act Copyright Act Cultural Property Export and Import Act Foreign Publishers Advertising Services Act Investment Canada Act Library and Archives of Canada Act Official Languages Act Radiocommunications Act Telecommunications Act
Human Resources and Social Development Canada	Workplace Health and Safety, Employment Standards and Industrial Relations Employment Insurance Canada Pension and Old Age Security	Canada Labor Code, Parts I, II and III Employment Insurance Act Canada Pension Plan Act Old Age Security Act
Indian and Northern Affairs Canada	Aboriginal affairs Northern resources development	Indian Act Indian Oil and Gas Act Indian lands Agreement Act Cree-Naskapi (of Quebec) Act Arctic Waters Pollution Prevention Act Canada Petroleum Resources Act Dominion Water Power Act MacKenzie Valley Resources Management Act Northwest Territories Act Northwest Territories Water Act Nunavut Act Territorial Lands Act Yukon Surface Rights Board Act

Table 1
Departments and their principal areas of regulation (*Continued*)

Department/agency	Area of regulation	Acts Administered
Justice Canada	Firearms control Official Languages Privacy	Firearms Act Official Languages Act Privacy Act
Treasury Board Secretariat	Financial administration, Official languages, User fees Lobbyists	Financial Administration Act Official Languages Act Federal Accountability Act User Fees Act Lobbying Act

failing of regulators is to underplay their authority by relying on informal suasion to seek negotiated solutions or voluntary actions from regulated industries. Others would support such pragmatic approaches by regulators who make appropriate use of discretion to achieve outcomes through the most efficient means.

Public response to proposals for regulatory reform is mixed. In general, groups devoted to issues of health, environment and social justice tend to be cautious about such changes that may lead to deregulation to which they are unalterably opposed.[13] Those with commercial interests are generally more supportive of proposals for reform because they expect to receive tangible benefits.

In seeking to follow the progress of the "smart regulation" reforms in Canada we were disappointed to learn that the last progress report on actions to implement recommendations of the External Advisory Committee on Smart Regulations was published in 2005[14] and that it is no longer available through Internet access. That report set out a number of important initiatives of widespread interest – for example, efforts to consolidate the work of federal Departments and Agencies on environmental assessments, work to improve the timeliness of reviews of pharmaceuticals and a proposal to develop a regulatory framework to strengthen economic development for First Nations.

The Smart Regulations report provides a sound and coherent intellectual foundation for regulatory reforms, some which have been taken by the Harper government and are described below. It would be helpful to demonstrate continuity of these actions with the Smart Regulation report and to adopt a systematic approach to reporting on progress. This would help Canadians to see an orderly implementation of an important strategy rather than a collection of worthwhile but separate projects.

BUDGET 2007 AND THE 2007 SPEECH FROM THE THRONE

Budget 2007

In the 2007 Budget[15] the Government of Canada announced a suite of measures to enhance the efficiency and effectiveness of its regulatory work. The centerpiece was a new Cabinet Directive on Streamlining Regulations[16] that came into effect in April 2007. The aim is to "make Canada a best-in-class regulator by ensuring that efficiency and effectiveness are key considerations in the development and implementation of regulations. It will improve timeliness by focusing on larger, more significant regulatory proposals, hold the government to account by establishing service standards, and create pressure for continual improvement through periodic reviews, all while ensuring that the safety of Canadians is protected."

The Government set aside $9 million over 2 years to assist in the implementation of this initiative. This description of a "performance-based" regulatory system has as its lead commitment "to protect and advance the public interest in health, safety and security, the quality of the environment and the social and economic well-being of Canadians." Enhanced monitoring and performance reporting will provide pressure for continuous improvement and adjustment of regulatory approaches including greater cooperation between orders of government.

The Streamlining Directive is the most comprehensive across-the-board-scheme put forward by a federal government to improve its regulatory system. It appears consistent with the approach recommended by the External Advisory Committee on Smart Regulations. The "proof of the pudding will be in the eating" and the promise of increased accountability, transparency and inclusiveness should enable early assessments of progress.

In addition to the systemic changes noted above three specific projects were also launched. They are:

- *Streamlining the Review of Natural Resource Projects* – major projects valued at over $300 billion are planned over the next decade, the majority involving the mining, transportation and energy sectors. The government is committed to halving the approval time from 4 years down to 2 and has created a Major Projects Office to spearhead the effort. A Committee of Deputy Ministers, chaired by the Deputy Minister of Natural Resources Canada, is leading this exercise. Under the current approach delays are attributed to a lack of coordination, transparency and accountability within the federal government. The objective is to reduce delays by having the Major Projects Office act as a single window on the federal regulatory

process and by making clear and public the accountability of individual regulatory departments and agencies. In April 2007 the Government set aside $60 million over 2 years for implementation-which has subsequently been increased to $150 million over 5 years.
- *Reducing the Paper Burden* – mirroring the initiative taken by the government of British Columbia, the federal government committed to conduct an inventory of its administrative and information requirements for business by September 2007 and reduce this demand by 20 per cent by November 2008. The most recent progress report on paper burden that we could locate dates from 2005 and is found on a paper burden web site that clearly pre-dates Budget 2007.[17]
- *Securities Regulation* – a new approach is proposed which is based more on principles and customized to the "unique make-up of Canada's capital markets." A common securities regulator was proposed, and a debate about the need for a single securities regulator continues in the country with advocates[18] that include the Federal Minister of Finance despite strong opposition from his provincial counterparts.[19]

The 2007 Speech from the Throne

In its 2007 Speech from the Throne[20] the Harper Government identified areas for action that will require significant support from its regulatory institutions:

- The promise to strengthen Canada's economic union raises expectations of federal action to reduce regulatory barriers to internal trade.
- A promise to improve the protection of cultural and intellectual property rights in Canada, including copyright reform.
- A promise to enact market choice in the barley trade while supporting supply management in other components of the agriculture sector
- New legislation and other actions to address violent crimes and crimes against property, including measures to address elder abuse and curb identity theft
- New national regulations on green house gas emissions and air pollution as well as establishment of a carbon emissions trading market. These initiatives will require very close cooperation with provincial jurisdictions to avoid real risks of duplication of efforts or worse, measures that work at cross-purposes.
- Tougher environmental enforcement that "will make polluters accountable"
- Measures to enhance the safety of food and consumer products. These will also require coordination with provinces to avoid working at cross-purposes in areas of shared jurisdiction such as food safety and animal health.

NEEDED: AN INVESTMENT IN HUMAN RESOURCES

If the Government is to advance this ambitious agenda for more efficient and effective regulations, policy and supporting procedural or structural reforms will need to be supported by a concurrent investment in the people who operate our regulatory institutions. In this we agree completely with Gaetan Lussier, the Chair of the Report of an External Advisory Committee on Smart Regulation,[21] who recommended "facilitating a profound change in the practices and culture of regulatory departments" in order to ensure "Canada's ability to innovate and provide citizens with high levels of protection."

It can be argued that previous reform efforts were limited by the lack of an appreciation of the need for cultural change – and agreement on what that might entail and what is required to achieve it. To change the culture of a single organization is difficult and time consuming. To do so across many departments and agencies requires a considerable investment in creativity, perseverance and stamina. Progress may be grudgingly slow but the ultimate benefits to Canadian society could be enormous.

The importance of a cadre of skilled regulatory personnel was recently noted by Pederson[22] with respect to regulatory institution and practices in the United States. The need goes beyond the careful recruitment, staffing and other procedural human resource management practices for which he made the case. It extends to the softer elements such as development of a shared *esprit de corps*, articulation of core values and ethics, development of strategic teams and alliances that span Departments, Agencies as well as jurisdictions that must work effectively together, and the development of a common language and understanding of the principles and practices of regulatory decision making in Canada.

Public Service Renewal and the Regulatory Community

The reasons for a major initiative led by Kevin Lynch, Clerk of the Privy Council to renew the Public Service of Canada[23] apply as much to the regulatory community as to other parts of government. Lynch quotes Prime Minister Harper as saying "effective government requires effective public servants."[24] This is especially true for the regulatory community. We see a particular need to build development and leadership programs for the regulatory profession that is rarely addressed in institutions of higher learning. We are pleased to note that "setting and enforcing the regulatory framework" is one of the five areas of the business of government mentioned in the First Report by the Prime Minister's Advisory Committee on the Public Service.[25]

Recruitment and Retention Needs Attention

Like other areas of the public service, regulatory institutions are going through a period of rapid and deep staff turnover that presents both challenges and opportunities. If the regulatory community is to seize this important renewal opportunity it will be important to build the image of a regulatory profession which provides some of the most critical services of Government, in a rapidly evolving and most challenging context. Far from offering stodgy bureaucratic careers, these institutions need to be recognized as offering some of the most exciting, dynamic and rewarding experiences in Government today. Leaders at all levels must articulate the sense of pride, accomplishment, personal growth and satisfaction that can be found with careers in the regulatory profession.

A Learning and Development Program

A strong learning and development program, while not a panacea, is essential to advance renewal within the regulatory community. Some promising steps have been taken in this area, notably:

- Work to address human resource needs of the regulatory and inspection community was launched in 1999 under the leadership of the Deputy Minister of Transport Canada. In 2005 this effort was broadened from its initial focus on operational personnel to include the employees who develop regulations. This renewed Community of Federal Regulators (CFR) led by the Deputy Minister of Health Canada has been promoting community development, learning and the exchanges of best practices.[26] As of December 2007, 14 regulatory Departments and Agencies (Table 2) had joined the initiative to develop their cadre of regulatory officials and leaders. The participating Departments and Agencies have mandates spanning health protection, occupational, transportation and nuclear safety and environmental protection. The Community has considerable room to grow if it were to include institutions that regulate commercial domains such as taxation, cross-border trade, agricultural commodities and communications.
- The Regulatory Affairs Division of the Treasury Board Secretariat (RAD-TBS, formerly of the Privy Council Office), is working in partnership with the Canada School of Public Service to develop a common core curriculum for regulators.
- The launching of a Centre of Regulatory Expertise (CORE) within the Treasury Board Secretariat to support Regulatory Departments and Agencies in areas such as cost-benefit analysis, performance measurement, evaluation and review and risk assessment.

Table 2
Membership in the community of Federal regulators as of December 2007

Agriculture and Agri-Food Canada
Canadian Food Inspection Agency
Canadian Nuclear Safety Commission
Citizenship and Immigration Canada
Environment Canada
Fisheries and Oceans Canada
Health Canada and the Pest Management Regulatory Agency
Human Resources and Social Development Canada
Indian and Northern Affairs Canada
Industry Canada
Justice Canada
Natural Resources Canada
Transport Canada
Treasury Board Secretariat

- The publication by RAD-TBS of new or updated guidelines for regulators on instrument choice, cost benefit analysis, consultations and international obligations and cooperation.[27]

STRENGTHS TO BUILD ON AND CHALLENGES TO FACE

Strengths To Build Upon

Key strengths of Canada's regulatory institutions are first, the values and traditions of a non-partisan professional public service, and secondly, the skills brought to regulatory affairs by personnel skilled in many specialized disciplines. Our Canadian context still favours pragmatic and inclusive approaches to problem solving.

1 PUBLIC SERVICE VALUES, TRADITIONS AND WORK EXPERIENCES

With its permanent, non-partisan public service that includes the most senior ranks, Canada stands apart from major competitors in the Americas, and from many other countries at a global level. Canadian Public Service core values and traditions were well described by a Deputy Minister's Task Force in 1996.[28] Canadian civil servants are trusted to be non-partisan in the exercise of the administrative discretion provided through legislation. The high costs of the litigious processes that have become a routine step in most regulatory decisions in the USA have generally been avoided in Canada by solving contentious issues through informal processes, dialogue and negotiations.

A less flattering view is offered by Grabosky and Brathwaite who in their book *Of Manners Gentle*[29] portray the relationships between Australian regulators and their business regulatees as "benign" and characterized by a preference for informal suasion over the formal use of the regulators' enforcement authority. Australian regulators explain these preferences as ways to make the most effective use of their authority. This debate on the appropriate balance between suasion and enforcement is not unfamiliar in the Canadian context, perhaps reflecting our shared governance heritage with Australia.

In fact, Canada has a governance and cultural platform that can support more adaptable regulatory processes than many other regimes. This can happen at different levels ranging from local environmental assessment and permit decisions to regional and national efforts to develop negotiated standards as in the case of Alberta's Clean Air Strategic Alliance[30] or to set out a path for future decision making as illustrated by the work of the Nuclear Waste Management Organization on disposal of used nuclear fuel.[31]

Regulators, *regulatees* and other interested parties must consider how to make the most of this fundamental governance advantage while avoiding the risks of "capture" of the regulators by regulated parties.

The effectiveness of this system requires that the principles and core values of the Public Service are not only understood, but are fully incorporated by regulators into their thinking and day to day practices. This requires the exercise of sophisticated judgment by regulators, senior civil servants and parliamentarians, and is instrumental in creating public confidence.

2 WELL TRAINED, DEDICATED AND EXPERIENCED EXPERTS

All fields of regulation (animal health, plant protection, food inspection, drugs and medical devices, taxes, immigration, communications, competition law, vehicle emissions, fuel quality, industrial pollutants to air and water, etc) require a cadre of capable and dedicated professionals. These professionals need to be experts in their respective disciplines and they also must recognize the impacts and consequences of their regulatory proposals on the operations of the sectors or industries they regulate. Regulators require extensive international networks in their field of work and the respect of their peers if they are to be influential in setting international norms and policies. A record of progressive actions by government allows regulators to be influential in these settings.

These are demanding specifications for qualified personnel that can only be met by sustained and well supported efforts to recruit, develop and retain the necessary people. Our universities and colleges will need to make a significant contribution to training and development in this specialized area.

ISSUES TO ADDRESS IN DEVELOPING REGULATORY PROFESSIONALS

Some of the basic learning needs for regulatory professionals can be met in traditional classroom and reading modes, and should be addressed in a core curriculum offered by institutions such as the Canada School of Public Service. These include topics such as the legal foundations for regulation, cabinet and other decision making processes to create regulations, applicable government policies and directives, theories and principles of instrument choice and uses and limitations of cost-benefit analysis.

Other areas for learning may be better served by experiential or action learning approaches – described as "Delta" learning by Paquet.[32] Methods range from the development and sharing of case studies to joint exploration of challenging issues by learning teams.

Three important challenges facing federal regulators in many institutions are particularly suitable for Delta learning:

- Addressing fragmentation
- Advancing our understanding of risk-based decision making
- Maintaining public confidence

These are key areas in which we need improved performance if the Government's goals of more effective and efficient regulation are to be realized. Hence we offer some perspectives on these challenges.

1 Fragmentation

Recommendations of the External Advisory Committee on Smart Regulations[33] called for increased national and international coherence amongst regulations. They sought improved coordination within the federal house, between Federal, Provincial and Territorial and Aboriginal jurisdictions, and with international initiatives.

The challenge here is to overcome various forms of fragmentation that can have a range of negative effects including unnecessary duplication, gaps in coverage of regulations or regulatory measures that are counter-productive or inefficient. Some instances of fragmentation are unique to Canada with its complex federation that brings federal, provincial, territorial, municipal and aboriginal governments into regulatory activities. Others are less obvious yet widespread and reflect specialized professional and sectoral niches within which practices and relationships have developed over many years, often isolated from outside influence or scrutiny by barriers of technology, language and expert cultures (consider such complex issues as animal health, vehicle emissions, telecommunications or drug and vaccine licensing).

Powerful cultures and traditions have developed around the professional disciplines and their associated niches of regulatory practice, comprising regulators, regulatees and other stakeholders. One positive result is that regulators understand and adapt to the needs of the regulated sectors. However, the existence of many separate decision making processes, often with their own specialized language, concepts and principles, can be a barrier to cooperation on issues that span sectors, jurisdictions and/or disciplines.

In the past the Government of Canada has addressed aspects of fragmentation by structural change. For example the government consolidated the work of federal pesticide regulators from a number of Departments into a single Pest Management Regulatory Agency reporting to the Minister of Health. Similarly the government consolidated food safety and other food inspection as well as animal and plant health inspection services in 1997 with the creation of the Canadian Food Inspection Agency reporting to the Minister of Agriculture. The federal government continues to seek ways to address thorny fragmentation challenges in areas such as environmental assessment and securities regulation.

Whatever the merits of past or future organizational consolidations, this chapter emphasizes the need for regulatory integration – through learning and the development of shared values, concepts and goals. The Government must foster a values-based alignment of efforts through learning and team building that places emphasis on common purpose, collaboration and serving the public interest.[34]

2 Decision Systems: Logic, Coherence and the Acceptable level of Risk

Regulatory decisions are based on logic and values that are intellectually challenging and fundamentally important – and yet are all too often overlooked or misunderstood in the public discourse. This topic is fraught with serious misconceptions even amongst practitioners of the regulatory and policy arts.

It is attractive and popular for all concerned to cite "science" as the basis for difficult regulatory decisions. Once duly informed by the available evidence, the regulator must usually decide what level of risk is acceptable. These are rarely if ever scientific decisions; rather, these decisions must take account of societal values and hence should be made by, or with the guidance from, elected officials supported by their senior policy advisors. This important principle is at times overlooked, with the risk that we may ask technical or scientific experts to make policy or political decisions.

In their analysis of risk assessments for the herbicide Alachlor, Brunk et al.[35] clearly demonstrated that subjective political or societal values can determine the outcome of supposedly "objective" science assessments. Using the same laboratory data Health Canada and Monsanto produced risks assessments that differed by up to six orders of magnitude (10^6). The chain of logic used in making the assessments required several assumptions to be made which did not involve questions of science or technology, but rather of policy. For example, should the assessors assume that agricultural workers would wear protective clothing? This is a policy question – should the government protect users who don't protect themselves?

A key lesson is that there is a need for risk assessors to consult with policy leaders on the non-science based values and assumptions that form part of such assessments. Decision makers need to ensure clarity and transparency about embedded values when considering the results of risk assessments.

Brunk has since identified a need for a policy framework to guide risk assessors with respect to non-scientific questions. Such frameworks will establish the degree of precaution to be exercised as decisions are required with respect to 1) who has the burden of proof (e.g. of harm or safety), and 2) what is the appropriate standard of proof, given the profile of the risk and the state of the science.[36] In our view, these fundamentally important insights warrant an update of the Government of Canada's guidance document on precautionary decision-making.[37]

This sort of rigorous scrutiny of the logic and principles supporting regulatory decisions is increasingly needed as new technologies and practices come under review. Regulators will be challenged over inconsistencies when products cut across expert and sectoral niches, or when new products or processes don't fit into established niches. Consider the case of a single biotechnology or nanotechnology that may produce products to be regulated as pesticides, pharmaceuticals, or other categories including novel ones.

3 Maintaining Public Confidence – guarding the public interest

If the Canadian regulatory regime is to continue to inspire confidence in Canadians and their trading partners as it undergoes reforms there are key issues that need attention.

A) ENGAGING CANADIANS: RISING EXPECTATIONS AND INNOVATIONS

Canadians need to be engaged in the setting of national standards and norms if the process and results are to have essential legitimacy. This requires regulators to be inclusive in their engagement of interest groups and scrupulous in ensuring transparency of process and accessibility of information. This is often a challenge given the unbalanced capacities of different communities to present their views. Not all interested parties such as First Nations, NGOs, business or the frequently unorganized and unaware risk-bearers, have the capacity to participate in what may be complex technical discussions. There is a need to support their participation in the dialogue by funding of parties, provision of expert help, creative use of the internet, or other means.. It also requires ongoing focus and emphasis on organizational values and ethics to ensure that the public interest is first and foremost in the minds of regulators.

Innovations in citizen engagement on issues like air pollution in Alberta (Clean Air Strategic Alliance),[38] remediation of the Tar Ponds in Sydney, Nova Scotia[39] and nuclear waste management at a national level[40] have set new standards that could strengthen the democratic base for decisions. There are important lessons to be learned from these constructive experiences.

B) BETTER UNDERSTANDING AND MANAGEMENT OF THE SCIENCE-POLICY INTERFACE

Disputes between experts and senior decision makers over regulatory decisions can arise from misunderstandings of decision-making such as those discussed previously on the case of Alachlor.[41] The respective roles of specialists/experts and senior decision makers (including Ministers and Deputy Ministers) need to be better explained to all concerned. Learning through dialogue is helpful, particularly where new risk management approaches are being introduced that may change long established practices.

C) IS IT POSSIBLE TO BE ENTREPRENEURIAL GUARDIANS?

Successful management of both public engagement and the science policy interface requires understanding and respect for key democratic and professional values of the public service. The need to respect these values while introducing new approaches to public administration was addressed by the landmark Deputy Minister's Task Force report "A Strong Foundation" – dealing with ethics and values in the public service.[42] Most pertinent is their thinking on the "New Public Administration" – and the potential for conflict with traditional and core values of the public service. Similar themes were explored by Jane Jacobs in her classic monograph "Systems of Survival"[43] in which she cautioned against perverse conflicts such as might arise in an effort to create "entrepreneurial guardians."

To achieve real improvements in efficiency and effectiveness innovative approaches to regulation must bridge conflicting pressures, retain appropriate checks and balances and avoid apparent or real conflicts of interest. "Capture" by vested interest is an occupational hazard which can result from losing a focus on serving the public interest as the bottom line.

CONCLUSION

This chapter has made mention of the many parties and interests affected by regulatory actions of government. While some laudable efforts are underway to improve regulatory practices, capacity and learning in the Federal Public Service and in provincial governments such as Nova Scotia[44] and Ontario,[45] much remains to be done to build a national "community of interest" where best practices might be located, lessons learned shared and intellectual capital pooled and nurtured. To paraphrase Clausewitz on war and generals, "Regulation is too important to be left to the regulators." What is needed is no less than to harness Canada's governmental and non-governmental intellectual capital in support of improved regulation. The limited number of people studying regulatory matters are scattered widely amongst universities, government departments, think tanks, NGOs, legal practices and the regulated industry sectors themselves. By drawing fully on this capacity Canada would improve its competitive position while advancing its regulatory goals.

Initiatives by successive Federal Governments including and subsequent to the Report of an External Advisory Committee on Smart Regulations[46] provide the ingredients to create a regulatory breakthrough.

There is a political appetite for more efficient regulations and at the same time for some important new and stronger regulations.

Within the Public Service there is a high level commitment to advance institutional renewal and to foster the human resources and leadership development required to develop and deliver better regulations. Initiatives are underway in a number of federal Departments and Agencies as part of a new Community of Federal Regulators, and through the Treasury Board Secretariat and the Canada School of Public Service to foster learning and development. At the same time potentially synergistic efforts are being developed by some provincial governments and universities

That said, these encouraging steps are just the beginning of a long voyage. To be truly successful this will need sustained effort and engagement by senior officials and parliamentarians. They must address the regulatory issues of the day and also make an investment in the development of future leaders and practitioners. The next generation, in a spirit of continuous improvement, should be more skilled in the art of regulation than their predecessors.

The rewards for this continued investment would be a significant competitive economic advantage for the country as well as the improved health, safety, security and environmental standards that Canadians expect and deserve.

ACKNOWLEDGEMENT

The authors acknowledge the helpful suggestions and feedback provided by Conrad Brunk, Bruce Doern, Bruce Dudley, Suzanne Legault, Marc Saner, David Zussman and several officials working on regulatory affairs for Departments and Agencies of the Federal Government.

NOTES

1 Bruce Doern, *Red Tape, Red Flags: Regulation for the Innovation Age* (Ottawa: The Conference Board of Canada, 2007).
2 Ibid.
3 External Advisory Committee on Smart Regulation, *Smart Regulation: A Regulatory Strategy for Canada*. Report to the Government of Canada, September 2004. Available at www.pco-bcp.gc.ca/smartreg-regint ; accessed 10 October 10 2007.
4 Department of Finance. *Budget 2007: Aspire to a stronger, safer, better Canada.* 19 March 2007. Available at http://www.budget.gc.ca/2007/news/newse.html; accessed 30 November 2007.
5 Government of Canada, *Cabinet Directive on Streamlining Regulation.* Available at http://www.regulation.gc.ca/directive/directive01-eng.asp; accessed 30 November 2007.
6 External Advisory Committee on Smart Regulation, *Smart Regulation.*
7 Australian Government Regulation Taskforce, *Rethinking Regulation: Report of the Task Force on Reducing Regulatory Burdens on Business.* Report to the Prime Minister and the Treasurer. Canberra: Australian Government Regulation Taskforce, April 2006.
8 Doern, *Red Tape, Red Flags: Regulations for the Innovation Age*, 16.
9 Eli Alboim, Personal communication based on public opinion surveys conducted for the secretariat of an inter-departmental committee on biotechnology circa 2005.
10 Andre Picard, "*Victims of HIV furious at acquittal of administrators in tainted-blood case*," Globe and Mail, 2 October 2007, A1; M.L. Benotto, *R. v. Armour Pharmaceutical Company.* Ontario Superior Court of Justice. Court File No. P51/04 2007-10-01. Available at http://www.canlii.org/en/on/onsc/doc/2007; accessed 10 October 2007.
11 Alan Fels, Seminar at the Canada School of Public Service, Spring 2007.
12 Peter Grabosky and John Brathwaite, *Of Manners Gentle: Enforcement Strategies of Australian Business Regulatory Agencies* (Oxford: Oxford University Press, 1986).
13 For an example of this perspective see an article by Paul Webster and John Cathro "Is 'smart regulation' dumb for Canada's wilderness areas?" *The Walrus*, November 2007, 40–42.
14 Privy Council Office, *Smart Regulation Report on Action and Plans.* Fall 2005 update. We were unable to locate this document on line through the advertised linkages, although a reference to it existed in a press release that was still available on 2 December 2007 at http://www.tbs-sct.gc.ca/media/nr-cp/2005/1028_e.asp.
15 Department of Finance, *Budget 2007.*
16 Government of Canada, *Cabinet Directive on Streamlining Regulation.* Available at http://www.regulation.gc.ca/directive/directive01-eng.asp ; accessed 22 November 2007.
17 The Reducing Paper Burden Website, available at http://www.reducingpaperburden.gc.ca/epic/site/pbri-iafp.nsf/en/Home; accessed 2 December 2007.
18 Diane Francis, "Canada's securities law is too lax," *National Post*, 12 August 2006, FP2; David Brown, Steve Foerester, Roger Martin and Hugh Segal, *Forward to Capital*

Markets and Sustainability: Investing in a Sustainable Future (Ottawa: National Round Table on the Environment and the Economy, 2007), 80. Available at http://www.nrtee-trnee.ca/eng/publications/capital-markets/index-capital-markets-eng.htm; accessed 2 December 2007.

19 Deirdre McMurdy, "Provinces won't give up their securities agencies without a bitter fight," *The Ottawa Citizen*, 24 October 2007, A5.

20 Government of Canada, *Strong Leadership: A Better Canada*. Speech From the Throne, 16 October 2007. Available at http://www.sft-ddt.gc.ca/eng/media.asp?id=1364; accessed 29 November 2007.

21 External Advisory Committee on Smart Regulation, *Smart Regulation*.

22 William F. Pederson, "Regulatory Reform and Government Management," in Michael McConkey and Patrice Dutil, eds., *Dreaming of the Regulatory Village*. (Toronto: Institute of Public Administration of Canada, 2006).

23 Kevin G. Lynch, *Fourteenth Annual Report to the Prime Minister on the Public Service of Canada* (Ottawa: Privy Council Office, 2007).

24 Stephen Harper, *Accountability and the Public Service*. Speech given on 23 March 2006.

25 Don Mazankowski and Paul Tellier, *The First Report by the Prime Minister's Advisory Committee on the Public Service* (Ottawa: Prime Minister's Advisory Committee on the Public Service, 30 March 2007).

26 Community of Federal Regulators. For additional information see http://www.cfr-crf.gc.ca/index_e.asp; accessed 30 November 2007.

27 Treasury Board Secretariat, Various guidelines available at www.regulation.gc.ca/documents/list-list-eng.asp; accessed 22 November 2007.

28 John C. Tait, *A Strong Foundation: Report of the Task Force on Public Service Values and Ethics* (Ottawa: Canadian Centre for Management Development, December 1996).

29 Grabosky and Brathwaite, *Of Manners Gentle*.

30 For an introduction to Alberta's Clean Air Strategic Alliance (CASA) via Alberta Environment please see: http://www3.gov.ab.ca/env/air/CASA/index.html; For a good example of its work please see a 2004 presentation to the NAFTA Council on Environmental Cooperation at www.cec.org/files/pdf/POLLUTANTS/Pres-Frank-Letchford_en.pdf; both sites accessed 30 November 2007.

31 Nuclear Waste Management Organization (NWMO), *Choosing a Way Forward: The Future Management of Canada's Used Nuclear Fuel*. Final Study. (Toronto: NWMO, November 2005), 451.

32 Gilles Paquet, *Savoirs, savoir-faire, savoir-être: in praise of professional wroughting and writing*. A think piece for campus 20/20 – An enquiry into the future of British Colombia's post-secondary education system, 2006. Available at http://www.campus2020.ca/EN/think_pieces/; accessed 3 December 2007.

33 External Advisory Committee on Smart Regulation, *Smart Regulation*.

34 Samy Watson, personal communication of an observation on three core elements of good public policy, 2006.

35 Conrad Brunk, Lawrence Haworth, and Brenda Lee, "Is Scientific Assessment of Risk Possible? Value Assumptions in the Canadian Alachlor Controversy," DIALOGUE (Canadian Philosophical Review) 30, no. 3 (Summer 1991): 235–48; C. G. Brunk, L. Haworth and B. Lee, *Value Assumptions in Risk Assessment: A case study of the Alachlor Controversy* (Waterloo, ONT: Wilfred Laurier Press, 1992).
36 Katherine Barrett and Conrad Brunk, *A Precautionary Framework for Biotechnology in Genetically Engineered Crops* (Binghamton, NY: The Haworth Press, 2007), 133–152.
37 Privy Council Office, *A Framework for the Application of Precaution in Science-Based Decision Making About Risk* (Ottawa: Privy Council Office, 2003). Available at http://www.pco-bcp.gc.ca/docs/InformationResources/Publications/precaution/Precaution_e.pdf; accessed 22 November 2007.
38 http://www3.gov.ab.ca/enu/air/CASA/index.html.
39 Joint Action Group – archived web site maintained by the Sydney Tar Ponds Agency at http://tarpondscleanup.ca/default.asp?T=2&M=73; accessed 31 November 2007.
40 Nuclear Waste Management Organization (NWMO), *Choosing a Way Forward*.
41 Brunk, Haworth, and Lee, "Is Scientific Assessment of Risk Possible?" and Brunk, Haworth, and Lee, *Value Assumptions in Risk Assessment*.
42 Tart, *A Strong Foundation*.
43 Jane Jacobs, *Systems of Survival: A Dialogue on the Moral Foundations of Commerce and Politics* (New York, NY: Vintage Books (Random House, Inc.), 1992).
44 Government of Nova Scotia. The Better Regulation Initiative. http://www.gov.ns.ca/betterregulation/; accessed 22 November 2007.
45 John Stager, *Modernizing Regulatory Compliance: The Ontario Experience*. A Presentation to the Community of Federal Regulators National Workshop, 7 November 2007.
46 External Advisory Committee on Smart Regulation, *Smart Regulation*.

5 A Little Imagination Required: How Canada Funds Territorial and Northern Aboriginal Governments

FRANCES ABELE
AND MICHAEL J. PRINCE

Three jurisdictional challenges shape governance and policy in Canada's North: maintenance of Canadian arctic sovereignty; the evolution of responsible government in the territories; and, the institutional realization of Aboriginal self-determination. All three challenges concern political structures and the process of intergovernmental relations, and all involve public issues of fundamental substance to Canadian nationhood. Indeed, these three jurisdictional challenges can be seen as the *other* three axes of Canadian federalism, entailing relations between the Canadian state and Aboriginal peoples; the Canadian south and northern political communities; and the Canadian nation and other circumpolar nations.[1]

The purpose of this chapter is, first, to examine the place of territorial governments, the newly formed Aboriginal governments, and the attendant "bridging" institutions, in the fiscal federation. In different ways, all of these institutions are still subject to the financial authority of the Minister of Indian Affairs and Northern Development. And, although all the governments (and their budgets) are relatively small, in their complexity and in the challenges they pose for the country, they represent a pivotal area of public policy. This is particularly evident in this, the International Polar Year,[2] and the year in which Canada's circumpolar neighbours have seen fit to challenge Canadian sovereignty in the North.

The second task of this chapter is to address major decisions taken by the Stephen Harper government concerning the role of the territories in the federation. In some respects, the Harper Conservatives have taken an approach that differs from that of the Paul Martin Liberal government. First, Prime Minister Harper began by explicitly agreeing that a vertical fiscal imbalance exists between Ottawa and the provinces and territories. When the Martin-appointed expert panel on intergovernmental finance reported,[3] Harper acted quickly to implement its recommendations for territorial financing. On the other hand, the Harper government's reaction to demands for province-like control of natural resource development from the two territories who still lack these powers (Northwest Territories and Yukon) are very similar to those of previous Liberal governments; there has been no action.

The Harper government abandoned the Kelowna Accord negotiated by the Martin government, thus walking away from a nascent approach to Aboriginal – Canada relations founded on comprehensive joint planning involving First Nations, Métis and Inuit and federal officials from a range of departments. Instead, the Harper Conservatives have returned to an earlier pattern of relationships, including distinguishing between on and off reserve programming and reverting to individual departmental management of the issue. This has had the effect of reducing federal attention to matters of northern Aboriginal governance, since there is only one reserve in the whole territorial north. Finally, the Harper government has emphasized the role of the military in protecting Canadian sovereignty in the North, with a gesture to territorial concerns in the announcement of construction of the long-desired deep harbour port in Nunavut. The use of defence expenditures for regional development has a long history in Canada, but there have not been substantial expenditures on defence infrastructure in northern Canada for many years. As the warming climate opens the Northwest Passage to increased commercial traffic, there will be stronger reasons to continue this pattern.

How Canada funds Territorial and Northern Aboriginal governments is significant for several reasons, some generic to any federation, others specific to this region. Watts identifies two reasons for the importance of fiscal relations that apply to all federations: "first, these resources enable or constrain governments in the exercise of their constitutionally assigned legislative and executive responsibilities; second, taxing powers and expenditures are themselves important instruments for affecting and regulating the economy."[4] Further reasons, particularly germane to the Canadian North, are the importance of expenditure and revenue powers for traditional renewable resource economies of hunting, fishing and trapping; for obtaining fair benefits to Northerners and other Canadians from the development of non-renewable resources; for preserving and promoting Indigenous languages and communities; for advancing responsible government in the Northwest Territories (NWT) and Nunavut;[5] for advancing self-determination and self-government for Aboriginal peoples by providing realistic support to Aboriginal governments; and, for giving expression to Canadian sovereignty in the arctic polar region.

Well-funded, adequately staffed and stable northern governments –along with a sophisticated, flexible and well-informed federal northern policy capacity – are the keys to the advancement of the Canadian national interest in northern affairs. In particular, it is essential that the new governing institutions created by modern Treaty negotiations develop in tandem with the evolving territorial institutions, and that together these governments have the knowledge and the means to address the increasingly pressing matters on northern policy agenda:

- Planning for adaptation to climate change, a long-term prospect with major dangers and some opportunities for innovation and growth;
- Improving the capacity of northern educational institutions to prepare all northerners for a full role in northern economic and political life;
- Developing northern research capacity in key areas (such as adaptation to climate change), potentially using research investments as a lever of economic development in each territory;
- Providing adequate housing, health care and social services in all northern communities; and
- Creating both regulatory capacity and economic plans that will respond to the rapidly accelerating interest of international corporations in the north's non-renewable resources, given accelerated global industrialization and the greater accessibility of these resources due to climate change.

These policy challenges are of course only partly a matter of adequate funding, and they are items for the federal as well as the territorial policy agenda. Inadequate funding for emergent northern governing institutions will make it difficult for these institutions to focus on the sharp challenges ahead, and to develop the personnel and analytical resources to deal with them.

There is also a need for visionary leadership in northern governments (both public and Aboriginal) and some inventive institutional development.[6] In 2003, the three northern territories signed the Northern Cooperation Accord, launching a new –pan-northern approach to addressing issues such as health care funding and formula financing that has proven effective. The federal response to this, under the previous Liberal government, was the Northern Strategy, which yielded some additional funding and the beginnings of a consolidated federal northern development policy. The Northern Strategy has been neither advanced nor abandoned by the Harper government. In 2007, the three northern premiers released a joint statement on their region's future in Confederation, *A Stronger North in a Better Canada*. Though very general, this statement may be the basis for a concerted and specific period of cooperative development planning by the territories.

Northern fiscal federalism, long characterized by nearly invisible bureaucratic struggles over inadequate transfers and marginal political attention in Ottawa, benefited from recent conflicts between provinces and the federal government over the existence or not of a fiscal imbalance and the preferred policy responses in equalization payments and other federal transfer programs to other governments. Indeed, we suggest that the territorial governments and their leaders have been effective participants in recent reviews of fiscal federalism, putting forward their concerns and offering reform options, most of which were adopted in one form or another by the recent changes to the Territorial Formula Financing (TFF) program. On the other hand, neither the NWT nor Nunavut has yet been successful in gaining a stronger purchase on the management of their economies through devolution of jurisdiction over natural resources, with the exception of jurisdiction over forestry and forest management in 1987.[7]

FISCAL FEDERALISM IN NORTHERN CANADA

Within Canada's contemporary federation, notable horizontal fiscal differences exist in spending demands and taxing capacities between the territories as a group and the provinces as a group of governments. The territories are by population the three smallest public governments within the federation. They have the highest per capita costs to build infrastructure and deliver programs, a consequence of their sparse, dispersed and relatively young populations,[8] relatively cold climates, and, especially for NWT and Nunavut, the high cost of transportation of virtually all goods. All have relatively large Aboriginal populations,[9] and in all three territories, political life and political institutions have been transformed in one generation by the processes set in place to respond to this fact. Each territory has been the site of distinctive processes of constitutional innovation, processes that have been at once intense and broadly democratic. This has altered the shape of the territorial governments, created a number of Aboriginal governments and, most interestingly of all, led to the development a number of bridging or hybrid institutions that are neither entirely public, nor entirely ethnic, governing forms.[10] Each territory also is home to heterogeneous non-Aboriginal populations, including strong francophone communities and a substantial proportion of recent immigrants.

The three territories share these factors, but there are significant differences among them. Of the three, Yukon has the most developed infrastructure: all Yukon communities are connected by roads, with the single exception of Old Crow in the far north; most Yukon communities are on an electrical grid, and all have high-speed internet connections. In contrast, although most NWT communities have high-speed Internet connections, over half of the communities are accessible only by air, water and, in some cases, winter road. There is as yet no electrical grid linking most communities. None of Nunavut's communities can be reached by road, though most communities do have Internet connections. For resupply, Nunavut relies upon a very short shipping season and air freight. The cost of living, and the cost of government, thus is highest, by far, in Nunavut, and lowest in the Yukon, with the Northwest Territories falling in the middle.

The territorial economies differ as well. All are comprised of a blend of public expenditures and employment, wages and profits from non-renewable resource development and tourism, and the fruits of traditional productive activity. Of these, only non-renewable resource development, tourism and associated service sector industries generate any substantial tax revenue. The blend differs across the territories, as does the relative revenue generated. Currently, the mining sector in the NWT and Yukon is booming. Nunavut, with the strongest traditional sector, is also developing a strong mining sector, with the prospect of diamond mining and more distantly, oil and gas production. In short, although the three territories have some basic characteristics (in having small dispersed populations, for example), the challenges they face vary in magnitude and sometimes, in type.

Federal-Territorial Fiscal Relations

The powers of the three territorial governments are defined by federal legislation, not by the Canadian constitution.[11] The federal legislation establishing the territories gives them powers very similar to those assigned by the British North America Act to the provinces. The exception to this rule is control over natural resources, a power retained by the federal order. Yukon gained control over oil and gas resources in 1993, and other minerals in 2003.[12] The NWT and Nunavut still lack province-like constitutional authority for natural resource development and management, though they have been lobbying vigorously for this. The lack of these powers produces an important jurisdictional imbalance, and the two easterly territories also lack access not only to royalties, but also economic development levers.[13]

These are important sources of fiscal asymmetry, but they are by no means the only ones.[14] Financial relations between Ottawa and the territories have evolved through a series of reforms that kept pace with progress towards the establishment of territorial administrations on the Westminster model. In 1978, for example, the territories were included in tax collection agreements for the first time, which led to the NWT government levying personal and corporate income taxes in 1979, and Yukon government in 1980.[15] Also in 1979, the Yukon government was granted responsible government, and the Northwest Territories Legislature met without the participation of the Commissioner.[16] In 1985, the process for transferring funds to the territories was changed. Before then, federal transfer payments were determined annually through consultation and negotiation among the Minister of Finance, the President of the Treasury Board, the Minister of Indian Affairs and Northern Development, and representatives from the territorial governments.[17] After 1985, the yearly budget negotiations were replaced by a more global and predictable, multi-year formula based upon actual past expenditures and eventually, past expenditures, rising public sector expenditures in the rest of Canada, and population.[18] These arrangements were referred to as the Formula Financing Agreements, recently replaced by the Territorial Financing Formula (TFF) which we discuss below.

Far more than any of the provinces, even the neediest "have-not" ones, Yukon, NWT and Nunavut are greatly dependent on federal transfer payments as a source of revenue each year, largely in the form of the TFF unconditional block grant. In 2007–08, as a share of territorial revenues, the TFF represented 59 per cent of revenues in Yukon, 63 per cent in NWT, and 81 per cent in Nunavut; as a portion of territorial expenditures, the shares are correspondingly even higher.

Other distinctive features of fiscal federalism in the North are that the Auditor General of Canada serves as the auditor of the public accounts and financial transactions in each of the territories; and, that powers for borrowing and investing money by the Yukon, NWT and Nunavut governments for territorial, municipal or local purposes, and the limits of such borrowing, are subject to approval by the federal cabinet.[19] These are indicators of limited and supervised financial decentralization exercised by the territorial governments in contrast to the provinces.

The most important difference between the provinces and territories in fiscal federalism, is that the NWT, Nunavut and Yukon are not part of the Equalization Program; the program that at present transfers to six so-called have-not provinces – Newfoundland and Labrador, Prince Edward Island, Nova Scotia, New Brunswick, Quebec, and Manitoba – fiscal resources enabling them to provide comparable levels of public services at comparable levels of taxation to a national average of fiscal capacity. In contrast, the territories receive "equalization-like" funds under the TFF with a grant formula based on fiscal capacity *and* expenditure needs, which is unique to the northern governments.

Chart 1 compares the TFF with the Equalization Program. While the TFF shares some features with Equalization, there are significant differences too. A basic distinction is that while Equalization is about transferring federal funds to certain provinces to help offset inequalities in provincial revenue capacities, the TFF is about transferring federal funds to all three territories to help offset differences in the high cost of providing essential public services in the unique circumstances in North.

In light of their obvious fiscal needs and the fact that Equalization predates the TFF by several decades, why are the NWT, Nunavut and Yukon not part of the Equalization Program? Equalization rests on the belief that provinces receiving payments to compensate for their relatively low revenue raising capacity will then have sufficient resources to provide reasonably comparable levels of public services at reasonably comparable levels of taxation. Implicit in this approach is that the per capita cost of providing public services is generally similar from one province to another. It is widely acknowledged, however, that the territories have widely differing costs of providing public services than do the provinces and so a transfer program is required that

Chart 1
Comparing the Equalization Program and Territorial Formula Financing

Parameters	Equalization	TFF
Origin	1957	1985
Constitutional status	Constitution Act, 1982, s. 36(2)	Administrative agreements until 2007, now legislated
Policy purpose and rationale	To address the large disparities in revenue capacity among provinces To ensure that provincial governments have sufficient revenues to provide reasonably comparable levels of public services at reasonably comparable levels of taxation.	To address the high expenditure costs in the North To provide territorial governments with the resources they need to deliver public services comparable to those that Canadians enjoy in the rest of Canada, taking into account the higher costs of services and unique circumstances in the North.
Formula design	Equalizing revenue capacities among provinces, no account of expenditure needs	Addressing both revenue capacities and expenditure needs of territories
Type of grant	Annual and unconditional	Annual and unconditional
Political salience	High visibility and awareness	Low visibility and little awareness
Review cycle	Usually every five years	Usually every five years
Funding source	Federal consolidated revenue fund	Federal consolidated revenue fund
Recipient jurisdictions	Presently 6 provinces (can vary over time)	All 3 territories continually
As a share of P/T expenditure budgets	Varies from about 20 to 30 per cent	Relatively high, between 62 to 90 per cent
Scale of federal transfer (millions of dollars in 2007–08)	$12,768	$2,212
Rate of change over past 15 years (1993–94 to 2007–08)	58.4 per cent	93.1 per cent

seeks to equalize somewhat disparities in the capacity of territories to provide public services comparable to those to other citizens in southern Canada, in a relatively expensive environment. To reflect the extraordinary costs of governance and public administration in the North, the TFF is designed to address both the limited revenue capacity and extraordinary expenditure needs of the territories.

With the provinces, the territories do participate in many of the other arrangements by which funds are transferred from Ottawa to other governments. Indeed, each territorial government participates in dozens of such federal programs.[20] Most of the linkages are multilateral agreements (federal/provincial/territorial), some are bilateral (federal-territorial) and others regional (between the federal government and the governments of the three territories). The main policy fields in which interaction occurs are environment, Indian affairs and northern development, health, social development and housing.

Most of the federal monies transferred to Yukon, NWT and Nunavut are unconditional, maximizing the territorial governments' potential to initiate policy dialogue and make policy choices important to local residents and communities. While the territorial governments have high financial dependence on Ottawa, they appear to enjoy a degree of policy and budgetary autonomy as a result of the general purpose nature of most of their transfer payments. The federal government sets no programmatic conditions on the TFF; payments are not tied to any specific public services. No matching funds are required. In this way, the purse strings have been decentralized.

The situation is, however, more complex than we have so far indicated. As a recent federal report notes: "Across the three territories, there are different fiscal arrangements and self-government agreements in place among the federal government, territorial governments, Inuit organizations, First nations, and Aboriginal organizations. The majority of the financial arrangements include sharing revenues (including resource revenues) among the First nations, Aboriginal governments and organizations, and the territorial and federal governments."[21] Since 1984, five comprehensive claims agreements (modern treaties) have been negotiated by Aboriginal peoples in the territorial north. There have been, in addition, ten self-government agreements, with more under negotiation. Most recently, in 2003, the Tlicho Dene signed the first combined self-government and comprehensive claims agreement in the territorial north. All of these agreements are intended to embody a stable and more just constitutional arrangement between Aboriginal collectivities and the citizens of Canada; all provide for the transfer of capital from federal to Aboriginal authorities. They contain, as well, a number of other fiscal arrangements that must be taken into account in understanding how Ottawa funds northern governments.

Aboriginal governments and fiscal relations

Since 1973, the federal government and relevant provincial jurisdictions have been engaged in negotiating modern treaties with Indigenous nations where no agreements existed, or where the legitimacy of existing agreements has been in dispute. In a parallel process linked to modern treaty negotiations,

Chart 2
Treaties and Self-Government Agreements in the Territorial North

Title	Date	Territory Covered
Historic Treaties		
Treaty 8	1899	Alberta, BC, NWT, Saskatchewan
Treaty 11	1921	NWT, Yukon, Nunavut
Modern Treaties (Final Comprehensive Land Claim Agreements)		
Inuvialuit	1984	NWT
Gwich'in	1992	NWT
Nunavut	1993	Nunavut
Sahtu Dene and Metis	1993	NWT
Council for Yukon Indians Umbrella Agreement	1993	Yukon
Vuntut Gwich'in First Nation	1993	
Nacho Nyak Dun	1993	
Teslin Tlingit Council	1993	
Champagne and Aishihik First Nations	1993	
Little Salmon/Carmacks First Nations	1997	
Selkirk First Nation	1997	
TR'ondök Hwëch'in	1998	
Ta'an Ksawch'an Council	2002	
Kluane First Nation	2003	
Kwanlin Dun First Nation	2004	
Carcross/Tagish First Nation	2005	
Tlicho Agreement	2005	NWT

in several places, self-government agreements are creating Aboriginal governments with separate funding but complex relations with provincial, territorial, and federal governments. This has resulted in treaties and self-government agreements in northern Quebec, Nunavut, parts of the Northwest Territories, Yukon, and parts of British Columbia.

All of the modern Treaties and self-government agreements contain financial provisions, and many also confer government-like obligations on the Aboriginal signatories. In general, fiscal relations between Canadian governments and Aboriginal governments include several elements:

- The clarification and identification of certain law making powers exclusively to Aboriginal governments, other powers shared, and many others remaining with the federal or provincial governments;

- Transfer of capital in compensation for lands ceded in modern treaties, typically over twenty years;
- Revenue raising powers allocated to Aboriginal governments;
- Federal loans for Aboriginal participation in treaty negotiations;
- Cost-sharing agreements between federal and territorial governments regarding Aboriginal-related programs and service provision;
- Equalization-like commitments in modern treaties with respect to ensuring service provision levels comparable to levels prevailing in the region;
- Compensation arrangements with third parties affected by land and resource settlements; and,
- Financial transfer arrangements with First Nations, or regional or national Aboriginal organizations, within or outside treaties.

Canada-Aboriginal fiscal relations share several policy and political characteristics with federal-provincial and federal-territorial fiscal relations. Both systems embody considerable technical complexity and some asymmetry in the number and types of financing formulas, programs, revenues and processes. Transfers not only distribute monies but are also expressions of multiple values. Beyond the technical and financial details, arrangements in both systems carry significant political symbolism, rooted in histories and strongly held conceptions of the federation, constitutional relationships and the country. Both systems are no strangers to political controversy and intergovernmental disputes, in large part because of the centrality of such arrangements to revenues and budgetary choices, the social policy union, constitutional law and politics. In both systems as well, the federal spending power looms large as a factor in the jurisdictions and finances of other governments. The stakes concern the capacity to govern and the intergovernmental balance of power and visibility.

In light of these considerations, Nunavut makes an interesting case. The Government of Nunavut (GN) is, of course, a public government, part of the same financial systems as the other two territories, and in financial matters, governed similarly. The GN serves the whole northern public, which is about 85 per cent Inuit and the remaining 15 per cent an extremely heterogeneous, "other." But Inuit are also beneficiaries under the Nunavut Agreement, and in this regard, they participate in the governance of Nunavut Tunngavik Inc., an organization formed to administer their entitlements and obligations under the modern treaty. NTI is funded in similar fashion to all other Aboriginal beneficiary organizations. There are several areas of overlapping jurisdiction between the GN and NTI (for example, concerning the monitoring of social well-being in the territory).

Under modern treaties and agreements signed in the North (and in British Columbia), the transfer of tax room and revenue sharing is on the rise as a feature of Aboriginal fiscal relations in Canada. Transfer of tax room involves a reduction of the federal and or provincial/territorial share of a specified tax base thus creating room for the Aboriginal government to collect a corresponding increased share. Land claims settled in the North with the Nunavut, Gwich'in, Sahtu, and the Dogrib include resource royalty sharing with the federal government respecting mineral, oil and gas royalties.

RECENT DEVELOPMENTS IN TERRITORIAL FORMULA FINANCING

The latest debate in Canada on a fiscal imbalance between levels of government began in earnest in 2002, prompted by a report commissioned by the Quebec government, and expanding into a series of commentaries and reports by the federal government, academics, think tanks, federal opposition parties, and, in various combinations, the provinces and territories. We need not examine the meaning, origins, scale and consequences of fiscal imbalances in the federation, as these issues are thoroughly analyzed elsewhere.[22] For present purposes, we focus on recent policy reviews commissioned by Ottawa and by the Council of the Federation, and on reforms introduced by the Martin and Harper governments as they relate to territorial fiscal arrangements.

Even before this latest debate on fiscal imbalance erupted, the territorial governments had serious concerns about the TFF, due to federal restraint measures applied to the transfer arrangement in the 1990s by the Mulroney and Chrétien governments. Specifically, the NWT, Nunavut and Yukon governments voiced concerns over the adequacy and complexity of the fiscal program, and that "financing levels no longer correspond to the 'expenditure needs gap' as defined in the original formula." As a result, "the TFF no longer meets its original objective of allowing the territories to keep pace with provincial expenditure growth."[23] During 2003, the territories, both individually and collectively, prepared a "business case" on the limitations of the TFF for Finance and Privy Council officials and were engaged in discussions on the TFF renewal in 2004. Even with enhancements in health and social transfers in the later 1990s and extra funding to the TFF announced in 2004, the territorial finance departments estimated an annual adequacy gap in federal transfer payments of $221 million in 2005–06.[24]

The Martin Liberal's New Framework on Territorial Financing

Following First Ministers' Meetings in September and October 2004, the Martin government announced a New Framework on the Equalization program as well as for the TFF. In brief, the main changes proposed for the TFF were as follows. First, the total 2004–05 TFF grant for all three territories was a funding floor of $1.9 billion, to be allocated according to the shares of each territory's 2004–05 TFF grant. This change increased total grants by $65 million over what would have been the case under the previous formula. Second, the total 2005–06 TFF grant was to be a fixed amount of $2 billion, a guaranteed increase of $89 million in grants of what had previously been announced. Third, the $2 billion total TFF entitlement was to be escalated at a growth rate of 3.5 per cent for the next 10 years. Fourth, the escalation rate and the TFF amounts were to be reviewed in March 2009. Finally, an independent panel would be established to advise on the allocation of the legislated amounts of Equalization and TFF transfers. The Martin government introduced a bill in late November 2004 to legislate these proposed changes. In March 2005, the federal finance minister, Ralph Goodale, established the Expert Panel on Equalization and Territorial Formula Financing (the O'Brien report, so named after the chair, Allen O'Brien).[25]

In a joint statement to the Expert Panel in June 2005, the territorial governments identified four main implications of the New Framework:

- The initial fixed amounts do not restore the adequacy of the TFF in relation to its original definition. Further, the allocation shares for 2005–06 do not reflect the full program responsibilities of the Yukon government, since the average of the TFF shares used to determine the allocation include a year for which the Yukon did not have devolution of resources.
- The fixed 3.5 per cent escalator after 2005–06 is inadequate compared to the population-adjusted expenditure base growth rate defined under the previous TFF. The TFF entitlements under the previous arrangements would increase at a more rapid rate because provincial/local government spending adjusted for territorial population growth has outpaced growth in eligible revenues. Indeed, territorial finance departments' forecast that the New Framework could provide less total funding by 2008–09 than would have been the case under the old TFF.
- Since the 3.5 per cent escalator is imposed for both the Equalization program and TFF, growth in per capita funding to the territories will be less than for the provinces. The reason is that the population growth rates in the territories are significantly higher than the population growth rates in Equalization-receiving provinces, and the escalator does not incorporate a population adjustment factor for the North's greater population growth.
- Setting a fixed amount for the total TFF creates a zero-sum game for the territories, whereby gains to one or two territories must necessarily come from another territory (or territories). In effect, each territory will share the revenue growth or losses of the other two territories.[26]

Evoking values of regional diversity, fiscal equity and Canadian citizenship, the territorial governments' fundamental contention was that the New Framework proposals for TFF would undermine the ability of the territories to have adequate fiscal resources to deliver comparable levels of services as the provinces while recognizing the exceptional conditions in the North. Added to these issues, the territories face issues of working out relations of tax policy coordination, tax revenue sharing and program transfer with First Nations and other Aboriginal governments and organizations; a pattern of relationships which are somewhat distinctive in each of the territories.[27] Gas tax funding and relationships with municipalities such as Whitehorse re: land development processes, climate change (urban transit, water and emergency issues) reflect emerging public government and funding issues; the majority of Northerners live in cities. Social issues such as homelessness, poverty and increasing substance abuse will require cooperation among all levels of governments in ways still to be determined.

That issues of financing Aboriginal governments in the North were not part of the terms of reference of the Expert Panel, prompted the Inuvialuit Regional Corporation in the Northwest Territories to offer comments and recommendations on the future fiscal arrangements between the federal government and territorial and northern Aboriginal governments. In short, the recommendations were that financing arrangements for the territorial government must recognize obligations to Aboriginal people; ensure that Aboriginal and territorial governments get a fair share of resource revenues; and the TFF be formula based, responding to expenditure needs and revenues.[28] Of great importance, according to the Inuvialuit Regional Corporation, is adequate financing of comprehensive claims and self-government agreements for Aboriginal peoples:

We believe that financing arrangements for territorial and Aboriginal governments are inadequate to meet the obligations agreed to by all three governments. The territorial and Aboriginal governments require financing arrangements, including access to own source revenues and transfers, sufficient to fully implement such agreements.

In particular, the territorial government cannot pass on a share of its revenue to Aboriginal government without that share being considered as part of their revenue capacity. This has forced the territorial government in proposing that either the federal government compensate for the loss of actual revenue or that Aboriginal governments receive a share that is directly related to responsibilities with a result of no net fiscal benefit. This arrangement does not recognize the status of an Aboriginal government in being distinct from the jurisdiction of other governments and would continue to perpetuate a dependency of Aboriginal peoples and their governments on the transfer payments from Canada or territorial governments.[29]

Shortly after the federal government established the Expert Panel, the Council of the Federation (the provincial and territorial premiers) created, in May 2005, an Advisory Panel on Fiscal Imbalance, co-chaired by Roger Gagne and Janice Stein, producing a final report in March 2006, while the Expert Panel's final report came out in June 2006.[30] By then, the Harper government was in place in Ottawa and in their April 2006 Speech from the Throne stated they would "respond to concerns about the fiscal imbalance and ... work to ensure fiscal arrangements in which all governments have access to the resources they need to meet their responsibilities."[31]

Table 1 summarizes the core ideas of the federally commissioned Expert Panel, the provincially and territorially commissioned Advisory Panel, and the Harper government's actions as demonstrated in their budgets, in regards to territorial fiscal relations and the TFF. Both panels gave concentrated attention to a similar range of issues of concern to territorial governments, although less so for the technical matters of fiscal arrangements between territorial and northern Aboriginal governments or federal-territorial-Aboriginal northern government funding relations. Overall, the panels' recommendations converged. In fact, the Council of the Federation endorsed the recommendations of the O'Brien report as regards the TFF, which in turn the Harper government readily and essentially adopted as reflected in the 2006 and 2007 budgets.[32] The two independent expert commissions enabled the territorial governments' interests a hearing in wider and more open forums than in the traditional executive federalism style of closed meetings between senior officials and the federal government dominating the outcome.[33] The territories succeeded in drawing attention to their concerns, in reframing the terms of the debate on fiscal relations in the North, and reversing core aspects of the New Framework unveiled in October 2004. Budgetary decisions in 2006 and 2007 mark the return to an agreed formulaic approach to determining entitlements, both for Equalization and the TFF, and away from the Martin government's confusing method of strident official denials of a fiscal imbalance even existing followed by several ad hoc and bilateral side deals on intergovernmental fiscal matters.[34]

Tables 2, 3 and 4 respectively show federal fiscal transfers to Yukon, NWT and Nunavut for the years 2005–06 to 2008–09.

For all three territorial governments, the TFF represents the vast share of federal transfers, accounting for 89 to 93 per cent of federal payments in 2008–09. New spending on the TFF by the Harper government totals $216 million by the end of 2008–09. Far behind financially are other programs, the most significant being for infrastructure. This funding reflects territorial shares of the Gas Tax Fund, the Building Canada Fund, the equal per capita jurisdiction funding, the Public Transit Fund and the Public Transit Capital Trust. The Canada Health Transfer and Canada Social Transfer, despite their huge symbolism and expenditure scale in southern Canada, are relatively minor sources of funding for the territories. In this respect, the hallmark of northern fiscal federalism is unconditional bloc grants, based on the federal spending power, with few cost-sharing obligations on the part of the territories.

Table 1
Reviewing and Reforming Federal-Territorial Fiscal Relations

Issue	Gagne-Stein Report	O'Brien Report	Federal Budgets 2006 and 2007
New Framework of October 2004	Return to a formula-based financing mechanism for each territory as previously	Replace the fixed pool under the New Framework with a principles-based formula with separate grants for each territory	Reinstated a principle-based and predictable formula for Territorial Formula Financing (TFF) with specific grants for each territory
Assessing and adjusting expenditure needs	Base on 2006–07 funding levels with future adjustments for each territory linked to per capita spending changes and relative population growth	Use 2005–06 funding levels, adjusted annually by relative population growth and comparable growth in the provinces, and using three-year moving averages	Certainty for 2006–07 payments and increased allocations of $115 million for 2007–08

Annual growth based on changes in provincial-local spending and relative growth in territorial population to that of Canada as a whole, using a three-year moving average for each territory |
| Determining and measuring revenue-raising capacity | Include only most significant tax and revenue sources | Establish a revenue block that includes 70% of measured revenue capacity in the formula, from seven of the largest territorial revenue sources | Representative tax system of seven revenue bases[1] |
| Natural resource control and revenues | Expedite transfer of responsibility for lands and resources and most of the revenues to territories | In principle, territories should see direct benefits from resources developments | Government will move ahead with negotiations to devolve onshore natural resource management and resource revenues to NWT |

Table 1
Reviewing and Reforming Federal-Territorial Fiscal Relations (*Continued*)

Issue	Gagne-Stein Report	O'Brien Report	Federal Budgets 2006 and 2007
Growth in revenues	Increase in revenues should not penalize territories overall	Exclude resource revenues from calculation of revenues for the TFF	Continue to treat natural resource revenues outside of TFF: 50% of resource revenues will be excluded from the offset calculation against the TFF
		Territories should realize net fiscal benefits from resource development	Improved incentives for territories to increase own revenue sources[2]
Other federal programs	Funding for territories be for actual demand and cost rather than per capita allocations	Notes that the territories have received significant new investments in recent years through other federal programs	Budget 2006 announced $308 million to address immediate needs for the territories for post-secondary education, public transit, affordable housing, and northern housing
	Exclude such funding from TFF calculations	Any increases in other federal transfers to the territories not be included in measure of territories' revenue capacity	Additional funds for climate change and infrastructure initiatives
Aboriginal affairs and relations	Future expenditure needs of territories should include new obligations from Aboriginal rights agreements	Strongly encourage governments and Aboriginal leaders to resume negotiations on devolution and resource revenue sharing agreements	$500 million fund over 10 years to mitigate negative impacts on local communities of Mackenzie Gas Project identified as a Aboriginal initiative
	Take into account Aboriginal rights in transfer of resource management		

Table 1
Reviewing and Reforming Federal-Territorial Fiscal Relations (Continued)

Issue	Gagne-Stein Report	O'Brien Report	Federal Budgets 2006 and 2007
Exceptional needs of Nunavut	Extraordinary investments for housing, infrastructure, and economic and social development	Undertake review of significant expenditure needs and higher public service provision costs	Specific measures included $200 million for affordable housing and $23 million for financial management systems in Nunavut.
		Any additional funding necessary for Nunavut's needs be provided through targeted programs rather than changes to the TFF formula	
Governance of fiscal federalism	Establish a FPT First Ministers' Fiscal Council and a Canadian Institute for Fiscal Information	TFF should be legislated rather than addressed through agreements	TFF payments legislated
		Annual reports to Parliament and a parliamentary review process prior to five-year renewals of TFF and other transfer programs	Borrowing limit for GNWT raised from $300 million to $500 million

[1] These are personal income, business income, tobacco, gasoline, diesel fuel, alcoholic beverages and payroll. A further 11 non-resource revenue bases (such as general sales tax, property tax, vehicle licences) are grouped into a revenue block, outside of the representative tax system, using actual revenues and a common escalator of 2 per cent for future years. This approach is consistent with the revenue coverage under the Equalization program

[2] Of every new dollar the territorial governments raise through their own-source revenues, 30 cents will not be considered in determining TFF entitlements. Natural resource revenues include royalties, licences, rents and fees from the development of oil and gas, minerals, forestry and water power.

Table 2
Federal Fiscal Transfers to Yukon, 2005–06 to 2008–09

	2005–06	2006–07	2007–08	2008–09
	(millions of dollars)			
Territorial Formula Financing[1]	495	514	540	561
Devolution Transfer Agreement Payment			4	
Canada Health Transfer	21	21	22	23
Canada Social Transfer[2]	9	9	10	10
New labour market training funding				0.5
Infrastructure	5	5	32	34
Canada ecoTrust			2	2
Total	530	549	609	630

[1] Includes supplementary payments in Budget 2005 and Budget 2006; excludes one-time adjustment to TFF in 2006–07.
[2] Includes transition CST protection payments in 2007–08.

Table 3
Federal Fiscal Transfers to the Northwest Territories, 2005–06 to 2008–09

	2005–06	2006–07	2007–08	2008–09
	(millions of dollars)			
Territorial Formula Financing[1]	728	753	788	783
Canada Health Transfer	20	17	19	20
Canada Social Transfer	7	6	13	14
New labour market training funding				0.6
Infrastructure	5	5	32	34
Canada ecoTrust			2	2
Total	760	780	854	853

Note: The Northwest Territories will also receive a corporate tax refund adjustment of $54 million in 2007–08.
[1] Includes supplementary payments in Budget 2005 and Budget 2006.

Table 4
Federal Fiscal Transfers to Nunavut, 2005–06 to 2008–09

	2005–06	2006–07	2007–08	2008–09
	(millions of dollars)			
Territorial Formula Financing[1]	812	839	893	942
Canada Health Transfer	22	23	24	25
Canada Social Transfer[2]	10	10	11	10
New labour market training funding				0.5
Infrastructure	5	5	32	34
Canada ecoTrust			2	2
Total	849	877	962	1,013

Note: The Northwest Territories will also receive a corporate tax refund adjustment of $54 million in 2007–08.
[2] Includes supplementary payments in Budget 2005 and Budget 2006.

CANADIAN ARCTIC SOVEREIGNTY AND HARPER'S NORTHERN AGENDA

"Exterior challenges to sovereignty come rarely to our country," wrote veteran political journalist Lawrence Martin in the summer of 2007, following on the spectacle of two Russian mini-submarines navigating under polar ice and leaving a Russian flag on the ocean sea floor. "When they do, they provide the governing party with an opportunity to gain public favour."[35] Martin added:

Mr Harper happens to be in office when the North finally looms high in the public consciousness, when it has taken on major significance, when it has become the new frontier. Previous governments have tried to stake a claim to a northern vision, but the timing was always premature. But now, with the combination of climate change, sovereignty challenges and renewed focus on resource riches, the moment is right. The North as the new frontier is the issue that can drive the public imagination, raise the patriotic pulse and give the Harper government a shot at a big legacy.[36]

Northern policy is likely to remain an enduring aspect of the next few years, for reasons having largely to do with climate change, the opening of northern seas to transportation, the international struggle over undersea resources, and the major social and economic development challenges faced by the north's relatively new governments. It is not clear that the Harper government will leave a "big legacy" in its responses to these challenges – nor it is obvious that the Harper initiatives will mesh well with longstanding northern priorities and plans.

The North is a hybrid policy domain with regional, constitutional, identity-based, and international attributes, in which external affairs and foreign policy, as Martin's observation suggests, is not usually the dominant concern.[37] According to Indian and Northern Affairs Canada (INAC), the long-term objective of northern policy is "the North as a self-sufficient, prosperous region in which Northerners manage their own affairs, enjoy a quality of life comparable to that enjoyed by other Canadians and make strong contributions to a dynamic, secure federation."[38] Expressed in INAC's departmental program activities, the federal government's northern agenda over the past several years focuses on the four components of governance, healthy communities, land and resources, and the northern economy.

In their 2005 founding policy document, the Conservative Party of Canada practically ignored the territorial governments and northern issues, mistakenly referring to the territories as recipients of the Equalization program and noticeably silent on the specific place of the territories in a more "open federalism" committed to the federal principle of division of powers. In their 2006 federal election platform, the Conservatives identified as part of their plan for promoting Canada's regions to "develop, together with northerners, both Aboriginal and non-Aboriginal, a northern vision to guide economic, social and environmental progress in the region."[39] This is language quite similar to expressions of northern policy in circulation in Ottawa since the 1980s. On mining, the Conservative plan committed to streamline federal regulatory processes, in particular "in the North for the oil and gas mining sectors."[40] The only other area of the Conservative's election platform which identified northern policy dealt with "defending Canada" and their intention in government to "increase the Canadian Forces' capacity to protect Canada's Arctic sovereignty and security."[41] On the issues of infrastructure, fiscal imbalance, and open federalism, the territorial and northern Aboriginal governments were absent.

The Russians are coming! And so are the Americans and Danes!

In a series of announcements over July and August 2007, Prime Minister Harper detailed elements of what he called his government's coastal security and Arctic security strategy, linking this plan to what he called the federal government's highest responsibility – "the defence of our nation's sovereignty. And in defending our nation's sovereignty, nothing is as fundamental as protecting Canada's territorial integrity: our borders; our airspace; and our waters."[42] He went on to note the growing importance of the North to Canada and by implication other nations: "The ongoing discovery of the North's resource riches – coupled with the potential impact of climate change – has made the region an area of increasing interest and concern. Canada has a choice when it comes to defending our sovereignty over the Arctic. We either use it or lose. And make no mistake; this Government intends to use it. Because Canada's Arctic is central to our identity as a northern nation. It is part of our history. And it represents tremendous potential of our future."[43]

Harper's Arctic security strategy for asserting jurisdiction through an enhanced military presence so far has four elements totaling about $8 billion in federal spending commitments over the next few decades:

1 To construct in Canada and deploy six to eight new Polar Class 5 Arctic Offshore patrol ships, equipped with new helicopters, with the ability to patrol the length of Northwest Passage during the summer months, when a Canadian naval presence is required, and its approaches year-round. The total cost is estimated at $3.1 billion for acquiring the ships and a further $4.3 billion for operations and maintenance over the 25 year lifespan of the ships.
2 Construction of a deep water port in the far North, established at Nanisivik inside the eastern entrance to the Northwest passage, to serve "as a forward operating base for the new patrol ships" allowing them to re-supply and re-fuel. As well as its prime military purpose, the deep-water port will have civilian and commercial shipping uses.[44] Preliminary estimates indicate a required investment of $100 million to complete this port and annual maintenance and operating costs of approximately $10 million.
3 Establishment of a Canadian Forces Arctic Training Centre in Resolute Bay envisaged as "a year-round multi-purpose facility supporting Arctic training and operations, accommodating up to 100 personnel. Training equipment and vehicles stationed at the site will also provide an increased capability and faster response time in support of regional military or civilian emergency operations."[45] Refurbishing costs are estimated at $4 million with an annual expenditure of $2 million for salaries, operations and maintenance.
4 Expansion of the Canadian Rangers by 900 members to 5,000 personnel, and modernization of their transport equipment, uniforms and weapons. Expansion of the Ranger Program (who are part-time reservists providing a military presence in remote and coastal communities) is approximately $12 million in annual additional costs, and the Ranger modernization project is estimated to cost $45 million.[46]

Harper situates his government's Arctic security strategy within a broader Northern Agenda that has four objectives:

- To encourage investment and adopt regulatory measures to complement the growing global demand for our northern energy and mineral resources;

- To vigorously protect Canadian sovereignty in the Arctic as international interest in the region increases;
- To end the paternalistic federal policies of the past so Northerners have more control over their own economic and political destiny, by strengthening federal-territorial fiscal and jurisdictional relations; and,
- To respond to the challenges of climate change in the North and make sure that its countless ecological wonders are protected for future generations.[47]

The October 16, 2007, Speech from the Throne "re-announced" these measures, adding specific promises to improve housing for First Nations and Inuit, build a "world-class" arctic research station, map the Arctic seabed, buy new arctic patrol ships, and expand both aerial surveillance and the Arctic Rangers.[48] These are all measures that are long overdue: the lack of adequate housing in Nunavut and in some parts of the Northwest Territories is major social problem; the other polar nations are well ahead of Canada in mapping the seabed, a measure required by the United Nations Convention on the Law of the Sea for nations wishing to confirm their sovereignty; and Canadian surveillance capacity in the Arctic is inadequate. If appropriate levels of spending are committed in these areas with some alacrity, there is indeed a chance that the Harper government will indeed be remembered for strength in northern policy.

To date, the distinctive features of the Conservative government's approach to northern affairs are the relatively cautious return to a more decentralized funding regime for territorial governments and an emphasis on the military – both features that are mandated both by current conditions and by the ideology of the government, including a commitment to a decentralized federation with a strong role for the federal government is certain restricted areas, such as defence. There has been less emphasis on the quiet spending of diplomatic affairs or scientific research in favour of spending meant to be seen and heard in the form of major capital projects for the Canadian Forces, linking regional measures with national goals of coastal security and economic development.

This is a policy domain also rich with symbolism that speechwriters and politicians cannot resist using. In announcing policies on and in the North, Harper has spoken of the Arctic as "the great Canadian frontier," central to "our identity as a northern nation" and part of our history; Northerners as "stewards of this magnificent land," this "vast storehouse of energy and mineral riches," this "precious reservoir of ecological and cultural treasures."[49] In the October 2007 Throne Speech, Canada is identified as "the Northern Star": "Like the North Star, Canada has been a guide to other nations; through difficult times, Canada has shone as an example of what a people joined in common purpose can achieve."[50]

Such rhetorical references reveal the presence of multiple political ideas in this policy domain that must be reconciled in some fashion over time. The rhetoric also emphasizes the Canadian-ness of the North in support of sovereignty claims to the Arctic, perhaps to build a broad and legitimate public interest in, and constituency for Northern policy as a whole and recent initiatives in the military-related component of this policy domain.

What is less clear is the extent to which the hoary visions of the current federal government (and many of its predecessors) respond to the actual needs and priorities of northerners. For example, the commitment to improve housing for those areas of the North, such as Nunavut, where the lack of adequate housing is an abiding source of serious social disorder, can only be realized with very substantial, sustained funding commitments. On another front, federal northern foreign policy seems to have dissolved into federal defence policy, leaving stranded the major diplomatic initiatives of the last two decades, to create a circumpolar governance regime and ignoring the importance of Greenland and Alaska to northern economic development. Even the location of the deep water port appears to have ignored northern needs for a port that will contribute to resupply where there are population concentrations.

CONCLUSIONS

The political project of redefining the terms and conditions of Canada's political communities is ongoing and nowhere more so than in the North, with the interplay of visions centred on the Canadian state, territorial governments, and Aboriginal nations. There is much unfinished constitutional business in re-confederating Canada. From our analysis in this chapter, we conclude that territorial leaders and officials deserve some credit for reforms to the TFF announced in recent federal budgets, reversing in large part the framework of reforms unveiled by the Martin government.

There remains, however, a structural imbalance in the distribution of expenditure and revenue powers of the territorial governments, resulting in a significant constraint on the autonomy of the territories and on their dependence upon federal transfer as a source of total territorial revenues. The federal Expert Panel commented that: "The goal of providing reasonably comparable public services to people in the territories has to be met through a combination of adequate federal support, active promotion of economic development in the territories, and sound financial management."[51] These are all worthwhile recommendations that require sustained action. Additionally, a satisfactory response must address the transfer of resource revenue powers to all three territories plus Aboriginal self-government agreements must have resource revenue sharing arrangements articulated with the resources and responsibilities of the federal government and the territorial governments; in essence, a trilateral form of fiscal equilibrium.

It is too early to gauge fully the consequences for territorial responsible government and for Aboriginal self-determination of the current emphasis on Arctic sovereignty with military measures for rallying Canadians against perceived foreign challenges. The tendency in Canada's political history, as Smiley has pointed out, is that one set of challenges crucial to the federation will "displace one or both of the others as a focus of public concern" although "the political cleavages formed in relation to whichever is at the centre of attention characteristically complicates divisions [and alliances] relevant to the other issues."[52] This analytical perspective suggests that a strong emphasis on Arctic sovereignty could well dislodge policy attention and action on the other major issues of nation-building in the North. Recent events in the Arctic make evident that the Harper government is determined to assert claims of Canadian sovereignty in the polar region. This growing military presence derives not from Russian submarines under the North Pole leaving a flag on the ocean floor, but rather to the Harper Conservatives' general prominence given to Arctic sovereignty and realization of issues of strategic economic and environmental importance in the region.

Putting greater stress on the sovereignty issue framed in this way, no doubt has implications for relations between Canada and the United States; federal and territorial governments; federal-Aboriginal, federal-Aboriginal-territorial, and territorial-Aboriginal relationships; and central heartland and coastal regions of Canada in regard to procurement contracts and economic development opportunities associated with recent military capital project announcements. A further inference is that with the federal government apparently preoccupied with Arctic sovereignty, the interests of northerners need expression, as effectively and vigorously as possible, by territorial and Aboriginal leaders, their governments and communities, supported by cooperation among public and indigenous governments, other premiers, and MPs and Senators representing the region.

NOTES

1 We call these the "other three axes of Canadian federalism" in relation to Smiley's paradigmatic analysis of the trilogy of spatially delineated forces facing Canadian nation-building – the relations between French and English; the central heartland and its eastern and western peripheries; and Canada and the United States. See D.V. Smiley, *Canada in Question: Federalism in the Eighties, Third Edition* (Toronto: McGraw-Hill Ryerson, 1980), chapter 8. The three axes we identify are "other" in that they receive relatively little attention in political science and studies of federalism, despite their importance and their role in the construction of identities both by northerners and southerners in Canada.
2 The 2007–09 International Polar Year (IPY) is an international research and research infrastructure development initiative, involving 33 countries. Hundreds of publicly funded research programs are currently underway. The first IPY occurred in 1882–3, and since then there have been three others, in 1932–1933, 1957–1958, and

2007–2008. Previous polar years were marked by concentration on meteorological and geophysical research; during the 2007–2009 IPY there has been an effort to broaden the disciplinary base (to include life sciences and social research, and also to include a broader range of educational activities.
3 Expert Panel on Equalization and Territorial Formula Financing, *Strengthening Canada's Territories and Putting Equalization Back on Track*. The Report of the Expert Panel on Equalization and Territorial Formula Financing (Ottawa: Finance Canada, 2006). Available at http://www.eqtf-pfft.ca
4 Ronald L. Watts, *Comparing Federal Systems, Second Edition* (Montreal & Kingston: McGill-Queen's University Press, 1998), 43.
5 Yukon has had responsible government (and party politics at the territorial level) since 1979.
6 Northwest Territories, Nunavut, and Yukon, *A Stronger North in a Better Canada*. Available at http://www.anorthernvision.ca/; accessed 31 January 2008. On the development of non-governmental northern policy capacity, see Frances Abele, *The Feasibility of a Northern Policy Research Institution*. Report for the Walter and Duncan Gordon Foundation, 2006.
7 Gurston Dacks, ed., *Devolution and Constitutional Development in the Canadian North* (Ottawa: Carleton University Press, 1990).
8 The greater part of the youthfulness of northern populations is due to higher than the Canadian average birth rates among Aboriginal communities. Yukon, with its smaller Aboriginal population, is beginning to confront the policy challenge of increasing proportion of retired and elder people.
9 Aboriginal people are approximately 20 per cent of the population of the Yukon, 50 per cent of the population of the Northwest Territories, and 85 per cent of the population of Nunavut.
10 Jack Hicks and Graham White, "Nunavut: Inuit Self-Determination Through a Land Claim and Public Government," in Jens Dahl, Jack Hicks and Peter Jull, eds., *Nunavut: Inuit Regain Control of Their Lands and Their Lives* (Copenhagen: IWGIA, 2000), 30–115; Jack Hicks and Graham White, "Building Nunavut Through Decentralization or Carpet-Bombing It Into Near Total Dysfunction? A Case Study in Organizational Engineering," Paper presented at the Annual Meeting of the Canadian Political Science Association, University of Western Ontario, London, Ontario, June 2005. available at http://www.cpsa-acsp.ca/papers-2005/Hicks.pdf.
11 Arguably, Nunavut Territory is at least a partial exception to this rule, as it was created pursuant to a provision in the constitutionally protected modern treaty (the Nunavut Agreement) ratified by the Inuit of Nunavut and the federal government in right of the Crown in 1992.
12 See http://www.ainc-inac.gc.ca/pr/pub/pni/pni06_e.html
13 In the past, federal – territorial Economic Development Agreements provided significant funding to the territories for strategic investment. These have no current parallel.
14 These examples are by no means exhaustive. Other asymmetric features include the distinctive role of the Territorial Commissioner as compared to the Lieutenant

Governors of the provinces; Yukon's power to make laws in relation to non-renewable natural resources, a power the other two territories lack; the legislative power of the NWT to levy a tax on furs or any portion of fur-bearing animals to be taken outside of the Territories; and the language rights for indigenous languages contained in the *Yukon Act, 2002* and the *Nunavut Act, 1993*.

15 Nunavut Territory was created in 1999 by division of the old Northwest Territories.
16 Bernard W. Funston, "Canada's North and Tomorrow's Federalism," in Ian Peach, ed., *Constructing Tomorrow's Federalism: New Routes to Effective Governance* (Winnipeg: University of Manitoba Press, 2007).
17 These annual payments were divided into operating and capital funds. The territorial governments could use the operating funds at their discretion, but major capital spending required approval by the federal Treasury Board.
18 Starting in 1985, the transfer of funds to the territorial governments came in the form of five year formula financing arrangements, based on 1982–83 actual expenditures escalated by growth in provincial and local government spending. The escalator was adjusted for population starting with the second five year formula financing agreement, which covered 1990–91 to 1994–95.
19 On the federal control of territorial government borrowing, see *Yukon Act, 2002*, sec. 23(2); *Northwest Territories Act, 1985*, sec. 20(2); *Nunavut Act, 1993*, sec. 27(2).
20 One of the authors has estimated in an earlier study that Yukon and the NWT governments were both involved in about 100 federal or intergovernmental programs. Michael J. Prince and Gary Juniper, *Public Power and the Public Purse: Governments, Budgets and Aboriginal Peoples in the Canadian North* (Ottawa: Report prepared for the Royal Commission on Aboriginal Peoples, 1997), chapter 2.
21 Expert Panel on Equalization and Territorial Formula Financing, *Strengthening Canada's Territories and Putting Equalization Back on Track,* The Report of the Expert Panel on Equalization and Territorial Formula Financing. (Ottawa: Finance Canada, 2006), 7. Available at http://www.eqtf-pfft.ca.
22 See Winer and Hettich in this volume, and Gilles Paquet, "Fiscal Imbalance as Government Failure," in Bruce Doern, ed. *How Ottawa Spends 2004–2005: Mandate Change in the Paul Martin Era* (Montreal: McGill-Queen's University Press, 2004), chapter 2; and Harvey Lazar, ed., *Canadian Fiscal Arrangements: What Works, What Might Work Better* (Kingston: Queen's University School of Policy Studies, Institute of Intergovernmental Relations, 2005).
23 Departments of Finance, Nunavut, the Northwest Territories, and Yukon, *Joint Territorial Submission to the Expert Panel on Equalization and Territorial Formula Financing*. (June 29, 2005), 3.
24 Departments of Finance, Nunavut, the Northwest Territories, and Yukon, *Joint Territorial Submission*, 7.
25 Expert Panel on Equalization and Territorial Formula Financing, *Strengthening Canada's Territories and Putting Equalization Back on Track*.
26 Departments of Finance, Nunavut, the Northwest Territories, and Yukon, *Joint Territorial Submission*, 5.

27 Departments of Finance, *Joint Territorial Submission*, 23–24 and 27 for a useful overview of the distinct arrangements across Yukon, NWT and Nunavut with respect to First Nation, Inuit and Aboriginal self-governments.
28 Nellie Cournoyea, Chair and CEO, Inuvialuit Regional Corporation, Letter to the Expert Panel on Equalization and Territorial Formula Financing, "Re: Recommendations for the Future Fiscal Arrangements between Canada and the Territories and Aboriginal Governments," (Inuvik, Nunavut: January 23, 2006).
29 Cournoyea, Chair and CEO, Inuvialuit Regional Corporation, Letter to the Expert Panel, 2.
30 Advisory Panel on Fiscal Imbalance, Roger Gagne and Janice Stein, co-chairs, Reconciling *the Irreconcilable: Addressing Canada's Fiscal Imbalance* (March 31, 2006). Available at http://councilofthefederation.ca.
31 Speech from the Throne, 4 April 2006.
32 The Council of the Federation, "Territorial Formula Financing," *Communiqué*, (St. John's, July 28, 2006). In part, the communiqué said: "Premiers reinforced their support for moving immediately to implement the recommendations of the Federal Expert Panel on Territorial Formula Financing."
33 Watts, *Comparing Federal Systems*, 51; also see Smiley, *Canada in Question*, chapters 3 and 5.
34 Paquet, "Fiscal Imbalance as Government Failure;" Andrew Teliszewsky and Christopher Stoney, "Addressing the Fiscal Imbalance through Asymmetrical Federalism: Dangerous Times for the Harper Government and for Canada," in Bruce Doern, ed., *How Ottawa Spends 2007–2008: The Harper Governments – Climate of Change* (Montreal: McGill-Queen's University Press, 2007), chapter 2.
35 Lawrence Martin, "Harper's golden opportunity in the Great White North," *The Globe and Mail*, 9 August 2007, A13.
36 Martin, "Harper's golden opportunity in the Great White North."
37 See Peter J. May, et al. "Policy Coherence and Component-Driven Policymaking: Arctic Policy in Canada and the United States," *The Policy Studies Journal* 33, no.1 (2005): 37–63; and, Robert F. Durant, "Agency Evolution, New Institutionalism and 'Hybrid' Policy Domains," *The Policy Studies Journal* 34, no. 4 (2006): 469–90.
38 Indian and Northern Affairs Canada, *2007–2008 Estimates, Plan and Priorities* (Ottawa: INAC, 2007), 38.
39 Conservative Party of Canada, *Stand Up for Canada: Conservative Party of Canada Federal Election Platform 2006* (Ottawa: Conservative Party of Canada, January 2006), 18.
40 Conservative Party of Canada, *Stand Up for Canada*, 19.
41 Conservative Party of Canada, *Stand Up for Canada*, 45.
42 Prime Minister's Office, "Prime Minister Stephen Harper announces new Arctic offshore patrol ships," (Esquimalt: July 9, 2007), 1–2.
43 Prime Minister's Office, "Prime Minister Stephen Harper announces new Arctic offshore patrol ships," 2.
44 Prime Minister's Office, "Prime Minister Stephen Harper announces new Arctic offshore patrol ships," 3.

45 Prime Minister's Office, "Prime Minister announces expansion of Canadian Forces facilities and operations in the Arctic," (Resolute Bay: August 10, 2007), 1.
46 Prime Minister's Office, "Backgrounder – Expanding Canadian Forces Operations in the Arctic," (Resolute Bay: August 10, 2007), 2.
47 Prime Ministers Office, "Prime Minister announces the expansion of Nahanni National Park Reserve," (Fort Simpson: August 8, 2007), 1–2. On this last objective, the Harper Cabinet, through an Order in Council, has substantially expanded the Nahanni National Park Reserve in the NWT, adding a further 5,400 square kilometers of land to the Park. This follows a 2003 agreement between Parks Canada and the Dehcho First Nations to protect the area by limiting the creation of new third party rights, such as to mineral claims. This latest announcement involves (1) protection of lands and wildlife (e.g., grizzly bears and herds of woodland caribou) by withdrawing additional land from future development; (2) respecting the rights of the Dehcho First Nations to continue to fish, hunt and trap on the lands; (3) recognize existing commercial interests and investments in the area; and (4) through public consultations, undertaken by Parks Canada, and other processes, determine land use policies for environmental, commercial, recreational and tourist purposes Prime Minister's Office, "Backgrounder- Protecting Canada's Ecological Treasures: Nahanni National Park Reserve Expansion," (Fort Simpson, NWT: August 8, 2007).
48 Canada, *Strong Leadership. A Better Canada.* Speech from the Throne, 16 October 2007.
49 Prime Minister's Office, "Prime Minister Stephen Harper announces new Arctic offshore patrol ships," 2; and "Prime Minister announces the expansion of Nahanni National Park Reserve," 1.
50 Speech from the Throne 2007, 16.
51 Expert Panel on Equalization and Territorial Formula Financing, *Strengthening Canada's Territories and Putting Equalization Back on Track,* 32–3. In fact, at their 2007 annual meeting, the western premiers issued a statement calling on the federal government to give the territories more jurisdictional powers and more funds through devolution agreements. See Katherine Harding, "Give North more money, western premiers tell Harper," *The Globe and Mail,* 6 July 2007, A4.
52 Smiley, *Canada in Question,* 185.

6 One Step Forward, Two Steps Back: Child Care Policy From Martin To Harper

CHERYL COLLIER
AND RIANNE MAHON

Child care policy was an important issue in the 2006 election, demarcating a clear difference between the Harper Conservatives and the other parties, including Martin's Liberals, on the role of government in general and the place of intergovernmental relations in social policy in particular. As child care was one of the Harper government's top five priorities, it was also one of the first areas where the new government acted quickly to establish a distinctive profile. Soon after the election, the Harper government announced its intention to withdraw from the bilateral Early Learning and Child Care agreements the Martin government had concluded with all ten provinces. It thus cleared the way for the implementation of its own child care policy: the "Universal Child Care Benefit" (UCCB), which provides $100 a month taxable dollars directly to families, for all children under six, and the Child Care Space Initiative (CCSI), which was to offer federal tax incentives to business and community groups, especially the former, to establish new spaces.

This is not the first time that child care has been in the political spotlight. It enjoyed a certain prominence in the 1984 election, where the parties were forced to position themselves on "women's issues", and again in 1993 when the Chrétien Liberal's gave it a prominent position in their "Red Book" of election promises. Its political stature stems in part from the complex of issues it potentially addresses: a "bridge" to gender equality; a means for alleviating child poverty (or, getting lone mothers off social assistance); a measure to help families to reconcile work and family life; and laying the foundations for lifelong learning. Solutions proposed vary with the way the issue is framed. Thus for instance, a focus on poverty reduction tends to suggest a more limited role for government, targeting poor families;[1] reconciliation, while broader (adult earner families) tends to focus only on the children of such families, while gender equality and early childhood development favour universality. Broader political value systems also enter into the picture: is child care primarily a family responsibility, preferably carried out in a home environment (i.e. the familialist arguments favoured today by social conservatives); a commodity offered on the market and subject to its laws of supply and demand (favoured by neo-liberals); or is it, like education, a public good, a stance more typical of social liberals and social democrats?

Divisions on these issues were reflected in the 2006 election debates. The Liberals, stressing child development, promised to build on the bilateral agreements that had involved a five year commitment to spend $5 billion on registered early learning and care programmes. In promising to extend these agreements for an additional five years, the Liberals proposed to establish the stable funding needed to provide affordable quality child care for pre-school children across Canada. They also promised capital funding, by making child care an eligible infrastructural investment under the Strategic Infrastructure Fund and the Municipal Rural Infrastructure Fund, thus recognizing child care as an essential element of the social infrastructure for Canadians living in big cities and rural municipalities alike. The NDP would have gone further, not only by increasing the federal government's financial contribution, but also by making child care a citizen right, like health care, by the promulgation of a federal child care act.

The Conservatives had a very different interpretation, one that clearly reflected the new party's ideological blend of neo-liberalism and social conservatism. The main proposal, the "choice in child care allowance" as the UCCB was called during the election, reflects this. The UCCB is designed to support families (i.e. mothers) who choose to remain at home as well as adult worker families – although its importance is more symbolic as the amount on offer ($100 per month, taxed if both parents are earning) is too little to make a real difference for most. The second component, the CCSI, marked an attempt to break with the pattern of federal-provincial relations that has been the foundation for much of Canada's social policies. Instead, for the first time, the federal government planned to offer incentives directly to employers[2] to establish new spaces. Both programmes reflected a clear shift in philosophy and both involved an attempt to break with the intergovernmental arrangements that have been a characteristic feature of Canada's post-war social policy regime.

This chapter will assess the Harper government's achievements in the field of early childhood education and care (ECEC), with particular emphasis on the implications for intergovernmental relations. We will begin with a brief reflection on the broader question of why intergovernmental relations matter in this field, not only in Canada but also in other OECD countries. Then, after reviewing the development of Canada's child care system, we will turn to examine two important initiatives that attempted to lay the foundations for a pan-Canadian system geared to establishing an accessible, affordable and universally available ECEC system, backed by mutually agreed procedures for assuring accountability. Against this backdrop, the final section will analyse the Harper government's ECEC plans and achievements.

EARLY CHILDHOOD EDUCATION AND CHILD CARE: WHY DO INTERGOVERNMENTAL RELATIONS MATTER?

Canadians may think it is only in federal systems like ours that child care policy becomes entangled in intergovernmental arrangements. Nevertheless the OECD's thematic review of early childhood education and care, *Starting Strong*,[3] made it clear that national-local arrangements are typical of this policy field for a number of reasons. First, child care programmes operate in a diversity of local contexts (and hence needs). Clearly sparsely populated areas encounter a different set of challenges to metropolitan areas. In addition, some places have substantial populations with diverse ethnic and linguistic backgrounds. Devolution to the local level allows for greater sensitivity to such needs.

Second, the field is simply too complex to manage adequately from above. Early childhood education and care is comprised of a broad range of programmes and arrangements – regulated centre-based and family child care, school-based kindergarten, independent preschools, drop-in centres, family resource centres with toy-lending libraries and other supports for home-based care, and a plethora of informal care arrangements including "kin care" (publicly supported in places like Alberta). As *Starting Strong II* noted, "the more numerous providers and fragmented provision patterns in the early childhood field make it difficult for central governments to ensure quality and a rational provision of services in the absence of devolved local management."[4] *Starting Strong II*, which makes a strong case for an integrated approach to ECEC, also adds that local authorities have often shown a greater willingness to pursue innovative experiments that cut across traditional divisions.[5] In Canada, Toronto and Vancouver stand out for their innovative efforts to develop a coherent system of ECEC services.[6]

Decentralisation also allows for greater involvement of parents and, more broadly, a democratic organization and management of ECEC services. In fact, one of the leading international experts in this field, Peter Moss, has made a strong pitch for ECEC as "sites of democratic practice." Clearly this is most likely to occur in ECEC systems that give local authorities an important role to play. Such an approach is even more important in neighbourhoods with diverse populations, where ECEC institutions can function as "spaces for participation and interculturalism ... based on the principle of democratic participation."[7] Like *Starting Strong*, however, Moss recognizes that local ECEC systems are best able to function this way when they form part of a supportive set of intergovernmental arrangements.

In other words, devolution functions best within a coherent national framework. For the authors of *Starting Strong II*, a strong national policy framework, which establishes a common vision, a coherent approach to funding, appropriate programme standards, and clear accountability procedures, is necessary to ensure equity and cohesion. In the absence of such a supportive legislative, administrative and fiscal framework, devolution will simply result in wide differences in access, affordability and quality. At the same time, it is important to strike a balance between the central government's capacity to establish the means to ensure equity and local authorities' scope for adaptation to local needs and for innovation.

What about federal systems? As Moss admits, research on ECEC governance needs to pay more attention to federal states, as the addition of another – and at least in Canada's case, very important – layer of government adds to the complexity. Given the historically weak ("creatures of the provinces") status of municipalities in Canada, the provinces are in a position directly and indirectly to impose substantial limits on local innovations. Federalism can lead to positive outcomes, however, if intergovernmental arrangements work within a framework that establishes common national standards "in particular in those areas that concern equity between families, and the right of children to provision and quality."[8] Canadian economist Thomas Courchene concurs. Agreeing that Canada needs to promote the development of a sustainable world-class *social* infrastructure to ensure equal opportunity to enable all Canadians to develop their capacities, Courchene argues that such a system will necessarily be led by provincial experimentation "*with the proviso that they are operating within nationally agreed-upon parameters.*"[9] In other words, in federal systems like Canada's where the key pieces of the ECEC puzzle come under provincial jurisdiction, the latter are likely to take the lead in setting standards, developing ECEC curricula and the like. Nevertheless, in the interest of equity, social cohesion and, according to Courchene, future national competitiveness, such experiments need to take place within a pan-Canadian framework that identifies the broad goals and provides the requisite financial support.

Provincial initiative within a nationally agreed framework is not enough, however. As Courchene and Moss both acknowledge, local level governments may lose out in federal systems, where the attention is focused on federal-provincial/state negotiations. For Courchene, it is a question of the necessity to integrate Canada's "global city regions" – i.e. cities like Toronto, Montreal and Vancouver – into "the structure and operations of fiscal and political federalism"[10] – if Canada is to be competitive in the global economy. Moss and the authors of *Starting Strong II*, would also argue that local authorities in smaller centres and sparsely populated areas need to be empowered to make choices that reflect distinct local needs and cultures. This is not currently the rule in Canada, where, for the most part, municipalities have been left out of the ECEC picture.[11]

CHILD CARE POLICY WITHIN THE POST-WAR SOCIAL POLICY ARCHITECTURE: FROM POVERTY TO GENDER EQUALITY TO POVERTY AGAIN

Starting Strong II singled Canada out as an example of a country where, in the absence of a coherent national framework, devolution (to the provincial level) has resulted in a system with significant differences in funding per child, programme standards and teacher requirements.[12] The Country Note went further, noting that the Canadian ECEC system was a "patchwork of uneconomic, fragmented services ..."[13] This patchwork, which left the majority of Canadian families reliant on what they could afford to purchase on the market, did not spring up overnight. Rather its development has occurred unevenly, with each lurch forward marked by the predominance of a particular way of framing the issue. In this section we will briefly review these developmental moments, with an eye to changing intergovernmental arrangements.

The federal government's first foray into the child care field occurred under the "exceptional" circumstances of the Second World War. The Dominion-Provincial wartime agreement on day care reached in 1942 made available federal support, on a 50–50 cost shared basis, to fund day nurseries for mothers working in war-related industries. Only two provinces – Ontario and Quebec[14] – participated and the growth in day care provision largely occurred in Toronto and Montreal. Viewed as exceptional, the arrangement was terminated at the end of the war. Instead of supporting working mothers whom, it was assumed, would return to their homes, the government adopted a system of family allowances, Canada's first universal social programme.[15] A monthly per-child amount, paid to mothers, the family allowance helped sustain the male breadwinner-female caregiver ideal of the post-war years. Such allowances need not be viewed as alternatives to child care. In fact, in Sweden which has one of the best developed child care systems, there is also a generous child allowance, in recognition of the principle of horizontal equity between those bearing the costs of raising children and those without such responsibilities. To this Guest would add administrative simplicity: "if the allowances were set at a defensible minimum they would replace all other allowances for children under a variety of income maintenance schemes such as social assistance, workers' compensation and unemployment insurance, etc. Such programmes could then develop their benefit schedules based on the income need of single persons or couples, leaving the family allowance system to take care of the needs of any children involved."[16] As we shall see, the idea of taking children off social assistance would reappear in the 1990s in the form of the National Child Benefit, but only certain families with dependent children were then understood to need support.

Families were assumed to provide care for young children in the home during the early years – and after school hours but the post-war return of women to the home was never as complete as expected. As early as the late 1950s the Women's Bureau of the federal Department of Labour began to document the rising need for day care.[17] The federal government's response came (belatedly) in the form of three programmes. Two of these, introduced in 1971, were within federal jurisdiction. Maternity (later expanded to parental) leave payments became part of the federally-run Unemployment Insurance programme while the Child Care Expense Deduction (CCED) permitted parents to deduct a specified amount from taxable income upon submission of child care receipts.[18] The third came as part of the Canada Assistance Plan (CAP), a cost-sharing programme with the provinces introduced in 1966. The inclusion of child care under CAP was not, however, motivated by women's rising labour force participation rates, nor even by the first stirrings of second wave feminism. Rather, its main purpose was poverty alleviation. Child care became an eligible service as a "remedial programme," targeting mothers in low income (often lone parent) families who "chose" work over social assistance.[19] Through CAP, the federal government agreed to fund 50 per cent of the fee subsidies made available to those in need or likely to become so. Federal support, focused on the demand not the supply side, was thus narrowly targeted at those who could pass a provincially administered means test.

There was another dimension to CAP that is often overlooked: the development of provincial administrative capacity. In the spirit of the times, CAP aimed to guarantee all Canadians, no matter where they lived, equivalent social rights, but it did so in a manner consistent with the post-war evolution of federalism, by strengthening provincial capacities to develop and manage the new programmes. CAP was thus designed to reinforce earlier initiatives, such as the system of equalisation payments to have-not provinces. Aware of on-going provincial inquiries that were redefining the relationship between provincial and municipal governments because of the latter's inability to meet the growing need for community services, such as child care, those who framed CAP recognised the need for additional measures.[20] In most provinces, strengthening provincial capacity meant centralisation of control to the provincial level. Only in Ontario and Alberta did the municipalities continue to be involved in managing child care and, as the 1970s drew to a close, even Alberta assumed control over child care for pre-school children.

A new reason for supporting child care, however, was soon on the agenda. In the name of gender equality, the Royal Commission on the Status of Women (1970) called for a universal child care programme. In other words, child care should not simply be viewed as a welfare service for low income families: all women needed access to child care in order to achieve equality of the sexes. While rejecting CAP's targeted approach to child care policy, the Commissioners did accept its assumption that the provinces were best placed to assume responsibility for planning the development of a network of child care centres, the establishment and enforcement of standards and the provision of information to parents. At the same time, the provinces could not do the job on their own. A National Day Care Act was needed to provide an appropriate framework and incentives for provincial action.

In the internal negotiations that followed the release of the Royal Commission's report, the idea of a separate child care act was ultimately dropped.[21] Instead, some modest improvements were introduced to CAP, notably through the addition of a "welfare services" option. If provinces chose the latter, federal funds could be used to cover operating costs and equipment and materials as well as fee subsidies. As such funding was only available to non profit providers, this created a modest bias in favour of the latter, which is still visible today. Seventy seven percent of all regulated child care operates under non-profit auspice in Canada. In addition, while universality was rejected, the definition of eligible families was expanded by allowing the introduction of a sliding fee scale. Provincial social assistance rates, adjusted to take family size into account, marked the turning point, after which families would have to pay a portion of the costs. This made it possible to extend fee subsidies well up into the middle class, for whom the cost of regulated child care was otherwise prohibitive. No province, however, took full advantage of this provision.[22]

By the early 1980s, the main features of Canada's child care governance structure had been established. The federal government was prepared to cover 50 per cent of eligible expenses, while the provinces were responsible for licensing and training, enforcement of standards and labour relations. The provinces were also free to develop additional financial support for capital and operating costs and the provision of wage subsidies. CAP did not identify any national standards and the provinces determined the rate of expansion, as well as the pattern of provision.[23] This left Canada with an uneven patchwork of child care as not all provinces were equally able and willing to expand regulated child care. This is reflected in the pattern of coverage to this day. According to Friendly and Beach,[24] Quebec has the highest rate of coverage (29.9 per cent) for children 0–12 in regulated care,[25] followed by Manitoba (14.3 per cent). Next come the three richest provinces – BC (13.7 per cent), Alberta (12.7 per cent) and Ontario (10.7 per cent).

Still motivated by the quest for gender equality, the inadequacies of this framework were highlighted in the report of the Abella Commission on

Equality in Employment (1984) and thoroughly documented in the Cooke Task Force on child care (1986). Set up under the Liberals, the Cooke Task Force reported to the then-recently elected Conservative government, but the latter had appointed its own Special Committee on Child Care, which ignored the voices of many who appeared before it and came up with the recommendations underlying the bill which the Conservatives eventually brought forward.[26] The latter was prepared to pass a child care act that would remove it from under the "welfare" shadow but this would have come at a price. Commercial providers would have become eligible for the full range of federal support and a cap would have been placed on federal contributions. The Conservatives' bill failed to get through parliament before the 1988 election and, given the widespread opposition it had aroused, the Mulroney government did not bother to revive it.

Two other elements of the Conservatives' child care policy did, however, make it through the House. The first, the Child Care Initiatives Fund, provided funding for innovative child care projects, with a particular emphasis on services for Aboriginal children, children with special needs, children of parents who do shift work or work part time, and children in rural areas. The second represented a blend of neo-liberal and social conservative ideas similar, in some ways, to those underlying the Harper government's "Universal Child Care Benefit." The Tories' refundable Child Tax Credit offered several billion dollars in tax assistance to lower and middle income parents. While this did provide some relief to those forced to rely on informal/unreceipted child care, it also offered just as much to traditional male breadwinner families, in line with the right wing, anti-feminist "family values" demands of REAL Women who formed a part of the Conservatives' constituency and had especially close ties with the Minister in charge, Jake Epp.[27]

Before the Tories lost power, they were able to introduce another measure marking a further step away from the spirit of the post-war social policy regime. In 1992, they announced a new Child Tax Benefit that would replace previous tax credits – and the family allowance programme.[28] While previous governments, including the Trudeau Liberals, had whittled away the substance of universality, the Mulroney government put an end to Canada's first universal social programme. As Guest notes, this signalled "a step back to the 19th century ... to a time when attempts were made to differentiate between the 'worthy' and 'unworthy' poor. The universal family allowance was predicated on the idea that all Canadian children were worthy of public support."[29] Ironically, the Harper government's "Universal Child Care Benefit" can be seen as a partial revival of the family allowance to the extent that it recognises that all parents with young children take on extra expenses and therefore deserve support, a point to which we shall return.

The victory of the Chrétien Liberals in 1993 seemed to promise another opportunity to develop ECEC as part of the basic social infrastructure. In response to mobilisation by feminists, child care advocates and their allies, the Liberal government had included a promise in its campaign "Red Book" to allocate $720 million for the creation of 150,000 new spaces over three years. The intent was that the federal government would cover 40 per cent of costs through CAP, matched by the provinces, which would leave parents to carry 20 per cent – precisely the division that the OECD would ultimately recommend. Although it initially looked as if the government would make good on its promise, in the increasingly harsh climate for social policy innovation, concern for gender equality was being eclipsed by child poverty.[30] To be sure, the 1994 Social Security Review saw child care in the context of women's labour market participation and child development as well as poverty alleviation, but the latter began to overshadow the former as fiscal austerity became the order of the day. This became clear in the February 1995 budget, which announced that CAP would be replaced by the new Canada Health and Social Transfer fund (CHST).[31] The latter was a block fund which let the provinces determine how to allocate the transfer payment, with no guarantee that any of it would be used for child care. Transfers to the provinces were also cut by approximately one third over three years. The final blow to hopes for the establishment of an adequately funded pan-Canadian child care programme came with the 1996 Speech from the Throne, when the federal government unilaterally declared it would not use its spending power to create new programmes in areas of exclusive provincial jurisdiction, without the consent of the majority of provinces.

As Bach and Phillips argued in an earlier issue of *How Ottawa Spends*, during the Chrétien Liberals' first term, there was "a clear shift from a designated federal funding role in child care services to one of income redistribution to poor families with children through the tax system. The prevailing paradigm at the federal level is now unequivocally provincial choice. Responsibility has been devolved not only from federal to provincial governments but from governments to parents."[32] Thus the CHST left it to the provinces to decide how to spend reduced federal transfers. The programme that replaced family allowances – the Child Tax Benefit, renamed the Canada Child Tax Benefit – was redesigned to focus on child poverty by "activating" parents. In this it was building on the earlier Mulroney government's initiative, which the Liberals took it one step further, negotiating an agreement – known as the National Child Benefit (NCB) – with all provinces (except Quebec), which sought to integrate federal and provincial/territorial systems. In addition to tax benefits reaching low and middle income families, the NCB included a supplement for low income families, whether their income was derived from work or social assistance. Child care was part of the package to the extent that the provinces were invited to claw back the equivalent amount from payments to social assistance recipients. The latter could then be reinvested in support services such as child care.

EARLY CHILDHOOD DEVELOPMENT FOR ALL?
FROM SUFA TO BILATERAL ACCORDS

In the late 1990s, the emphasis began to shift again, this time from child poverty to the promotion of early childhood development, aided by the work of experts in the field like Fraser Mustard. This new perspective was reflected in the 1997 National Children's Agenda, which outlined the federal, provincial and territorial government's agreement to work together to develop a comprehensive, cross-sectoral and long term strategy to ensure that all Canada's children would have the best possible opportunity to develop to their full potential. As the communiqué issued by the First Ministers in September 2000 noted: "The early years of life are critical in the development and future well-being of the child, establishing the foundation for competence and coping skills that will affect learning, behaviour and health ... New evidence has shown that development from the prenatal period to age six is rapid and dramatic and shapes long-term outcomes. Intervening early to promote child development during this critical period can have long-term benefits that can extend throughout children's lives."[33]

The first two initiatives pertinent to ECEC – the Early Childhood Development initiative (2000) and the Multilateral Framework Agreement on Early Learning and Child Care (2004) – were launched as part of the new agenda were negotiated through the Social Union Framework Agreement (SUFA).[34] SUFA was an intergovernmental agreement concluded in 1999 to permit the renewal of Canada's social programmes and to re-establish a stable and sustainable basis for financing them. Like the post-war initiatives, it promised programmes of comparable quality irrespective of where one lived in Canada. Also like the post-war arrangements, municipalities had no place at the table.[35] SUFA differed from post-war arrangements in several important respects, however. First, it represented a codification of the federal government's self-imposed limitation on the use of its spending power: new programmes could only be launched with the assent of the majority of provinces. Second, it looked to a new accountability mechanism – public reporting on agreed performance indicators – to fill the gap. Each government, however, only undertook to report to "its" public, not to all Canadians and especially not to the federal government.

The Early Childhood Development Initiative, which involved a federal commitment of $2.2 billion over 5 years beginning in 2000–2, included the "strengthening of early childhood development, learning and care" as one of four areas where the provinces and territories could spend the new federal funds.[36] True to SUFA, the agreement committed the participating governments to monitor and report back to their respective publics, using eleven indicators in the four domains. In negotiating the deal, however, the federal government had backed off from its original aim of requiring the provinces and territories to invest in all four areas, in order to get them to sign on.[37] With no requirement to spend on ECEC, however, less than ten percent of the over $300 million in federal funds originally disbursed were used for child care. Only six of the thirteen governments invested in child care in the first years of the programme and none of the biggest – Ontario, Alberta and British Columbia – did so.

The Liberal government's commitment to ECEC was more strongly reflected in the second agreement, concluded in 2003. The multilateral framework agreement committed the federal government to transferring $1.05 billion to the provinces and territories over five years, with the explicit aim of improving access to affordable, provincially/territorially regulated ECEC programmes for children under six. Nevertheless, the agreement did not require matching provincial/territorial investment. The provincial and territorial governments were also free to select from a broad menu of ECEC expenditures.[38] These included demand-side measures more typical of a market oriented model – information provision, fee subsidies, quality assurance – and the kind of supply-side measures associated with ECEC as a key part of the social infrastructure – capital and operating grants, training and professional development, and wage enhancements. The Multilateral Framework Agreement did, however, commit all governments to report annually on their investments, specifying investments to improve availability, affordability and quality. The website directs interested parties to each government's ELCC website but a visit to these suggests that the agreement by each party to make public annual reports has been difficult to maintain.[39]

In the fall of 2004, the OECD's Starting Strong team issued the country note on Canada's ECEC system, to which we referred above. Reflecting on the Multilateral Framework Agreement, the report noted that "federal funding has begun to have a significant impact since 2003/4, and is stimulating a renewal of ECEC services *in several provinces*."[40] In other words, some progress had been made but not sufficient to ensure that all Canada's children had access to affordable quality ECEC. In addition to recommending a substantial increase in public funding under a transparent and accountable system, the report called for a strengthening of intergovernmental arrangements. The aim should be to establish a national quality framework, comprised of "a statement of the values and goals that should guide early childhood centres; a summary of programme standards ... an outline of the knowledge, skills, dispositions and values that children at different ages can be expected to master across broad development areas; and ... pedagogical guidelines outlining the processes through which children achieve these goals ..."[41]

The report also recommended the establishment of a federal secretariat responsible for young children, which could support the work of the provinces and territories. The latter, in turn, should be encouraged to work with major stakeholders to develop ECEC strategies "with priority targets, benchmark and timelines, and with guaranteed budgets to fund appropriate governance and expansion."[42] In addition, the Starting Strong team made a plea for the development and co-construction of appropriate ECEC services for Aboriginal children, including those living off-reserve in Canada's major urban areas.[43] Last but not least, it suggested that managerial structures be strengthened not only at the provincial/territorial level but also on the ground. For, "at the ground level, expert managers or pedagogical advisors are also needed to map services, to create networks (especially across dispersed settlements), to ensure monitoring and to organise the support services that centres and staff need."[44]

The OECD country note was released in October 2004, the same month that the federal government announced its intention to "establish the foundations of a truly national system of early learning and child care." In February 2005, the federal, provincial and territorial governments reached an agreement on the "QUAD" principles that were to govern the system:

- *Quality* defined as 'evidence based practices, including provincial/territorial regulations and monitoring, appropriate complement of staff and child care providers; education and support for early childhood education and care centres; and the promotion of community partnerships;
- *Universally inclusive*[45] – responsive without discrimination, inclusive of children with special needs, Aboriginal children and children with various cultural and linguistic circumstances;
- *Accessible* – broadly available and affordable to all, with includes a flexible range of options for families and enhanced operating funds and/or fee subsidies;
- *Developmental* – to strengthen the learning and developmental component across Canada to meet more fully the cognitive, physical, emotional and social development needs of children by investing in evidence-based practices.

The federal budget allocated $5 billion to be spent over a five year period to develop the foundations for a pan-Canadian QUAD-based ECEC system. Unlike the Early Childhood Development initiative and the multilateral framework agreement, however, the federal government was unable to reach a multilateral agreement. Instead, it was forced to negotiate on a bilateral basis, reaching agreements with all ten provinces.

All ten agreements referred to the QUAD principles and all agreed to report to their respective publics, as well as to exchange information with an eye to contributing to the development of a pan-Canadian quality framework. Moreover, for the first time in over a decade, Quebec was included. Yet there were important limitations. Only two agreements made it clear that the funds would only be invested in non-profit operations while three explicitly stated their intention to fund commercial operations, despite the fact that study after study has confirmed that non-profit operations are much more likely to provide quality care then their commercial counterparts.[46] Only three agreements specified that investments could include innovative programmes in the formal school system – a move which could do much to bridge the divide between child care and pre-school education.[47] Moreover, while eight provinces made a commitment only to invest in regulated ECEC programmes, two did not.[48] One of these was Quebec, which, as noted earlier, was already well ahead of the rest of the country in establishing a coherent, accessible ECEC system.[49] The other, however, was New Brunswick, which has one of the weakest records in this field.

Thus the ECEC agreements negotiated by the Liberal government[50] built on the foundations laid in the multilateral framework agreement. They went beyond the latter in that they succeeded in including Quebec, which had stayed outside SUFA. Yet there was a price – while QUAD appeared in all agreements, the bilateral accords permitted a greater degree of variation, thus perpetuating the patchwork character of the system.

CHOICE IN CHILD CARE WITH LESS OPTIONS: A RETURN TO NEO-LIBERALISM UNDER THE HARPER CONSERVATIVES

Even though the Liberal bilateral agreements failed to incorporate "best practices" in policy and thus largely reinforced provincial diversity in child care programme delivery, they accounted for the largest increase in federal child care expenditure to date and offered some hope that a national programme could materialize under the QUAD umbrella. Any progress made toward a national vision of child care was, however, quickly extinguished once the Harper Conservatives took office in 2006 and implemented its vision of a federal child care plan. Under the pledge to "help parents with the cost of raising their children,"[51] the new government's vision combined a social conservative focus on the family (the "Universal Child Care Benefit") with a neo-liberal emphasis on private sector provision of new child care spaces (the "child care spaces initiative"). In addition, both new programs aimed to by-pass traditional intergovernmental channels, marking a pronounced change in direction from the previous Liberal regime.

As noted in the introduction, the newly-elected Conservative government moved quickly to establish their new child care plan, announcing the Universal Child Care Benefit in the May 2006 Budget. The UCCB payment of $100 per month, per child under the age of six, taxable to the lower-income spouse in a household, did not provide child care per se. Although the allowance *could* be used by parents to offset child care costs if desired, the $1,200 per year provided was insufficient. After tax it could amount to as little as $600 a year, while actual child care costs could run upwards of $8,000 per year on average for children under the age of three and approximately $3,500 for before and after-school care.[52]

The UCCB was, moreover, available to all eligible families, including those with a stay-at-home parent. In this sense, it might best be viewed as a return to the (taxable version of the) universal family allowance eliminated by an earlier Conservative government in 1992, rather than a child care programme. In fact, the UCCB's monthly $100 payment per child would have represented a significant increase in the family allowance had the FA not been cancelled by the Mulroney Conservatives and continued unchanged to the present day.[53] The new benefit was not, however, as widely distributed as the older family allowance as it only applied to children under the age of six, whereas the latter was available to dependent children under age 18.

The cost of the UCCB was high – approximately $2.4 billion per year. The Conservative government argued that, to pay for the benefit, it had to cancel the Liberal bilateral deals negotiated in 2005. This was a popular decision, particularly with social conservatives who saw supports for regulated child care (included in the Liberal deals) as encouragements to parents "to spend less time with their children."[54] The partisan child care debate during the 2006 election was often cast as one between supporters for families who chose to care for their own children versus those who chose to work, leaving their children with outside caregivers.[55] The UCCB was presented as a solution to this dichotomy, allowing parents to "choose" where to spend the money instead of the state "dictating" how that money should be spent – a solution deemed unfair to single breadwinner families.

The second element of the Conservative's child care plan announced in the 2006 Budget planned to offer tax incentives to businesses and communities to create 25,000 child care spaces per year through the Child Care Spaces Initiative. Incentives of up to $10,000 per space created would be offered under a total commitment of $250 million per year. Despite the fact that some provincial jurisdictions had failed to kick-start business provision of child care space delivery through similar plans in the past, the federal government announced its intention to implement the CCSI beginning in 2007.

One of the main reasons for directly engaging the private sector and communities in child care delivery was to bypass traditional federal/provincial negotiations and to produce a specifically federal solution to the need for more child care spaces across the country. This decision reflected Stephen Harper's approach to intergovernmental relations, which he called "open federalism." Open federalism aimed more strictly to adhere to the traditional constitutional separation of powers between the federal and provincial levels of government.[56] As such, the Conservatives sought to avoid federal directives to the provinces in areas of provincial responsibility. In effect, this meant moving further away from the creation of a truly pan-Canadian child care programme.

In many ways, the Harper approach to child care was reminiscent of the Mulroney Conservatives during the late 1980s. To be sure, there are differences in the Mulroney and Harper child care plans. The Mulroney government's legislation, while falling well short of what the broad coalition of child care advocates had called for, did entail dedicated child care federal transfers to the provinces. Yet it is the similarities that are particularly striking. Both embraced a distinct blend of social conservatism and neo-liberalism and both sought to change intergovernmental relations. Thus, Susan Phillips argued that the Mulroney Conservative government viewed child care "as primarily a private issue of parental choice" and that its unwillingness to provide national level standards demonstrated a preference for "decentralized federalism because it carefully avoids interfering at the provincial jurisdiction."[57] These ideological differences in approaches to child care would become more apparent later in the life of the Harper minority government.

POLICY LEARNING THROUGH CONSULTATION: CHILD CARE CHANGES IN THE 2007 BUDGET

While the Harper government was quick to implement the first part of its "child care" plan, before implementing the CCSI, the government agreed to consult the various stakeholders. Human Resources and Social Development Canada held consultations with close to 300 child care stakeholders, representing over 200 organizations across the country during the summer and fall of 2006. The government saw these consultations as a way to better understand how to deliver the CCSI and, in particular, how to ensure that employer-sponsored child care was successful.[58] Yet instead of providing solutions on how to best operationalize business involvement in the CCSI, the key message delivered to civil servants during the consultation process was that businesses were not interested in creating child care spaces. "There is much scepticism about the effectiveness of tax credits and other financial supports in providing an adequate incentive for employers to create child care spaces. This concern was raised by all stakeholders, including employers, child care providers as well as provinces that have attempted to encourage employer-sponsored child care with limited success."[59]

Despite the presence of substantial opposition to the main thrust of the CCSI, Human Resources Minister Diane Finley announced the creation of a Ministerial Advisory Committee during the HRSDC consultation process to continue to explore how to make employer-sponsored child care a reality. In September 2006, the Ministerial Advisory Committee on the Government of Canada's Child Care Spaces Initiative began this task with a briefing of the HRSDC consultations and then moved ahead with its own research into Canada's child care needs through child care site visits, report reviews and strategy sessions. Its work was concluded in January 2007 with the release of a series of 10 recommendations aimed at persuading employers to create child care spaces, even while acknowledging the business community's lack of interest in the proposition.

Interestingly, all of the Advisory Committee's recommendations were "focused on actions that are within Federal jurisdiction" while also recognizing "the lead role played by provincial, territorial *and municipal* governments in regulating, funding and in some cases, operating child care."[60] This recognition of the role of municipal governments in child care delivery was likely influenced by the presence of Advisory Committee Chair Gordon Chong, a former Toronto city councillor. Chong himself acknowledged that his "understanding of municipal government add[ed] richness and depth to the discussion about child care spaces development and sustainability."[61] One of the Advisory Committee's more innovative recommendations involved the creation of a Child Care Spaces Investment Fund managed by a third party that would distribute money to eligible applicants who would create new high quality child care spaces.[62] This fund could have become a vehicle for distributing federal money directly to municipalities thereby further altering the intergovernmental nature of child care provision in the country. This recommendation, like others made by the Advisory Committee, was ignored by the Conservative government, which delayed releasing the report until after the March 2007 Budget.[63] In the end, the Conservatives did accept the fact that businesses were not keen on creating or running child care centres, prompting significant changes to the CCSI that were included in the 2007 Budget.

Consultations with child care stakeholders held throughout 2006, particularly with provincial and municipal levels of government, not only pointed to potential problems with business involvement, but also highlighted concerns with the Conservative government's plan to abandon established multilateral and bilateral funding arrangements struck between the provinces and the federal Liberals between 2003 and 2005. One of the concerns was sustainability: many jurisdictions had extensive child care plans already in place and the abrupt ending of essentially all stable and incremental ECEC funding would seriously undermine those plans. Another was the importance of quality as well as quantity of child care space delivery, a point that was strongly communicated to the Conservative government. These consultations also underscored the point made in the OECD report, that local community involvement was essential to ensure high quality child care delivery.

Accordingly, the Spring 2007 Budget reflected a significant shift in the Conservatives' child care plans. The UCCB would remain intact, but the $250 million originally earmarked to provide tax incentives for employer-created child care was instead offered up to the provinces to create the child care spaces.[64] With the cancellation of the Liberal bilateral deals still in effect, critics quickly pointed out that the $250 million divvied up to the provinces on a per capita basis would constitute significantly less funding than was originally promised under the former agreements. For example, Ontario would receive $97 million under the Conservative plan, over $350 million less than they would have received under the Liberal bilateral agreement for 2007–08.[65]

The $250 million provincial transfer would first appear as a one-time transition payment in 2007–08. Starting in 2008–09, the $250 million is to be distributed through the renewed Canada Social Transfer.[66] This transfer payment is projected to grow over time through an annual 3 per cent escalator beginning in 2009–10– a new addition to the CST. Provincial and territorial governments are also to be required to report to their citizens on their specific child care space expenditures, although the extent of this reporting was still part of on-going bilateral discussions with federal bureaucrats at time of writing. The fact that those discussions are being conducted on a bilateral basis, rather than the multilateralism of the accords struck under SUFA, suggests that the reporting criteria are even less likely to be "national" in focus. In fact, new HRSDC Minister Monte Solberg insisted that reporting criteria should be flexible so that the government would refrain from establishing national level standards. "Every province is so different," he was quoted as saying in a 2007 media interview. "You know having the same standards for downtown Toronto or Nunavut just doesn't make any sense."[67] Neverthelss, the intergovernmental framework remains federal/provincial/territorial. Toronto, like all other municipalities, continues to be treated as invisible partners to their provinces, if that.

Further changes were made to the CST in the 2007 Budget to increase transparency in provincial and territorial expenditures, ostensibly to make it easier to determine whether or not provincial and territorial governments were actually spending the federal transfer on ECEC programmes. CST payments would be provided on an equal per capita basis and the federal government pledged to delineate CST allocations based on 2007–08 provincial-territorial spending patterns. Based on these patterns, 25 per cent of the CST would be allocated for post-secondary education, 9 per cent for "support for children," and the remaining 66 per cent for other social programmes.[68] Although this change will allow for some minimal level of transparency non-existent under the CHST, it will only make it possible to identify whether or not a province fails to spend the minimum amount "earmarked" under these percentages. For example, there is still no way of clearly determining exactly how much of the 9 per cent in transfers for "support for children" would actually go toward child care space provision. In this respect, it is not all that different from the Liberals' early childhood development initiative. The Liberal government, however, learned that if it wanted to promote the development of ECEC, it had to find a way to ensure that federal funds would be used for that purpose.[69]

Along with the $250 million transfer to the provinces for child care space creation, the Conservatives announced that $850 million in provincial ECEC transfers negotiated during the ECDI and the MFA in 2000 and 2003 would also continue under the CST until 2013–14. This transfer is also to be subject to the annual 3 per cent escalator. Clearly the message from the provinces

> Federal ELCC Support in Budget 2007
>
> - $2.4 billion Universal Child Care Benefit
> - $250 million transfer to the provinces and territories for child care space creation
> - $850 million transfer to the provinces MFA ECC Agreements to 2013/14
> - $1.5 billion New Child Tax Credit
> - $695 million in recognition of child care expenses through the child care expense deduction (first established in 1971).

that stable ECEC funding was essential to maintain has gotten through to the minority government, forcing it to revisit the established intergovernmental ECEC model. The Harper government's strong adherence to decentralized federalism means, however, that not only would a patchwork of services continue, but also that the kind of balance between federal, provincial/territorial and municipal governments discussed in the first section is unlikely to be achieved. The addition of a new $1.5 billion child tax benefit harkened back to the tax-based child care programmes of the Mulroney Conservatives and further solidified the Harper government's neo-liberal approach to child care delivery. Alongside the continuation of the $695 million child care expense deduction programme and the $2.4 billion UCCB, it showed that on balance the Conservatives still prefer to transfer more money directly to the private sphere (families and business) rather than to the public (the provinces and territories) (See Box 1).

CONCLUSIONS

The story of child care policy in Canada, especially over the last two decades, clearly illustrates distinct policy approaches of different governments as well as strong elements of continuity. While Liberal governments have at times seemed poised to establish a publicly-supported pan-Canadian child care system, the policies of the Mulroney and Harper governments have reflected a blend of social conservatism and neo-liberalism. Changes of government have thus contributed to uneven lurches in ECEC policy progress, at times moving one step forward, at others, two steps back. All the while, the existing intergovernmental arrangements that have governed the policy field since the mid-1960s have remained remarkably resilient. The federal government has continued to influence ECEC policy via transfers to the provinces and individuals, as well as acting within its own jurisdiction, mainly through the use of the tax instrument. More broadly, successive federal governments have failed to establish the conditions for universal access or setting national standards. This has resulted in a patchwork of provision as intergovernmental relations have reinforced the principal role of the provinces and territories. In the process, municipalities have been left out of the intergovernmental decision-making framework and in most provinces have no official role. In turn, families have been left to rely on the uneven market for child care.

At the beginning of the new century, it looked as if the federal government, concerned to promote early learning and child care, was prepared to take more of a leadership role. The Multilateral Framework Agreement sought provincial and territorial commitment to the principles of affordability, access and quality, while the bilateral agreements negotiated under the Martin government attempted to enshrine the QUAD principles. The victory of the Harper government put an end to that. Motivated by a blend of neo-liberalism and social conservatism, the Harper government tried to avoid intergovernmental transfers in favour of transfers to the private sectors – to families via the UCCB and to businesses via the CSSI – thus emphasizing an individual family/market-based approach to child care policy. It succeeded with the "family-centred" UCCB, but was forced to recognise that, on their own, incentives to business would not solve the problem of inadequate number (and quality) of child care spaces. Transfers to the provinces will continue, albeit at a rate much lower than the Liberal plan.

While the Harper government may think the subject closed, the opposition parties have not abandoned the idea of a pan-Canadian child care policy framework. On My 17, 2006 New Democratic MP, Denise Savoie, introduced private member's Bill C-303, An Early Learning and Child Care Act. The bill was noteworthy in that it garnered the support of all three opposition parties, with New Democrat Olivia Chow, Liberal Ruby Dhalla and Bloc member Vivian Barbot joining forces to compel a parliamentary vote on the bill in May 2007.[70] More specifically, Bill C-303 calls for the introduction of a pan-Canadian child care system with dedicated federal funding. If it were to pass third reading, Bill C-303 would establish strict federal criteria for transfers to the provinces and territories. Those refusing to meet the criteria would forfeit the transfer payments (although in recognition of its superior child care system, the Quebec government would be permitted to opt out). While the minority Conservative government has threatened to ignore the Bill even if it managed to become law, it has the potential to reignite the child care debate.

NOTES

1 This is not always the case. Campaign 2000, which was created to end child poverty in Canada, favours universal child care.
2 Communities were mentioned too but as approximately 80 per cent of regulated child care spaces are provided by non-profit operators, the only "new(er)" element for them would have been the establishment of a direct relationship with the federal

government. (In the 1970s, the federal OFY and LIP programmes funded a number of community-based child care initiatives.)
3 In 1998, the OECD charged its Education branch (now Directorate) with the task of examining early childhood education and care programmes in member countries as part of its push to promote "life long learning". While not among the 12 countries that participated in the first round, Canada did participate in the second. For more on *Starting Strong*, see Mahon (2006; 2007).
4 OECD, *Starting Strong II: Early Childhood Education and Care* (Paris: OECD, 2006), 50.
5 OECD, *Starting Strong II*, 51.
6 Rianne Mahon (with Jane Jenson and Katherine Mortimer), *Learning from Each Other: Early Learning and Child Care Experiences in Canadian cities*, Study commissioned by the cities of Toronto and Vancouver and Social Development Canada (Toronto: 2006).
7 Peter Moss, *Bringing Politics into the Nursery: Early Childhood Education as a Democratic Practice*. Working papers in Early Childhood Development. (The Hague: Bernard Van Leer Foundation, June 2007), 13.
8 Moss, *Bringing Politics into the Nursery*, 10.
9 Thomas Courchene, "Canada as a 'State of Mind' in the Knowledge Era," *Policy Options*, July /August 2007, 60. Emphasis added.
10 Courchene, "Canada as a 'State of Mind' in the Knowledge Era," 61.
11 Jane Jenson and Rianne Mahon, *Child Care in Toronto: Can Intergovernmental Relations Respond to Children's Needs?* (Ottawa: Canadian Policy Research Networks), Project F-62.
12 OECD, *Starting Strong II*, 52.
13 OECD, *Early Childhood Education and Care Policy: Canada Country Note* (Paris: OECD 2004), 6.
14 According to Tom Langford, Alberta contemplated joining in but decided against it. See his unpublished manuscript on the history of child care policy in Alberta. British Columbia also considered it in 1944, but the criteria for joining – 75 per cent of mothers using the services had to be working in war-related industries – were too stringent for BC at the time. See Marcy Cohen et al., *Cuz There Ain't No Daycare for Almost None, She Said: A Book about Daycare in BC* (Vancouver: Press Gang Publishers, 1973).
15 There were other rationales too behind the adoption of the family allowance programme, from the short-run objective of maintaining wartime wage controls to Keynesian demand stimulation to avert the expected post-war depression. Nonetheless, the assumption that the male breadwinner family would become the norm again ran through the Marsh report as well as the deliberations of the post-war reconstruction planning committee. It should be noted that the family allowance programme adopted offered compensation well below the level recommended in the Marsh Report – a grand design for Canada's post-war social architecture that was only gradually realized. See Dennis Guest's entry on this subject in the Canadian Encyclopedia Historica for a good brief overview – www.thecanadianencyclopedia.com.

16 Dennis Guest, "Family Allowance," in *The Canadian Encyclopedia Historica*. Available at www.thecanadianencyclopedia.com ; accessed 26 January 2008, 1.
17 Alvin Finkel, "'Even the Little Children Cooperated': Family Strategies, Childcare Discourse and Social Welfare Debates, 1945–1975," *Labour/le Travail* 36 (Fall 1995): 91–118; and Rianne Mahon "The Never Ending Story: The Struggle for Universal Child Care Policy in the 1970s," *Canadian Historical Review* 81, no. 4 (2000): 582–615.
18 The CCED is more favourable to higher income earners, though receipts are hard to come by. Even today the vast majority of non-parental child care is provided by the informal sector, where receipts are often not available.
19 Unlike the American programme of the time, the federal government explicitly rejected the push by some provinces to introduce workfare, upholding instead a mother's right to choose whether to work or to remain on social assistance.
20 The Department of Health and Welfare's files explicitly refer to the Boucher inquiry in Quebec, the Byrne Commission in New Brunswick and the Michener inquiry in Manitoba.
21 Mahon, "The Never Ending Story."
22 For more detail see Cooke Task Force, *Report of the Task Force on Child Care* (Ottawa: Supply and Services Canada, 1986).
23 Some provinces favoured family-based day care whereas others put greater emphasis on centre-based care. In addition, although the welfare service route offered more generous terms, provinces could still support the development of a for-profit based system by choosing the original funding route. Today three provinces – Alberta, Newfoundland and New Brunswick – have a high proportion of commercial operations.
24 Martha Friendly and Jane Beach, *Early Childhood Education and Care in Canada 2004* Child Care Resource and Research Unit, 2005 (Toronto)
25 In the late 1990s, Quebec adopted a universal "$5 a day" child care programme, which rapidly pushed it ahead of all the other provinces and inspired child care advocates in the rest of Canada to renew the struggle for universal child care. For more on the development of Quebec's programme see Jane Jenson, "Against the Current: Child Care and Family Policy in Quebec," in Sonya Michel and Rianne Mahon, eds., *Child Care Policy at the Crossroads: Gender and Welfare State Restructuring*. (New York: Routledge, 2002).
26 See Martha Friendly, *Child Care Policy in Canada: Putting the Pieces Together* (Don Mills: Addison-Wesley, 1994).
27 Kate Teghtsoonian, "Neo-Conservative Ideology and Opposition to Federal Regulation of Child Care: Services in the United States and Canada," *Canadian Journal of Political Science* 36, no. 1 (1993): 97–122.
28 The Liberal government began to chip away at universality when it made family allowances taxable in 1972. In 1978 the Trudeau government cut family allowances from an average of $28 per month to $20 and introduced the first refundable Child Tax Credit for low and modest income families. The Mulroney government ended any semblance of universality by requiring upper income parents to repay all of their benefit.

29 Guest, *Family Allowance*, 3.
30 Wendy McKeen, *Money in Their Own Name: Feminism and the Shaping of Canadian Social Policy* (Toronto: University of Toronto Press, 2004).
31 Note, in 2004, the fund was split into the Canada Health Transfer and the Canada Social Transfer.
32 Sandra Bach and Susan Phillips, "Constructing a New Social Contract: Child Care Beyond Infancy?" in Gene Swimmer, ed., *How Ottawa Spends 1997–98* (Ottawa: Carleton University Press, 1998), 254–5.
33 Canadian Intergovernmental Conference Secretariat, "First ministers' Communiqué on Early Childhood Development," News Release, Ref: 800-038/005, 11 September 2000.
34 Quebec remained outside SUFA and these two agreements in part because its child care programme put it well ahead of the other provinces.
35 The issue of municipal involvement was raised by the Coffey-McCain report, commissioned by the City of Toronto, which called upon the federal government to utilize SUFA to establish a child care partnership with municipalities, modeled on the recent housing initiative, Supporting Community Partnerships. The possibility of direct municipal involvement was also raised in the report of the Liberal caucus social policy committee, which issued a forceful call for a new national child care programme.
36 The other areas were: promotion of healthy pregnancy, birth and infancy; improvement of parent and family supports; and strengthening community capacities.
37 Charles Coffey and Margaret Norrie McCain, *Final Report of the Commission on Early Learning and Child Care for the City of Toronto* (Toronto: City of Toronto, 2002). Available at www.toronto.ca/children/report/elcc.pdf; accessed 26 January 2008.
38 Investment in the formal school system – i.e. kindergarten – was however explicitly ruled out, thus perpetuating the division between child care and education.
39 On 14 May 2007, Susan Bailey reported for Canadian Press that not only were numerous provincial reports "months or even years overdue" but so too were the federal government's 2004–5 and 2005–6 reports. We found the same when we checked the federal site as well as several of the provinces', August 2007.
40 OECD, *Early Childhood Education and Care Policy*, 6. Emphasis added.
41 OECD, *Early Childhood Education and Care Policy*, 11.
42 OECD, *Early Childhood Education and Care Policy*, 6.
43 Some initial steps had been taken. In 1995, $72 million was put into a First Nations/Inuit child care initiative to fund and establish child care programmes in cooperation with First Nations and Inuit groups. In 1999, the Aboriginal Head Start programme was extended to on-reserve First Nations.
44 OECD, *Early Childhood Education and Care Policy*, 11.
45 Note the federal government sought to enshrine the principle of universality but this was watered down to "universally inclusive" during negotiations with the provinces in the fall of 2004.
46 See for example H. Goelman et al., *You Bet I Care: Caring and Learning Environments: Quality in Child Care Centres Across Canada* (Guelph: Centre for Family, Work and

Well-being, University of Guelph, 2000); Gordon Cleveland and Michael Krashinsky, *The Quality Gap: A Study of Non-Profit and Commercial Child Care Centres in Canada* (Toronto: Department of Management and Economics Working Paper, University of Toronto, 2005); and Christa Japel, Richard E. Tremblay and Sylvana Coté, "Quality Counts! Assessing the Quality of Daycare Services Using the Quebec Longitudinal Study of Child Development," *Choices* 11, no.15 (2005). The provinces committed to non-profit provision were Saskatchewan and Manitoba. Alberta, British Columbia and New Brunswick made clear their intention to fund commercial provision. In the former provinces, commercial provision accounts for the lion's share.

47 These were Ontario, whose "Best Start" programme sought to link preschool child care to the school system; Saskatchewan, where there is growing interest in establishing four year old kindergarten programmes; and British Columbia.

48 Alberta, moreover, explicitly included subsidies to families with stay-at-home parents/mothers. A report in the *Edmonton Journal* noted that in 2006, the province spent only $118 million of the $147 million budgeted in the bilateral agreement. The representative for Alberta Children's Services noted that "fewer families took advantage of provincial programmes, *mainly the offer of $100 a month for stay-at-home parents who want to put their children in play schools*" ("Day care plan good stop-gap," 4 May 2007, emphasis added).

49 The Martin government was defeated before it could turn most of these agreements from agreements in principle to full-fledged agreements, backed by provincial plans. Quebec's was one that did not make it past that stage.

50 Only three of the provinces – Manitoba, Saskatchewan and Ontario – had finalized the agreements by the time the election was called. All agreements, moreover, allowed either party to withdraw after giving advance notice.

51 Quoted in Gloria Galloway, "Cities blasts Harper over waiting times," *The Globe and Mail*, 9 January 2007, A4.

52 This amount was calculated in Paul Kershaw, "Measuring Up: Family Benefits in British Columbia and Alberta in International Perspective," *Choices* 13, no. 2 (2007), from unpublished child care operating fund data in British Columbia (fn 19, p. 35).

53 Based on calculations using the CPI and 1991 as a base year, the family allowance for 2006 would have been $46.50 per month if it had continued along its original path. The 2006 UCCB is more than double that amount.

54 A founder of the Advocates for Child Care Choice quoted in the Globe and Mail and cited in the Canadian Centre for Policy Alternatives (2006) Editorial "Conservative child-care plan comes at high price" http://policyalternatives.ca/Editorials/w006/02/Editorial1299/index.cfm?pa+da794529 (accessed August 16, 2007).

55 Kershaw, "Measuring Up," 5.

56 Thomas Courchene, "A Blueprint for Fiscal Federalism," *Policy Options*, April 2007, 16. Open federalism also included a commitment to address the issue of fiscal imbalance between and among federal and provincial levels of government.

57 Susan Phillips, "Rock-a-Bye, Brian: The National Strategy on Child Care," in Katherine Graham, ed., *How Ottawa Spends 1990–91* (Ottawa: Carleton University Press, 1991), 180 and 169.
58 Human Resources and Social Development Canada (HRSDC), *What We've Heard: Summary of Consultations on the Child Care Spaces Initiative* 2007 (Ottawa: HRSDC, 2007). Available at www.hrsdc.gc.ca/cgi-bin/hrsdc-rhdsc/print/print.asp?Page _Url+/enpublic_consultations; accessed 26 January 2008.
59 HRSDC, *What We've Heard*, 4.
60 Ministerial Advisory Committee on the Government of Canada's Child Care Spaces Initiative, *Child Care Spaces Recommendations: Supporting Canadian Children and Families: Addressing the Gap Between the Supply and Demand for High Quality Child Care: A Report Submitted to the Honourable Monte Solberg, PC, MP Minister of Human Resources and Social Development* (Ottawa: HRSDC, 2007), 1. Emphasis added.
61 Ministerial Advisory Committee on the Government of Canada's Child Care Spaces Initiative, *Child Care Spaces Recommendations*, 27.
62 Ministerial Advisory Committee on the Government of Canada's Child Care Spaces Initiative, *Child Care Spaces Recommendations*, 2.
63 Jennifer Ditchburn, "Report: Tories need to collect child care data," *Halifax Chronicle Herald*, 13 April 2007, A11.
64 The Conservatives stressed that the 25 per cent investment tax credit to businesses that create new workplace child care spaces up to $10,000 per space would still be available but no specific money was earmarked for the plan in the 2007 Budget (Budget 2007, Chapter 4).
65 Calculations made by the Child Care Advocacy Association of Canada. Similar calculations are also available for all 13 provincial and territorial governments. See www.childcareadvocacy.ca/resources/pdf/Financial_reality_behind_spaces_initiative:Oct06.pdf .
66 The original CST legislation was set to expire at the end of 2007/08.
67 Quoted in the National Post, April 2, 2007.
68 Department of Finance, *Budget 2007* (Ottawa: Department of Finance, 2007), chapter 4.
69 On-going bilateral consultations at time of writing had the potential to clarify this, but the lack of provincial accountability under the 2003 MFA mentioned above, alongside unwillingness to establish national standards, indicates that this was unlikely.
70 Carol Goar, "Women MPs blur party lines," *Toronto Star*, 9 May 2007.

7 Telecommunications Policy: What a Difference a Minister Can Make

RICHARD SCHULTZ

> It was, and is, natural that senior bureaucrats would have their own methods of gaining approval for the decisions they both needed and wanted. A new minister is ... not only vulnerable but, indeed almost without protection.
>
> Flora Macdonald[1]

> ...basic reforms in our policy process should ensure effective ministerial control over the civil service and the regulatory system.
>
> Lloyd Axworthy[2]

> That would be courageous, Minister, very courageous.
>
> Sir Humphrey Appleby, *Yes Minister*

Notwithstanding the rhetoric over the past 40 years about "the information highway" and "telecommunications as the railways of the future" or the actual tectonic, transformative shifts in public policy governing the market structure of the industry in the past two decades, telecommunications has largely been the neglected step-child as far as elected policy-makers are concerned. The major policy changes that have occurred have been, for the most part, bureaucratically shaped and determined while political authorities have played primarily a reactive, legitimating role for decisions made by others. This is true even for the 1993 *Telecommunications Act* which did not substantially affect the policy directions pursued by the CRTC since it gained jurisdiction over telecommunications in 1976.

The political-bureaucratic dynamic in the telecommunications sector dramatically changed with the election of the Conservative government of Stephen Harper in January 2006, particularly with the appointment of Maxime Bernier as Minister of Industry, the department with responsibility for telecommunications. Telecommunications was not one of the vaunted five priorities of the new government. Indeed, telecommunications did not even merit a mention in the Conservative Party's electoral manifesto, "Stand Up for Canada." However, in one of his first public appearances as minister, Bernier made it clear that he had his own agenda: "As many of you may know, our new government has five priorities, but I can assure you that telecommunications is at the top of my action list."[3]

The minister's personal commitment to that agenda was soon apparent. He exploited the two major avenues, other than legislative changes, open to political authorities to influence regulatory decision-making. One, which is more traditional, is to act on appeals to the Cabinet on specific decisions. In the case of the CRTC's telecommunications decisions, the appeal mechanism permits Cabinet both to send back decisions for reconsideration and to "vary or rescind" such decisions.[4] The second, which is both more exceptional, and, in the case of telecommunications, more recent, dating from 1993, is the power to issue a policy direction on broad policy matters.

Between March 2006 and April 2007, Bernier was successful in obtaining cabinet approval first, for fundamentally changing two major decisions of the CRTC through the appeal process and secondly, for imposing a major policy direction on the CRTC, the first since cabinet was authorized to do so in the 1993 legislation.[5] These initiatives arguably not only represented the most profound policy changes to the regulatory regime since the introduction of competition in 1979, and its extension in 1992 and 1994, but established, for the first time, that elected authorities, not appointed officials, were responsible for policy decisions. That Bernier was able to overcome doubts from some of his cabinet colleagues, including the Prime Minister and his senior political advisors and especially the determined opposition from both his departmental officials and those in the Privy Council Office, including the Clerk, reflected not only his determination but also his political skill. For the first time in the past forty years of federal regulation of telecommunications and a dozen ministers, a minister had made a policy difference.

In changing fundamentally the CRTC decisions on the regulation of local telephone service and offering telephone service over the Internet, Bernier, with the support of his colleagues, rejected continued detailed regulation of the incumbent telephone companies, the former monopolies, and in effect imposed deregulation on these services. The major direction which cabinet sent to the CRTC substantially re-interpreted, some would argue re-wrote, the policy objectives of the *Telecommunications Act* such that the regulator was ordered to henceforth give market forces primacy in its regulatory decisions. This was a fundamental re-ordering of the objectives of telecommunications regulation.

This chapter will analyse the policy outcomes and the political processes that resulted in the Minister of Industry successfully imposing his preferred policies on the CRTC. In particular, sections below will analyse the specific processes that led to fundamental changes for the CRTC's decisions on Voice over the Internet Protocol (VOIP) and forbearance of local telephone regulation as well as that for the policy direction imposed on the CRTC. Before turning to those specific decisions, it is necessary to provide background as to the conditions that provided the opportunity for Bernier to be the first minister responsible for telecommunications who successfully imposed his policy preferences on the regulator.

PART ONE: BACKGROUND

There is no evidence that Maxime Bernier came to the position of Industry Minister with any prior knowledge of, or even familiarity with, telecommunications or indeed, notwithstanding his subsequent claim, with an agenda for the sector. What he did bring, however, was a philosophical outlook that would allow him to adopt, and aggressively pursue, an inter-related set of policy prescriptions for telecommunications. Bernier was/is a quintessential example of what Donald Savoie in his four-fold characterization of Canadian cabinet ministers, would categorize as a "mission" participant, that is one who brings "to the cabinet table strongly held views and they usually do not avoid confrontation if their views are challenged." Such ministers "are particularly tenacious in pushing their causes or their point of view and they are likely to keep on trying long after other ministers would have given up."[6]

In Bernier's case, his sense of mission was clearly ideologically inspired. He is a staunch advocate of free market principles, inspired in part by his roots in the Beauce region of Quebec and reflected in his position, prior to his election in 2006, as Executive Vice President of the libertarian think-tank, the Montreal Economic Institute, which promotes the values of limited government and the primacy of free market principles. Bernier, in his first speeches as a minister, emphasized that he saw himself as a defender of economic freedom and open competition who embraced "... the spirit of entrepreneurship and all it stands for – individual freedom, self-reliance, responsibility and autonomy."[7] Subsequently, in his first speech on telecommunications, Bernier signalled to all the importance he attached to his principles: "I came to this portfolio from the private sector with a strong appreciation for the benefits of markets and their ability to deliver results ... The record is clear around the globe. Economic freedom benefits individuals, communities and countries ... Countries where economic freedom flourishes – countries that are open to business and entrepreneurship – are countries that have faster-rising standards of living."[8]

A clear, even if ideologically coherent, set of policy predispositions, as other reformers have learned, does not guarantee policy success, however, especially when confronted by determined opposition from both those actors who benefit from the policy status quo and more significantly the architects of the existing policy regime. Nor does an ideology automatically provide a specific prescription for a new set of policies, something that Bernier undeniably was lacking, not surprisingly given his limited familiarity with the telecommunications sector. Before turning in the next section to the process employed and the specific actions that Bernier took to impose his policy preferences on the telecommunications sector, it is necessary to discuss both of the above aspects: opposition to change, especially from the CRTC, and the emergence of a new set of policy initiatives.

Bernier faced a formidable opponent to his potential agenda in the Canadian Radio-television and Telecommunications Commission (CRTC). Since acquiring jurisdiction over telecommunications in 1976, while it had rivals, especially from first the Department of Communications and, after that department was disbanded, from Industry Canada, it had become the dominant force in shaping the telecommunications regulatory policy regime. Without any overt political direction or guidance, for example, it had radically redefined legislative provisions dating from 1906 to permit competition in the terminal equipment and long distance telecommunications markets.[9]

The only direct political intervention in the telecommunications regulatory system, and it was a mixed blessing, was the *Telecommunications Act* passed in 1993. The new statute had three positive features. The first was that it empowered the CRTC, when the Commission deemed that competitive conditions merited it, to forbear, or conditionally refrain, from exercising its powers to regulate rates and other aspects of market behaviour. The second was that it permitted the CRTC to develop alternative methods for regulating telecommunications rates and services instead of relying on the traditional, and much criticized, detailed and time-consuming rate of return regulatory method. The third was that the cabinet was given the authority "... to issue to the Commission directions of general application on broad policy matters with respect to the Canadian telecommunications policy objectives," i.e. a policy direction power.[10]

Far less positive was the statutory statement of policy objectives to guide the CRTC in its regulatory decision-making:

7. It is hereby affirmed that telecommunications performs an essential role in the maintenance of Canada's identity and sovereignty and that the Canadian telecommunications policy has as its objectives
(a) to facilitate the orderly development throughout Canada of a telecommunications system that serves to safeguard, enrich and strengthen the social and economic fabric of Canada and its regions;
(b) to render reliable and affordable telecommunications services of high quality accessible to Canadians in both urban and rural areas in all regions of Canada;
(c) to enhance the efficiency and competitiveness, at the national and international levels, of Canadian telecommunications;
(d) to promote the ownership and control of Canadian carriers by Canadians;

(e) to promote the use of Canadian transmission facilities for telecommunications within Canada and between Canada and points outside Canada;
(f) to foster increased reliance on market forces for the provision of telecommunications services and to ensure that regulation, where required, is efficient and effective;
(g) to stimulate research and development in Canada in the field of telecommunications and to encourage innovation in the provision of telecommunications services;
(h) to respond to the economic and social requirements of users of telecommunications services; and
(i) to contribute to the protection of the privacy of persons.[11]

The problems with this statement are two-fold. The first is that, given the pro-competition decisions that had been taken by the CRTC prior to 1993, the legislation did not provide a clear statement of what the "endpoint" or ultimate policy objective was to be. This contrasted sharply, for example, with the new transportation policy which had been passed by the same Conservative government only six years earlier.[12] The more serious problem with the new telecommunications policy objectives, identified by both the Senate Committee which made an extensive study of the proposed legislation and various witnesses who appeared before it, was that it contained little more than a grocery list of ambiguous, unranked, and potentially conflicting goals that could provide little concrete guidance for the CRTC in its decision-making.[13]

The concern over a lack of either a clear statement of a primary objective or a ranking of the alternative objectives, however, was immediately mitigated by the actions of the CRTC following enactment of the new statute. It made it clear that, whatever the provisions of its governing statute, the CRTC had one over-riding objective, the promotion of competition. Two years after the *Telecommunications Act* was passed, for example, the CRTC declared that, regardless of the language of S.7, henceforth it would pursue one primary objective: the promotion of competition. It justified this by noting that the environment within which telecommunications services are provided is changing "... in ways that outpace the ability of regulators to recognize and define, let alone control. [Consequently, in a competitive world, what] ultimately emerges will be determined by the demands of users and the willingness of suppliers to take risks. The role of the Commission should be to ensure that the right economic and technical conditions for open access are in place."[14] Such an approach was necessary, the Commission concluded, because "market forces allow for greater choice and supplier responsiveness and ensure that user applications, not regulators, drive supply considerations."[15] In hindsight, if the Commission had remained committed to this philosophy there would have been no conflict with Bernier.

In the years immediately following, the Commission, through the use of its forbearance powers and substitution of new price setting instruments, as well as other decisions, appeared to be fully committed to giving full effect to its pro-competitive philosophy.[16] In 1994, it deregulated both the terminal attachment and wireline sectors which it deemed to be sufficiently competitive. In 1998 it stopped regulating the incumbent firms' long distance retail rates. One measure of the success of the new policy was that over the years incumbents increasingly lost market share to the new competitors, especially, but not solely, in the business wireline markets, such that by the millennium their share was approaching one third both in terms of revenues and minutes, a remarkable development given that competition had been permitted in 1992 and effectively only begun in 1994.[17] The Commission also deregulated retail Internet services of the incumbents and then of the cable companies, a development which would subsequently have significant ramifications. Furthermore, after calling for applications for local service competition in 1994, the Commission in 1997 established its regulatory rules for such competition as they applied to the incumbent firms. This competition, however, was slow to develop and was concentrated in the urban business market sector.

In 1997, however, a warning sign appeared that caused apprehension amongst the traditional telephone companies or incumbent local exchange carriers (ILECs) as they had become known. The cause was the release by the CRTC of its "Vision Statement."[18] Although rather anodyne in most respects, several aspects were troubling to the incumbent firms. The first was the CRTC's statement that its mandate was to "regulate and supervise" both the broadcasting and telecommunications systems. Although this was correct for the former, the telecommunications legislation gave it no such role for the latter. In broadcasting, "supervision" was central to the CRTC's role as a planning, sectoral managing agency but no such role was envisioned at least by Parliament for the telecommunications sector.[19] The incumbents were also concerned by the CRTC's reference to regulating "communications services" a term not found in its legislative mandates. The concern was caused by the Commission's insistence that such services be responsive to social values and the emphasis it placed on Canadian content in such services.

Although the incumbent firms did not explicitly criticize the Commission's statement, through their traditional consortium, Stentor, they immediately issued a policy statement that sought to remind the CRTC that government communications policy "... increasingly seeks to rely on market forces to achieve its objectives."[20] Concerned that the Commission seemed to be backing away from a commitment to moving toward a fully competitive market as its ultimate objective, through its suggestion that its role included "supervision," Stentor recommended to the Commission and the Government the elimination of economic regulation, which it insisted should be narrowly defined, by the end of 2001 and that at that time "pricing and entry issues in the communications industry ... be dealt with under the *Competition Act*."[21] As for any suggestion that social objectives be pursued in the telecommunications sector, as far as Stentor was concerned, this was a matter best left to industry self-regulation.

What transformed the apprehension of the incumbent telephone companies into a bitter conflict with the CRTC were several decisions after 2001 that had direct implications for the local exchange market which, as indicated above, was not only the last major market not yet significantly competitive-incumbents' local market shares ranged from 94 per cent to 100 per cent up to 2002 – but was also the single richest market segment accounting for approximately 30 per cent of telco revenues. The conflict was intensified because, as a result of technological developments, potential local competition was soon to become real as cable companies such as Rogers, Shaw and Videotron entered the local telephone market.

It was not initially specific decisions per se in this period that antagonized the incumbent telcos but rather the emergence of a new explicit philosophy that, for the incumbents, indicated that the CRTC was abandoning its stated commitment to allowing market forces to work. The commission was now concerned about "sustainable" competition, perhaps not a surprising development given the bursting of the dot-com bubble in the late 1990s which had dramatic consequences for telecommunications firms in the US and elsewhere. In Canada, for example, new entrants diminished from 28 to 2 in just a few years. As a consequence, the CRTC interpreted its governing statute as mandating a responsibility to be "fair" to new competitors. It made this explicit in a 2002 decision where it stated that its objective was "… to balance the interests of the three main stakeholders in telecommunications markets, i.e. customers, competitors and incumbent telephone companies."[22]

The issue came to a head in 2004 when the CRTC, in response to a request from Bell Canada filed in late 2003 for information concerning how the CRTC intended to regulate cable company-provided local telephone services, indicated that it intended to regulate voice communications services using Internet Protocol (VOIP) as local exchange services which therefore would be subject to the framework governing local competition.[23] This would mean asymmetrical regulation in that the tariffs and service conditions for similar services provided by the ILECs would be subject to regulatory approval, and a concomitant extended public process, while those provided by its competitors would not. Furthermore the incumbents were worried about how the "fairness" doctrine would work out in this area. For them, the fear was that the CRTC's regulatory approach would represent the worst of all possible developments. The CRTC, having embraced competition in principle, having encouraged entry into the local market, was now not only not going to be neutral and not let market forces work, it would "manage" the competitive process in such a manner as to protect the new entrants in the name of fairness.

As the CRTC's approach became evident with its initial position and then subsequent decision on VOIP in 2005, the ILECs had few options. The first was to exercise their right to appeal to Cabinet to vary or overturn CRTC decisions. This would in fact be employed when the CRTC's VOIP decision was announced, as we shall see in the next section. The second was to request informally that the CRTC reconsider its underlying approach. The Commission showed no willingness, however, to undertake an internal review and when approached by the telcos to participate in a non-governmental external policy review, the Chair abruptly dismissed the idea.

Although the other ILECs were resigned to waiting for the right opportunity for a Cabinet appeal, Bell Canada decided it could not afford to wait. Its economic performance was languishing for a number of reasons. It had suffered the most from long distance competition and was a relatively weaker competitor compared to Rogers and TELUS in the wireless sector. It had also made major telecommunications as well as non-telephone-related acquisitions that had imposed significant costs without a corresponding payback. Furthermore, it was now facing competitive inroads in its home territory from TELUS, especially in the business and wireless sectors. Its share price was not performing as well as its competitors and in fact the company was soon to become a takeover candidate.

Faced with these negative economic circumstances, Bell concluded that it could not simply wait for the cable companies to enter the local telephone market under favourable regulatory circumstances and then hope that it could successfully appeal to Cabinet to overturn any CRTC decision. Consequently it decided in 2004, during the CRTC's proceeding but prior to its decision on VOIP, to wage, single-handedly, an intense lobbying campaign at the highest governmental levels to persuade the Government to do what the CRTC had refused to do, namely review its preferred policy approach on local competition, especially its emphasis on "fairness" for the new entrants. Much to the surprise of its erstwhile allies and its competitors, not to mention the CRTC and indeed the Minister of Industry and his department, the Bell campaign was successful.

On February 23, 2005, the Minister of Finance, in his budget, surprised the telecommunications sector with the following announcement: "The Government recognizes the critical importance of the telecommunications sector to Canada's future well-being and the need for a modern policy framework. To ensure the telecommunications industry continues to support Canada's long-term competitiveness, the Government intends to appoint a panel of eminent Canadians to review Canada's telecommunications policy and regulatory framework. Reporting to the Minister of Industry, the panel will be asked to make recommendations before the end of the year on how to move Canada to a modern telecommunications framework in a manner that benefits Canadian industry and consumers."[24]

Initially this policy review had little support from either other industry players or especially from the CRTC and the Minister of Industry and his department.

Despite the initial scepticism within and outside the government, in April 2005, the then Liberal Minister of Industry, David Emerson, announced the appointment of the three members of the Telecommunications Policy Review Panel. Although the Panel had a three part mandate, including access to telecommunications services and the adoption of information and communications technologies, for our purposes the central aspect pertained to telecom regulation:

The existing regulatory regime was designed to facilitate the introduction of competition into an industry previously structured around monopolies. The development and deployment of advanced technology, such as Internet Protocol-based services, high-speed Internet access and wireless broadband communications, combined with maturing consumer demand, have had a profound effect on the telecommunication industry and have started to change the shape and structure of the industry. Governments face the challenge of regulating the industry as it exists today and protecting the interests of its users, while at the same time not standing in the way of progress or restricting the benefits and adoption of advanced telecommunications networks and services.

The panel is asked to make recommendations on how to implement an efficient, fair, functional and forward-looking regulatory framework that serves Canadian consumers and businesses, and that can adapt to a changing technological landscape.

Less than two months later an extensive consultation paper was released and what followed over the next eight months was the most comprehensive public review of Canadian telecommunications policy in the country's history.[25]

In March 2006, the Review Panel issued its report. The core of the Panel's philosophy of the purpose of telecommunications regulation was set out in the following statement:

- Market forces should be relied upon to the maximum extent feasible as the means of achieving Canada's telecommunications policy objectives.
- Regulatory and other government measures should be adopted only where market forces are unlikely to achieve a telecommunications policy objective within a reasonable time frame, and only where the costs of regulation do not outweigh the benefits.
- Regulatory and other government measures should be efficient and proportionate to their purpose and should only minimally interfere with the operation of market forces to meet the objectives.[26]

The report went on to make 127 recommendations including over 50 that set out the details as to how to change the current regulatory restrictions on competition so as to give effect to the core philosophy. The Panel was particularly critical of the CRTC's "balancing" approach:

The Commission's goal appears to have been to promote the financial viability of competitors to the ILECs, in order to ultimately provide consumers with the benefits of increased competition. Application of the doctrine has resulted in a new, high level of regulatory intervention aimed at shaping the structure of markets, rather than allowing market forces to determine the success or failure of different service providers. The relative degree of intervention by the CRTC on behalf of new entrants has been very substantial and has led to the imposition of extensive constraints by the CRTC on the activities of the major suppliers of many telecommunications services, the ILECs.[27]

The Panel recommended that the current presumption that the CRTC should regulate unless it decides to forbear "... should be replaced with a legislative presumption that services will not be regulated except in specified circumstances designed to protect end-users or maintain competitive markets."[28] More significantly, although the Panel recommended fundamental legislative changes, in the interim, it recommended that the Cabinet exercise its direction power acquired in the 1993 *Telecommunications Act* to order the CRTC to give effect to the Panel's recommendations by giving primary emphasis in its regulatory decision-making to para 7(f) and 7(c) cited above.

Although appointed by a Liberal Minister, the Panel's report was delivered to the new Conservative Industry Minister, Maxime Bernier, little more than a month after he had been appointed. He had already decided, according to one source, to concentrate on the telecommunications component of Industry Canada's wide-ranging portfolio. The report's pro-market, deregulatory core clearly matched the Minister's philosophical preferences. More importantly, it gave him a concrete detailed set of recommendations that easily translated into a personal policy agenda. According to another source who met with the Minister shortly after the Panel's report was released, the Minister acknowledged that, armed with the Panel's recommendations, he, both a novice MP and Minister, could make his mark and he intended to do so.[29] All that was needed was an opening that he could rush through.

In fact that opening was on his desk the day he was appointed, in the form of an appeal to Cabinet from the ILECs against the CRTC's decision on telephone service employing Voice over the Internet Protocol (VOIP). A second opening came less than a month later when the same companies appealed to Cabinet to send back for reconsideration by the CRTC its April decision regarding forbearance from regulation in the local service area. Both openings would provide the opportunity Bernier sought to pursue his newly developed policy agenda. On the other side of that opening, however, was considerable opposition not lacking in resources: from the CRTC, the affected companies which included the major cable companies such as Rogers, Shaw and Videotron which presumably did not lack political support and from opposition Members of Parliament in a minority government situation. Most importantly, the Minister confronted determined opposition from his own department officials, some cabinet colleagues, the PMO and especially the PCO. It is to the ministerial initiatives and how he overcame the extensive opposition that we now turn.

PART TWO: OVERTURNING THE VOIP DECISION

To paraphrase Wilde's character Lady Bracknall in *The Importance of Being Ernest,* for the CRTC to misread one signal from the Government may be regarded as a misfortune; to ignore two looks like carelessness. Yet this is what happened in 2006 when the CRTC, either through carelessness, or hubris, chose to ignore two direct policy signals from the Government. For an agency that often stated that it was only filling a policy vacuum that elected authorities had created and would not correct, its rejection of the clearly articulated governmental preferences enabled not only the Government, acting at the request of the Minister of Industry, to impose a comprehensive policy shift on the regulator but, by so doing, to alter fundamentally the political-bureaucratic relationship that had been the norm for the previous thirty years. The CRTC's response to the Minister and the Government would constitute a monumental policy blunder which, it is arguable, was the key to Bernier's success in pursuing his agenda.

The first opening was created by the CRTC's 2005 decision on how to regulate VOIP telecommunications services. Although the convergence of telecommunications and computers had long been anticipated, and in fact had already had a profound impact on telecommunications switching and transmission systems, as well as terminal equipment, the impact on the telecommunications market structure had been less profound. All players- incumbent carriers, new entrants, potential alternative service providers such as cable systems, and customers- were waiting for the emergence of computer-based telecommunications which would allow for full competition to develop in the single largest market segment- the local business and especially residential market, the so-called "last mile" in telecommunications.

Notwithstanding the fact that the CRTC had opened the local market to competition or the availability of a computer-based telecommunications service such as that provided by Skype or Vonage, there was very little local service competition in Canada prior to 2004.[30] VOIP promised to change radically the nature of such competition at least for most Canadians with access to high speed broadband telecommunications. For the ILECs, the assumption was that the entry of cable into the local and long distance telecommunications markets would radically change the competitive environment. Unlike the existing competition which offered only one service, the cable companies such as Rogers, Videotron and Shaw were well-financed and experienced competitors who would be able to have a significant competitive edge in that they could offer a bundle of services that included cable television, local, long distance, wireless and broadband services. The problem for the ILECs was that the CRTC quickly established that it did not share their assumption that "cable changes everything."

Anticipating the growth of VOIP services, both Bell Canada and one of its competitors, Call-Net, had requested clarification of the regulatory rules that would govern the provision of VOIP services. In response in April 2004, the CRTC issued a preliminary statement on those rules.[31] For our purposes the most important was its preference to make the provision of VOIP services by the ILECs subject to the existing regulatory framework, namely the filing of tariffs for approval by the Commission to ensure that rates were "just and reasonable", the statutory requirement dating from 1906 and carried forward in the 1993 *Telecommunications Act*. New entrants, known either as Competitive Local Exchange Carriers (CLECS) or resellers would be exempted from price approval. The CRTC then initiated a public proceeding to develop its proposed rules for VOIP.

In May 2005, the CRTC announced the rules that would be imposed on VOIP services.[32] In this decision a divided CRTC rejected the ILEC position that VOIP services were revolutionary new services which should not be regulated through tariff approval and other requirements.[33] The CRTC adopted the view that such services, rather than being uniquely novel, simply marked "another step in the evolution of telecommunications networks" and were not a substitute for primary local exchange services. It went on to state: "Examples of earlier evolutionary steps include electromechanical step-by-step switching and digital switching technologies. In each case, technological advances have increased the ability of networks to carry greater amounts of voice traffic at lower per unit costs."[34] It was on this basis that the Commission imposed an asymmetrical regulatory regime for VOIP services whereby it would continue to regulate the prices and service conditions for such services offered by the ILECs but forebear from regulating the CLECs and resellers on the grounds that they did not have any market power as new entrants. This would give the cable companies especially a very significant competitive advantage. Included in the regulatory rules were the so-called "winback rules" which prohibited an ILEC from initiating contact with a residential customer which it had lost to a competitor initially for a period of three months but then changed to twelve months. These rules were justified by the Commission on the grounds that they would prevent anti-competitive behaviour by the ILECs before a market had "matured" and permit new competitors "a reasonable opportunity to demonstrate the quality and reliability of their services and that it should have a minimal impact on the marketing ability of the ILECs."[35]

Less than two months after the CRTC's decision, the ILECs filed an appeal to the Cabinet to overturn the CRTC's decision with respect to the asymmetric regulatory requirements as well the winback rules.[36] As a result of the volatile political situation facing the minority Liberal Government which would lead to the election call for January 2006, there was no action on the appeal. Weeks after his appointment, at a lunch with members of the Policy Review Panel attended as well by departmental officials, the VOIP appeal was discussed. Departmental officials discouraged Bernier from entertaining the appeal on the grounds that it "would be too technical and difficult ... to explain to other cabinet ministers why they should take the extremely unusual step- and political risk- of overturning the regulator's decision."[37] Panel members, however, advanced a fundamentally different perspective, specifically that the central issue was not how complex the matter was but that VOIP and its regulation or non-regulation represented the type of issue that they believed their report's recommendations addressed. For the Panel members, VOIP was not an extension of traditional services but was exactly the type of novel breakthrough technology that should not be regulated by anything other than market forces.

Over the objections of his officials, Bernier decided to support the appeal but only to the extent of persuading Cabinet in May 2006 to send the decision back to the CRTC for reconsideration.[38] The grounds for the requested reconsideration are important, especially in light of the CRTC's subsequent action. The Order in Council noted that para 7 (f) of the statement of telecommunications policy objectives- found above- required the CRTC "to foster increased reliance on competition and to ensure that regulation, where required, is efficient and effective" and that VOIP technology, contrary to the CRTC's evolutionary stance "has transformed the nature and extent of competition in telecommunications markets." The Order also took note of the Telecom Policy Review Panel's report which recommended the maximum reliance on competition as possible to achieve the telecom policy objectives and indicated that the Government was undertaking a review of telecom policy in light of the Panel's recommendations. Finally, the Order referred to another related appeal- to be discussed below- on forbearance from regulation of retail local exchange services. In short, the Government could not be clearer in signalling its objectives and preferences to the CRTC.

Just in case the CRTC did not "get" the message, in June 2006, Bernier announced that Cabinet was prepared to employ for the first time the power found in the *Telecommunications Act* to issue a policy direction to the CRTC. Although we will leave a discussion of the details of, and the debates over, this direction to the next section, the main point was that it ordered the CRTC to give a fundamental priority to market forces in its deliberations and to regulate only when absolutely necessary. The direction, Bernier argued, indicated that the Cabinet had rejected the CRTC's current approach and embraced that recommended by the Policy Review Panel.

After receiving comments from interested parties, in September 2006 the CRTC announced that it was reaffirming its original decision although it was prepared to conduct a future proceeding to re-assess its specific requirement that it would not consider forbearance until an ILEC had lost 25 per cent of its market to competitors.[39] What was particularly notable about the decision was that the Commission made no reference whatsoever to the factors that the Cabinet had included in the send-back order. It was as if they either did not exist, or were simply irrelevant or could not be referred to as being beyond its legislative mandate, a course it had adopted previously. The Commission was content simply to note that "its determinations in the Decision are consistent with its statutory obligations."[40]

The consequences of the CRTC's response for both its decision and its relationship with political authorities, especially Bernier, were dramatic and immediate. Bernier viewed both the confirmation of its initial decision and its total disregard for the reasons Cabinet had sent back the issue for reconsideration as arrogant and a wilful dismissal of political policy direction. Convinced that this was evidence that the CRTC was currently out of control and "did not get it," Bernier easily persuaded his cabinet colleagues that a Liberal-appointed commission was not sympathetic to the "new" government's policy direction in telecommunications.[41]

Two specific consequences flowed from the CRTC's action. The first was that, little more than two months after the CRTC's "reconsideration", Bernier convinced Cabinet to vary the original decision. On the basis of Bernier's submission that the CRTC's decision was antithetical to the general economic policies and preferences of the Government as well as its approach to telecommunications specifically, the Commission was ordered to end the asymmetrical regulation of VOIP services provided through any broadband Internet connection by forbearing from regulating those services provided by the ILECs.[42] Bernier's argument was that barriers to entry in this market were low and consequently, "in a competitive sector, there is no reason to regulate some companies while others can offer the service they want at the prices they want. It is time to have a level playing field from which customers and small businesses can benefit."[43] The result was a major victory for both the ILECs and for Bernier. For Bernier it was not only his first real victory in reaching his goal of imposing a policy agenda based on deregulation but more importantly it reinforced his own commitment and strengthened his case with his cabinet colleagues that the policy direction he had released in June should be authorized. That he was to win this battle was perhaps the more enduring consequence of the first round in his battle with the CRTC. It is to the politics of the direction that we now turn.

PART THREE: FIRST POLICY DIRECTION TO THE CRTC

When Bernier indicated that he wished to proceed with the Review Panel's recommendation that the Government should not wait for legislative changes to the CRTC's policy mandate but, in the interim, issue a direction outlining its policy philosophy and priorities, departmental officials balked. Despite the fact that from 1976 on they had sought such a power, once granted in 1993, they were extremely reluctant to exploit it. As they had on previous occasions when interested parties had requested the Minister to use the direction power, his officials cautioned that it was too untested and, if used, might open up a Pandora's Box as parliamentarians, since they had to be consulted on its use, would seize the opportunity to demand that the whole legislation be revisited. They cautioned that the Government would not want to entertain such a development.

Bernier was not persuaded but conceded that, given the minority government situation, he would not be able to proceed with fundamental legislative changes. Despite an unenthusiastic cabinet memorandum drafted by his officials, he adopted a second-best approach, namely to convince his cabinet colleagues that a direction, roughly along the lines proposed by the Review Panel, should complement the request that the CRTC reconsider its VOIP decision. Although it is clear that Bernier was committed to the direction in principle as the right thing to do until new legislation could be passed, the original level of commitment of his colleagues to the direction beyond acting as an obvious signal to the CRTC is not clear.

When, on behalf of the Government, he announced the direction, Bernier promoted it in terms of his personal philosophy. He argued that "it is not the role of government to decide how this increasingly complex market should evolve. It is you- producers and consumers. Likewise our role is not to decide which technology is better and should be permitted to grow faster. That is up to the marketplace to decide ... Our government is committed to modernizing the way the telecommunications industry is being regulated in Canada."[44]

The direction tabled in the House of Commons on June 13, 2006 profoundly challenged the existing policy mandate of the CRTC found in s. 7 of the *Telecommunications Act* cited earlier. Given the complexity of the policy shift proposed, it is necessary to provide the major sections of the direction:

1. In exercising its powers and performing its duties under the *Telecommunications Act*, the Canadian Radio-television and Telecommunications Commission shall interpret and implement the Canadian telecommunications policy objectives set out in section 7, and particularly in paragraphs 7(c) and (f), in accordance with the following principles:
   (a) the CRTC should
   (i) rely on market forces to the maximum extent feasible as the means of achieving the telecommunications policy objectives, and
   (ii) when relying on regulation, use measures that are efficient and proportionate to their purpose and that interfere with the operation of competitive market forces to the minimum extent necessary to meet the policy objectives;

(b) when it is determined that regulatory measures are required, then that regulatory measure should satisfy the following criteria:
   (i) each regulatory measure should specify the telecommunications policy objective that is advanced by the measure and demonstrate compliance with this policy direction,
   (ii) economic regulation, when required, should neither deter efficient competitive entry nor promote inefficient entry,
   (iii) regulatory measures designed to advance non-economic objectives of regulation should, to the greatest extent possible, be implemented in a symmetrical and competitively neutral manner, and
   (iv) interconnection arrangements and access regimes, including access to buildings, in-building wiring and support structures, should, to the greatest extent possible, be technologically and competitively neutral, in order to enable competition from new technologies and not to artificially favour either Canadian carriers or resellers;
(c) in order to promote efficient, informed and timely operations the Commission should adopt the following operational practices:
   (i) provide for maximum efficiency in regulation by using only tariff approval measures that are as minimally intrusive and as minimally onerous as possible,
   (ii) with a view to providing increased incentives for innovation, investment in and construction of competing telecommunications network facilities, conduct a review of its regulatory framework regarding mandated access to wholesale services, in order to determine the extent to which mandated access to wholesale services that are not essential services should be phased out and the appropriate pricing of mandated services to encourage investment and innovation in network infrastructure,
   (iii) maintain and publish service performance standards for the various forms of regulatory proceedings it undertakes to ensure that regulatory measures, when required, are efficient, and
   (iv) continue to explore and implement new approaches for streamlining its regulatory process to enhance the efficiency and effectiveness of regulatory measures;[45]

It is obvious, compared to S. 7 of the *Telecommunications Act*, this direction was not a simple reordering of the existing policy statement but rather a fundamental recasting and, as such, it was not clear whether such an expansive use of the power was originally contemplated. However, although several parties raised the issue of its legality in the comments they filed as part of the compulsory public process, this did not become a major issue in subsequent parts of the process.

The process following the issuance of a direction is two-fold. The first is that public comments are solicited. The second stage, and as Bernier's officials advised him the potentially more contentious, is that the direction must be tabled before Parliament and cannot be acted upon until after 40 sitting days. With regard to the first consultation stage, over sixty comments were filed with the Industry Department and while most were tangential to the purposes of this chapter, two are relevant. The first was that, while the ILECs were naturally supportive of the direction, TELUS was concerned that it might be too permissive in that it stated that the CRTC "should" do what was ordered rather than "shall" as the Review Panel suggested. Furthermore, TELUS was concerned that two clauses from the Panel's proposed direction were not included and argued that they should be. The two clauses were interpreted as providing for timely regulation where necessary and reviews that had to demonstrate significant market power. Absent these provisions, TELUS argued, it was possible that the CRTC might become "overly slow or cautious" in forbearing from regulation and ultimately undermine the reliance on market forces which was the central objective of the direction.[46]

For their part, the major cable companies which would be most affected by the Cabinet's VOIP decision did not believe they could reject outright the basic principles of the proposed direction. Consequently, they endorsed it in principle while arguing that it needed amendments to ensure that the Review Panel's safeguards against abuse of significant market power where in place.[47] They urged the Government to adopt a transitional period, citing the Panel's call for a period of 12 to 18 months, to permit the creation of an institutional framework and enforcement mechanisms necessary for full competition. Furthermore, they suggested that the Government must ensure that the direction was legal. As they noted, while the Cabinet "can use a policy direction to clarify the policy objectives in section 7 ..., it cannot use it to amend the substantive provisions of the *Act*."[48] They cautioned the Government that a direction that suggested the CRTC should regulate as if its legislation has been amended "could lead to serious legal issues which would unnecessarily divert attention from the central goal of promoting the transition from monopoly to competition in all telecommunications markets."

The most significant source of opposition to the proposed direction was the one most feared by Bernier's officials, namely Opposition Members of Parliament. By law, Bernier had to table the direction before the House and Senate and give both bodies 40 sitting days to respond. The direction had been tabled June 13, but the clock did not start until Parliament resumed sitting which was in September. Consequently on October 19 and 24, the House Committee on Industry, Science and Technology heard from panels of witnesses drawn from those who had made submissions during the summer to the Cabinet who both supported and opposed the direction.[49] Consequently Opposition members of the committee who were in the majority decided that it should recommend delay in the implementation of the direction for six months, until March 1, 2007, to allow for further study and to hear from more witnesses.[50] This motion was opposed by the Government members. As indicated this was the type of reaction that Industry Canada officials feared.

To understand the next development it is important to recall that subsequent to the issuance of the direction in June, the CRTC had reaffirmed its original decision on VOIP services. It is not clear whether the direction was originally meant primarily as a signal from the Government to the CRTC as to the direction it expected it to take. Nor is it clear that, faced with what it considered an acceptable response from the CRTC, the Cabinet would have proceeded further with the direction. All that changed, however, with the CRTC's action, which paid no heed to either the Cabinet's arguments requesting the reconsideration, or the draft direction that the Commission should go into a different policy direction.

For Bernier, the CRTC's decision was all the evidence he needed that it "just did not get it" and was obstructionist. In terms of the direction, the CRTC's action was clearly a monumental error. Bernier was able to exploit the CRTC's response not only, as seen, to persuade Cabinet to significantly amend the original decision but to convince his colleagues to ignore the Opposition parties' recommendation for a delay. Consequently on December 14, 2006, reflecting the statutory minimum of 40 sitting days that the direction had to be before the House, Cabinet issued an order directing the CRTC to implement the revised telecommunications policy objectives. Bernier maintained that Cabinet was simply following the letter of the law which did not require that it had to act on what members of Parliament, even the majority of a House committee, had recommended. To follow the House Industry Committee's majority recommendation for further study, it was argued, "would mean that the benefits of an updated regulatory regime that relies on market forces would be postponed. The power to issue directions was designed to be an instrument to provide timely guidance to the regulator. Issuing a policy direction formally states the government's vision and enables timely change towards more market-oriented regulation in advance of any legislative changes, which would inevitably take more time."[51] Bernier had won again, ignoring or overriding the fears and advice of his departmental officials, and the CRTC had lost again. In terms of his personal agenda he was now 2 and 0. He was not finished, however, and in his third battle he would encounter the most strenuous opposition to date, opposition that came not surprisingly just from some industry players, his officials and the CRTC, but from the most senior levels of the government in both the PMO and PCO.

PART FOUR: DEREGULATING LOCAL SERVICES

In April 2006, the CRTC issued its decision setting out how and when it would forbear from regulating the ILECs providing local retail exchange services.[52] This was a major decision that would determine the nature of local telephone competition and was closely linked to the VOIP decision which was then under appeal and about to be referred back to the Commission. For our purposes, the two central contestable parts of the regulatory framework were the stipulation of a very strict five component test before forbearance could be considered and the requirement that the ILECs would be subject to a series of marketing restrictions including existing "winback rules" that prohibited them from contacting customers they had lost to competitors. The only gain from the ILECs perspective on the latter was the reduction from twelve to three months of the prohibition, although even this period was unacceptable to them. The forbearance test included requirements that an ILEC would have to lose a 25 per cent market share in a specific geographic market to competitors and meet wholesale quality of service requirements for the previous six months before the CRTC would consider forbearance.

On May 12, 2006, the ILECs appealed to the Cabinet seeking to have the decision referred back to the Commission with the requirement that the CRTC must reconsider its decision in light of the report from the Telecommunications Policy Review Panel.[53] Bernier's actions on this appeal would be the most controversial of the three issues he confronted and would see him involved in two intersecting conflicts, one with the House Standing Committee on Industry, Science and Technology while the other was with his own officials, the PCO and the PMO as well as some of his cabinet colleagues. That Bernier was able eventually to impose his preferred outcome illustrates his remarkable determination to give effect to his philosophical/ideological approach to markets.

The first stage in the appeal process was a comment period on the petition which occurred over the summer of 2006. Comments were submitted by the major cable companies as well as the ILECs' two telecommunications competitors. All comments urged the Cabinet to reject the petition. As the joint cable company submission argued "this is an inappropriate case to refer back to the Commission for reconsideration." They went on to make an argument that began to resonate in some Ottawa circles: the Cabinet appeal power, they argued "is an extraordinary one that ought to be exercised in the clearest of cases. To exercise it frequently will do a disservice to the integrity of the Commission as an independent, *quasi-judicial*, expert tribunal. This is not a case that justifies extraordinary intervention."[54]

In developing his response, Bernier encountered sustained opposition from departmental officials who felt that he was going too far in his attempt to impose his vision on the CRTC. According to several sources, at one point he complained that drafts of the cabinet memorandum to be submitted in his name contained more arguments opposed to his recommendation than supporting ones. On several occasions he was told that Cabinet did not have the legal authority to pursue the course that he preferred. He was only able to overcome this argument by obtaining independent legal opinions from outside the department that confirmed his position. When Bernier persisted in his approach, departmental officials, according to several sources, then sought external support, primarily from the Privy Council Office to defeat their minister.

This departmental lobbying of PCO was successful to a point. When Bernier presented his preferred response to the appeal, PCO was able to persuade the PMO and then Cabinet that Bernier should have to undertake an additional public consultation. PCO claimed that that the proposed order to the CRTC on the forbearance decision would have to be published in the *Canada Gazette* which made a public comment period mandatory before Cabinet could proceed with it. As specialists in the "machinery of government," this was apparently a persuasive argument for the Prime Minister and his Office. Such a requirement was unprecedented, however, in the history of Cabinet appeals of regulatory decisions and was particularly notable because it had not been required for the Order overturning parts of the CRTC's VOIP decision. The one consolation Bernier received was that almost simultaneously Cabinet approved the order directing the CRTC on the telecommunications policy objectives discussed in the previous section.

The result was Bernier's announcement on December 11, 2006 of the proposed order to vary the CRTC's decision to accelerate deregulation of the local service market by, among other measures, removing the 25 per cent market share loss requirement and substituting the requirement that there be at least two independently-owned facilities based providers in specified local business markets and three in residential markets to justify forbearance. In addition the Order would relax the quality of service requirements and most significantly end the "winback" rules and other marketing restrictions.[55]

During the next month, Industry Canada received more than 35 submissions on the proposed order from corporations and consumer groups as well as dozens of letters and emails from individuals. In addition the House of Commons Industry Committee held a series of meetings to consider these submissions as well as to invite interested parties to appear before it to address both the forbearance order and the general issue of deregulating local telecommunications. The opposition members of the committee, who were a majority, did not hide the fact that they were extremely upset by Bernier's ignoring their original recommendation to the House of Commons that the policy objectives order be suspended until March 2007.

Consequently, starting in late January and continuing to late March, the House Industry Committee held a wide-ranging series of meetings on the topic of "the deregulation of telecommunications" with the Cabinet's proposed order on the forbearance appeal as the central, but not sole, concern.[56] Among the witnesses were the ILEC's, the CLECs especially the cable companies, other new entrants, user groups and consumer groups as well as the Vice Chair of the CRTC and the Commissioner of Competition Policy. A review of the testimony finds that while the ILECs had no problems with the order, surprisingly the CLECs did not object to it in principle but rather argued against some of the specifics, especially the removal of the winback provisions, and contended that the order was unnecessary because the market was in fact changing in ways preferred by the order.

One of the more important points of debate was that referred to earlier, namely the justification for, and impact on, the CRTC as an independent expert body. When Richard French, then Vice Chair-Telecommunications appeared before the Committee, he did not challenge the legality of the order or the recent cabinet orders, but did note that, in response to a question about how the recent ministerial activities "relate in terms of their interaction with the CRTC," that "there is no precedent for this degree of initiative on the part of the political executive."[57] Others were far more explicit in their criticisms. A witness from Cogeco, a Quebec-based cable company, now offering VOIP services, made the following statement: "let me voice our deep concern that political decision-making now appears to be Canadian telecommunications, taking precedence over quasi-judicial decision-making by the independent administrative body formally entrusted by Parliament with the job of ruling on telecommunications issues ... As a result independent fact-finding, proper evidentiary assessment and due process have all taken a beating, in our view, with a resulting loss of trust in the due process."[58] This witness went on to argue, as did others, that rather than employing such ad hoc ministerial interventions, the Government should move forward with new telecommunications legislation.

One of the members of the Telecom Policy Review Panel, while supporting both the cabinet's two appeal orders and the direction as being consistent with the Panel's recommendations, nevertheless did state that he did not think that "anyone in a modern industrialized democracy believes that the political arm of government should regularly interfere with the decision-making process of an independent, professional telecommunications regulator ... Over the long term, government and parliament should develop clearer policy directions which should then be administered by an independent professional regulator, and that should be done in legislation."[59]

The outcome of the parliamentary hearings is perhaps less significant substantively, in part because it was rather predictable, than for what it represented in terms of developing opposition to Bernier's initiative. On March 30th, the Committee made the following report to the House of Commons: the Committee "recommends that the Minister of Industry withdraws the order varying Telecom Decision CRTC 2006–15 and table in Parliament a comprehensive package of policy, statutory and regulatory reforms to modernize the telecommunications services industry."[60] It is perhaps significant that, notwithstanding the fact that the Conservative members of the Committee had consistently defended the initiative during the hearings, and voted against the recommendation, they did not, as they had with the Committee's recommendation that the policy direction be delayed, file a dissenting report.

This may suggest that their enthusiasm for the Minister's agenda was diminishing but this cannot be substantiated.

Bernier and the Government could ignore the House Committee recommendation, as they did in the case of the policy direction, and as we shall see, they would in this case. What Bernier could not ignore was the growing opposition to the proposed order within both the political and bureaucratic arms of the Government. As noted earlier, PCO, both in response to departmental, and increasingly their own, concerns, had imposed the unprecedented requirement that Bernier publish his proposed order in the Canada Gazette thereby creating an opportunity for public criticisms to be expressed and of course postponing imposition of the order.

While the public and parliamentary processes were proceeding, Bernier was repeatedly required to defend his order before several Cabinet Committees. In those meetings he encountered opposition from some of his colleagues as the public confrontation grew. Some of the opposition, while framed in terms of specific problems of timing and concern that a non-priority item was deflecting the Government from its course and its message, undoubtedly reflected personal rivalries and perhaps some jealousy that such a novice minister was getting such press- good or bad. In response to other criticisms that he was being somewhat dogmatic in his defence of markets, Bernier relented and accepted recommendations that a consumer complaints agency be established within the CRTC, the subject of the second direction referred to earlier in the chapter, and that legislation be introduced, as proposed by the Review Panel, that the Competition Bureau be empowered to impose significant administrative fines for anti-competitive behaviour.

Most importantly was the opposition growing within the bureaucracy, up to and including the Clerk of the PCO. Senior bureaucrats were apprehensive about Bernier's apparently routine willingness to ride roughshod over his departmental advisors. More importantly, there was a growing concern that echoed comments made in the Industry Committee that Bernier, solely or primarily for philosophical reasons, was undermining the role of the CRTC as an important, widely-respected, bureaucratic institution. While the CRTC had not helped its cause and consequently the central bureaucrats could not intervene on its behalf on the VOIP and policy direction decisions, now there was a belief that Bernier was going too far.

Bernier's most compelling argument had been that the CRTC "just didn't get it." For PCO actors, however, this was arguably changing. A new Chair, Konrad von Finckenstein, someone with an excellent reputation within the bureaucracy, both within Foreign Affairs and then as Commissioner of Competition Policy, had been appointed in late January. Given his experience, especially with competition policy, it was argued he should be given some time because he was exactly the type of person to redirect the Commission to reflect the philosophy and policy thrust of both the Telecom Policy Review Panel and the Minister. Furthermore another "safe hand" was about to be appointed as Secretary General and there would soon be vacancies amongst the Commissioners. Surely the Government, it was argued, would be able, in short order, to put its stamp on the Commission.

Although Bernier was not happy that he had to submit the proposed order to public consultation, he assumed that the required 30 day period into January 2007 would not be problematic. Furthermore, he was confident that the repeated Cabinet Committee deliberations would not have a negative impact on the process. As the latter and especially the House Committee hearings dragged on into late March, he increasingly became concerned. The reason for this was that the Government was required by law to deal with the CRTC appeal within a year and the final date was looming, namely April 5, 2007. He remained confident, however, that Cabinet would take up the order before that date.

As that date came closer, Ottawa witnessed one of those marvellous, surely unanticipated, bureaucratic coincidences worthy of *Yes Minister*. On March 27, just nine days before the deadline, the CRTC announced that it was granting TELUS's request from October 19, 2006 to forbear from regulating its local service offerings in Fort McMurray, Alberta. Although he did not take part in the decision, Konrad von Finckenstein, the new Chair, declared in the accompanying press release that the "decision reflects our commitment to act quickly to bring the benefits of competition to Canadians."[61]

Cabinet was meeting that same day to take its decision on Bernier's requested order. For the relevant PCO and PMO officers, here was sufficient proof that the CRTC did indeed finally "get it." The Prime Minister was informed of the CRTC's decision and, as a result, Bernier went to the Cabinet meeting only to discover that his item, approval of the order, had been lifted from the agenda. Following the Cabinet meeting, Bernier returned to his office but he was not yet prepared to concede defeat. He ordered his political staff to contact senior Bell and TELUS officers to inform them of the situation and to tell them that, unless they were able to give him some help quickly, the order was doomed and the decision would stand.

Both companies immediately issued press releases critical of the CRTC's decision. TELUS said that it was "extremely disappointed" by the CRTC's decision because it said that "the conditions for deregulation they set out are unattainable in any practical sense and ... their decision runs entirely contrary to the government's direction." The release went on to argue that "It is imperative that the Government immediately reverse today's CRTC decision and continue to deregulate local phone service ... by implementing the test for deregulation proposed" in the December draft order.[62] For its part, Bell Canada declared that the CRTC's decision "is not forbearance." Bell claimed that the decision "confirms that the CRTC's original framework ... is fundamentally flawed and cannot lead to timely meaningful forbearance in any market." Like TELUS Bell called on the Government to move on the draft order "that will bring the full, benefits of open competition to consumers."[63]

In another of those coincidences that can mark the policy process, Bernier was scheduled to meet with Prime Minister Harper the afternoon of his Cabinet setback. Armed with the two press releases, he persuaded the Prime Minister that the need for the order amending the CRTC's forbearance decision was in fact as strong as ever. As a consequence, Harper instructed officials in both the PMO and the PCO that, unless they had substantive problems with the order, he was authorizing Bernier to announce that the Government was varying the CRTC's decision in accordance with the December draft order. Both agencies in effect capitulated.

On April 4th, one day before the legal deadline, Bernier made the announcement that the Cabinet had opted to rewrite fundamentally the CRTC's original decision and invited the ILEC's to file for forbearance in a number of major urban markets.[64] Furthermore, it ordered the CRTC to treat each application on a priority basis and to issue a decision within no more than 120 days after receipt of an application. This order was undoubtedly the most comprehensive variance of a CRTC decision since the Commission was given responsibility for telecommunications in 1976. As far as the recommendation from the House Industry Committee was concerned, the Minister was content simply to state that he "had the opportunity to hear the views of a wide variety of stakeholders, other experts, and members of parliament."[65]

CONCLUSION

Three weeks after the Cabinet order, the new Chair of the CRTC, after describing Bernier as "a fervent believer in free markets [who] does not hesitate to express his views forcefully and to pursue his objectives," made the following statement: "the message is clear: the government wants to move quickly toward more reliance on market forces in telecom services, less regulation and smarter regulation. I welcome the clarity and I welcome the variation order. While it isn't precisely what we have chosen to do, it is a feasible alternative and you can be sure that we are going to implement it in a way that captures the spirit as well as the letter of what the government has said it wants to accomplish."[66] This gracious "concession" speech concluded the twelve month series of battles that had been fought following the appointment of Maxime Bernier as Minister of Industry, battles that the Minister had clearly won. No minister responsible for telecommunications in the previous thirty years had had the impact that Bernier had. It is true that he could not have pursued his agenda, furnished by the Telecom Policy Review Panel, without the lobbying efforts of Bell and TELUS, which provided both the opportunity for ministerial intervention through their regulatory appeals and especially through the former's call for the wide-ranging telecommunications policy review. No clearer sign of their role in the process was shown than in the last of Bernier's three battles when they issued press releases attacking, and thereby undermining, the CRTC's recent forbearance decision.

Notwithstanding the importance of the corporate lobbying for the outcomes analysed in this chapter, to this observer Bernier is the primary factor in explaining those outcomes. Other ministers have had preferences in the past but none have been willing to pursue those preferences as energetically or consistently as Bernier. Previous ministers would simply bemoan the fact that they did not have sufficient control and ask for remedial relief which was not forthcoming. Shaped by both his fervent, ideological belief in markets and his personal ambition to make his mark, Bernier successfully overcame opposition from his own officials, those at most senior levels of the bureaucracy and even amongst his cabinet colleagues. Rather than being dissuaded from acting because such action was "courageous", he acted with determination both to change telecommunications policy and to recast the political-bureaucratic dynamic which had seen the CRTC as the driver of that policy for the previous thirty years.

Where other ministers before him had decried the dominant policy role that the CRTC had assumed and talked about the necessity to ensure that ministers were the policy-makers, he acted to reverse the roles and establish the principle. Unfortunately, we will never know whether he would have been able to deliver on the other components of the action plan developed by the Telecom Policy Review Panel because, after little more than a year and a half as Industry Minister, Bernier was rewarded for his performance by being promoted to Minister of Foreign Affairs. What can be said, however, is that, in the short time he was Minister responsible for telecommunications, he decidedly made a difference that other ministers, past and present, can only envy.

ACKNOWLEDGEMENTS

The author would like to thank three confidential informants and especially Ian Scott, Hudson Janisch, Bruce Doern and Allan Maslove for their insights, comments and assistance in writing this paper. In particular, he would like to express his deepest gratitude to Alan Hamilton, of TELUS, who provided a full set of public documents including parliamentary reports, CRTC decisions and newspaper commentary, without which the paper could not have been written.

NOTES

1 Flora MacDonald, "The Minister and the Mandarins," *Policy Options* 1, no. 3 (1980): 29.

2. Lloyd Axworthy, "Control of Policy," *Policy Options*, April 1985, 20.
3. The Honourable Maxime Bernier, Minister of Industry, "Speaking Points," 2006 Canadian Telecom Summit, Toronto, 13 June 2006, 1.
4. On the various "political appeal" mechanisms available to Cabinet see Richard Schultz "Regulatory Agencies and the Canadian Political System," in Kenneth Kernaghan, ed., *Public Administration in Canada: Selected Readings*, 3rd ed. (Toronto: Methuen, 1977); and Hudson Janisch, "Policy Making in Regulation," *Osgoode Hall Law Journal* 17 (1979).
5. The Cabinet, at the same time as it issued its variance of the forbearance decision, also issued a second direction to the CRTC to create an agency to deal with consumer complaints in the telecommunications sector. This direction was not particularly controversial and therefore is only discussed in passing below. For information on the direction see "Order requiring the Canadian Radio-television and Telecommunications Commission to Report to the Governor in Council on Consumer Complaints," P.C. 2007–0533. Available at http://strategis.ic.gc.ca/epic/site/smt-gst.nsf/en/sf08753e.html; accessed 27 January 2008.
6. Donald Savoie, *The Politics of Public Spending in Canada* (Toronto: University of Toronto Press: 1990),190–191. The other three categories are status, policy and process participants.
7. The Honourable Maxime Bernier, Minister of Industry, "Speaking Points," Economic Club of Toronto, 15 November 2006, 1.
8. The Honourable Maxime Bernier, Minister of Industry, "Speaking Points," 2006 Canadian Telecom Summit, Toronto, June 13, 2006, 3.
9. G. Bruce Doern, "Regulating on the Run: The Transformation of the CRTC as a Regulatory Institution," *Canadian Public Administration* 40, no. 3 (1997): 516–38; and Richard J. Schultz, "Still Standing: The CRTC, 1976–1996," in G. Bruce Doern et al., eds., *Changing the Rules: Canadian Regulatory Regimes and Institutions* (Toronto: University of Toronto Press, 1993).
10. *Telecommunications Act*, Statutes of Canada 1993, c.38, s. 8.
11. *Telecommunications Act*, Statutes of Canada 1993, c.38, s. 8.
12. *National Transportation Act*, 1987 Statutes of Canada, Vol. 1, c. 34.
13. Senate of Canada, Standing Committee on Transport and Communications, *Report on the Subject matter of Bill C-62, An Act respecting Telecommunications*, Third Session, Thirty-Fourth Parliament, June 1993.
14. Telecom Decision CRTC 94–19, (33).
15. Telecom Decision CRTC 94–19, (13).
16. For an overview to 1997 see Richard Schultz "Governing in a Gale…," in Dale Orr and Thomas A. Wilson, eds., *The Electronic Village: Policy Issues of the Information Economy* (Toronto: C.D.Howe Institute, 1998).
17. For details see, CRTC, *Report to the Governor in Council: Status of Competition in Canadian Telecommunications Markets*, various years starting in 2001.
18. CRTC, "From Vision to Results at the CRTC," (Ottawa: CRTC, 1997).

19 On the difference between policing, the traditional regulatory role, and regulatory planning see Richard Schultz and Alan Alexandroff, *Economic Regulation and the Federal System* (Toronto: University of Toronto Press, 1985).
20 Stentor, "Competition and Regulation in the Canadian Communications Market," (Ottawa: Stentor,1998), 3.
21 Stentor, "Competition and Regulation in the Canadian Communications Market," 26.
22 CRTC, "Regulatory Framework for the Second Price Cap Period," Telecom Decision CRTC 2003–34, May 30, 2002, para. 99.
23 CRTC, 'Regulatory framework for voice communications services using Internet Protocol," CRTC Public Notice CRTC 2004–2, Ottawa, 7, April 2004.
24 Department of Finance, "Budget 2005– Budget Plan: *Chapter 4 - A Productive, Growing and Sustainable Economy: More Efficient and Effective Markets*;" available at http://www.fin.gc.ca/budget05/bp/bpc4ee.htm, accessed 23 October 2007.
25 Full details of the Panel's work and its results can be found at http://www.telecomreview.ca.
26 Telecommunications Policy Review Panel, *Final Report 2006* (Ottawa: Industry Canada, 2006) Executive Summary, 4.
27 Telecommunications Policy Review Panel, *Final Report 2006*, 3–8.
28 Telecommunications Policy Review Panel, *Final Report 2006*, 3–8.
29 Confidential interview. A published version of this meeting is provided by Simon Tuck, "How telecom reform topped Bernier's agenda," *Globe and Mail*, 14 December 2006, B9.
30 See CRTC Report to the Governor in Council on the Status of Competition in Telecommunications Markets, 31 October 2005 which stated that the ILECs retained 97 per cent of the local residential telephone market and 87 per cent of the local business market in 2004.
31 CRTC, "Regulatory framework for voice communications services using Internet Protocol," CRTC Public Notice CRTC 2004–2, Ottawa, 7, April 2004
32 CRTC, "Regulatory framework for voice communications services using Internet Protocol," CRTC Telecom Decision 2005–28, Ottawa, 12 May 2005.
33 The Vice-Chair Broadcasting and another member dissented from the decision with both arguing that ILEC VOIP services should not be regulated if those of their competitors were not. See CRTC, "Regulatory framework for voice communications services using Internet Protocol," CRTC Telecom Decision 2005–28, 63–6.
34 CRTC, "Regulatory framework for voice communications services using Internet Protocol," CRTC Telecom Decision 2005–28, para 18.
35 CRTC, "Regulatory framework for voice communications services using Internet Protocol," CRTC Telecom Decision 2005–28, paras 243–8.
36 The ILEC petition, dated July 28, 2005, as well as comments from other parties can be found at http://strategis.ic.gc.ca/epic/site/smt-gst.nsf/en/sf06105e.html.
37 Tuck, "How telecom reform topped Bernier's agenda," FN 24. The essence of this part of the report was confirmed in a confidential interview by one of the Panel members who attended the lunch.

38 Privy Council, Order-in-Council P.C, 2006–305, May 4, 2006.
39 CRTC, "Reconsideration of Regulatory framework for voice communications services using Internet Protocol," Telecom Decision CRTC 2006–53, Ottawa, 1 September 2006.
40 CRTC, "Reconsideration of Regulatory framework for voice communications services using Internet Protocol," Telecom Decision CRTC 2006–53, para 77.
41 Bernier knew that this message would resonate with Harper because of his general comments to this effect during the election. See Tom Flanagan, *Harper's Team: Behind the Scenes in the Conservative Rise to Power* (Montreal: McGill-Queen's University Press, 2007), 262.
42 "Order Varying Telecom Decision CRTC 2005–28," *Canada Gazette* 140, no. 24, (29 November 2006), available at http://canadagazette.gc.ca/partII/2006/20061129/html/sor288-e.html; accessed 27 January 2008.
43 The Honourable Maxime Bernier, Minister of Industry, "Speaking Points," The Economic Club of Toronto. 15 November 2006.
44 The Honourable Maxime Bernier, Minister of Industry, "Speaking Points," 2006 Canadian Telecom Summit, Toronto, 13 June 2006, 1.
45 "Order under Section 8 of the Telecommunications Act – Policy Direction to the Canadian Radio-television and Telecommunications Commission," *Canada Gazette Part 1*, Vol. 140, no. 24 (17 June 2006).
46 See the Comments filed by TELUS, 16 August 2006, esp. pages 5–10. Available at http://strategis.ic.gc.ca/epic/site/smt-gst.nsf/en/sf08689e.html; accessed 1 November 2007.
47 Representations of Cogeco Cable Inc., Quebecor Media Inc., Rogers Communications Inc. and Shaw Communications Inc. 16 August 2006. Available at http://strategis.ic.gc.ca/epic/site/smt-gst.nsf/en/sf08689e.html; accessed 27 January 2008.
48 Representations of Cogeco Cable Inc., Quebecor Media Inc., Rogers Communications Inc. and Shaw Communications Inc. 16 August 2006, 5.
49 See House of Commons, 39th Parliament, 1st Session, Standing Committee on Industry, Science and Technology, Evidence, 19 and 24 October 2006.
50 See House of Commons, 39th Parliament, 1st Session, Standing Committee on Industry, Science and Technology, Evidence 26 October 2006 and Third Report to the House of Commons.
51 "Order issuing a Direction to the CRTC on Implementing the Canadian Telecommunications Policy Objectives," Regulatory Impact Analysis Statement. *Canada Gazette Part II* 140, no. 26 (14 December 2006), 2347.
52 CRTC, "Forbearance from the regulation of retail local exchange services," Telecom Decision CRTC 2006–15, Ottawa, 6 April 2006.
53 "Petition to the Governor in Council to refer Telecom Decision 2006–15 ... back to the Canadian Radio-television and Telecommunications Commission for reconsideration," available at http://strategis.ic.gc.ca/epic/site/smt-gst.nsf/en/sf08628e.html; accessed 27 January 2008.

54 Submission of Cogeco Cable Inc., Quebecor Media Inc., and Rogers Communications Inc. "in the Matter of Canada Gazette Notice No. DGTP-007–2006 ...." available at http://strategis.ic.gc.ca/epic/site/smt-gst.nsf/en/sf08628e.html; accessed 27 January 2008.
55 The proposed order is available at http://canadagazette.gc.ca/partI/2006/20061216/html/regle6-e.html; accessed 27 January 2008.
56 Full information on the witnesses, their evidence and questions can be found at http://cmte.parl.gc.ca/cmte/CommitteeList.aspx?Lang=1&parlseS=391&jnt=0&selid=e21_&com=10476; accessed 27 January 2008.
57 Richard French, "Evidence," House of Commons Standing Committee on Industry, Science and Technology" (hereafter as INDU) No. 41, Ist session, 39th Parliament, 5 February 2007, at 3:46 pm.
58 Mr Yves Mayrand, "Evidence," INDU, 7 February 2007 at 3:50 pm.
59 Hank Intven, "Evidence," INDU, 12 February 2007, at 3:48 pm. For similar arguments, see the evidence of Michael Janigan from the Public Interest Advocacy Centre given at INDU, 26 February 2007 at 3:50 pm.
60 INDU, *Sixth Report*, 30 March 2007.
61 CRTC, "CRTC to deregulate local telephony in the Fort McMurray residential market," News release, 27 March 2007.
62 TELUS News release, "TELUS comments on CRTC refusal to deregulate local phone market in Fort McMurray," 27 March 2007.
63 Bell Canada Enterprises, News Release. "Bell Canada comments on CRTC's announcement with respect to Fort McMurray," 27 March 2007.
64 "Order Varying Telecom Decision 2006–15," P.C. 2007–532, April 4, 2007. *Canada Gazette* 141, no. 8 (18 April 2007).
65 "Order Varying Telecom Decision 2006–15," P.C. 2007–532, 11.
66 Konrad von Finckenstein, "Notes for an Address to the 2007 Telecommunications Invitational Forum," Montebello Quebec, 25 April 2007, 1.

8 How Ottawa Doesn't Spend: The Rapid Appearance and Disappearance – and Possible Reappearance – of the Federal Social Economy Initiative

EDWARD T. JACKSON

Cell-phone static crackled on the conference call. "We did some things well; but other things really didn't work," said one caller. On a sunny day in late August 2007, leading Ontario activists from cooperatives and credit unions, non-profit agencies, and francophone organizations had come together to evaluate their collective efforts of two years earlier on the federal Social Economy Initiative. Their organizations had formed a consortium to implement the new program. However, the Paul Martin government fell in late 2005, and the newly elected Conservatives terminated the Initiative. Quebec was funded before the cuts were made, but Ontario and the rest of Canada got nothing except some research money. Conference-call participants agreed: they hadn't built sufficient political leverage to force the federal government, under either major party, to protect this program and bring it to implementation. The Ontario activists vowed to deal with this weakness, and be prepared for the next opportunity in the political cycle to secure significant public resources for the social economy sector.[1]

That same week, across the Atlantic, the United Kingdom Government of Gordon Brown and the Labour Party released the report of a year-long review on the third sector. After a decade of successive governments led by Tony Blair actively supporting social enterprise across the UK, through grants, loans and better access to business advice – as well as regulations creating an entirely new category of non-profit business enterprise with unique tax benefits and funding for sector-wide intermediaries and networking – the government moved to strengthen the broader non-profit and charitable sector by endowing community foundations with new funds, investing in community-based asset-building, supporting youth volunteering, promoting public awareness of social-purpose businesses, funding third-sector infrastructure, and strengthening the relationship between the sector and all levels of government. These measures totalled more than $1 billion in new spending, to be coordinated by an Office of the Third Sector.[2] Canadian social-economy activists looked at this British policy initiative with envy – but also with renewed inspiration that their own work would soon bear fruit of this kind. Or would it?

INTRODUCTION

What was the Government of Canada's Social Economy Initiative (SEI), what were its origins, how did it die – and why, in fact, does it matter anyway? Moreover, what are the chances that this policy initiative could actually reappear, in some form, in the future? Involving only $132 million in federal spending, the SEI was small by any measure, dwarfed by the "big politics" issues of the day, including the war in Afghanistan, the "fiscal imbalance" and climate change. But when the program was announced in the federal budget of 2004, it had the personal support of Prime Minister Paul Martin. And even after it died of natural causes, the SEI left a legacy of both disappointment and hope among the non-state actors that had supported it. Most of all, it appears, the initiative sparked a learning process – primarily a political education – among the leaders of the social enterprise sector. Where the SEI failed (with a couple of important exceptions) to deliver real financial resources to the sector, it may well have generated political learning that could influence the policy process in the years ahead.

CONTEXT

Civil society is "the arena, outside of the family, the state, and the market where people associate to advance common interests."[3] Over the past decade, against a backdrop of intensifying economic globalization, and concern over the limits of the welfare state, the "new public management" has made room for civil society as a policy partner for the state, as well as a service-delivery agent.[4] Governments have also experimented with strategies to more effectively engage citizens in the policy process, as well as working more systematically with networks of other policy actors inside and outside government.[5] For their part, citizens can participate in (all, some, or only one of) six stages of the policy process: problem identification, priority setting, policy formulation and design, passage of policy instruments, implementation and evaluation; at each stage, there are different combinations of types of citizen involvement, as well as a variety of political institutions, in play.[6]

Viewed from another angle, in the context of pursuing policy reform, the policy implementation process can be seen to rely on a series of major strategic tasks. These include: legitimization, resource accumulation, organizational design and modification, mobilizing resources and actions, and monitoring progress.[7] Failure to address any one of these tasks in robust fashion could result in the failure of the reform. Furthermore, public policy has a spatial dimension; its boundaries are socially constructed and contested. Political actors negotiate "over the (re)-allocation of policy responsibilities to another or new scale;" a process known as "rescaling."[8]

Arising from experience in France, Belgium and other European countries, as well as in Quebec, the social economy (*économie sociale*) comprises non-profit and cooperative enterprises that pursue both commercial and social (and also often environmental) objectives, as well as the community-based and sector-wide organizations that support these social businesses.[9] In English-speaking Canada, this sector is known as community economic development (CED), a concept that involves place-based strategies to generate local businesses and jobs and social justice. Social enterprises are often small and fragile, and the local organizations and national networks supporting them have been typically fragmented and under-financed.[10] Like other elements in civil society in Canada, the social economy sector relies on government for more than half its income. Yet it chafes at the unpredictable, short-term, project-driven nature of state support.[11] Nonetheless, over the past decade, the sector has grown, enhanced its internal connectivity and coherence, and built greater professional capacity. Moreover, through an alliance of leaders of both économie sociale in Quebec and CED in the rest of Canada, the sector has sought to strengthen its position vis à vis the federal government.

Moreover, as they have slowly (and unevenly) moved toward the policy mainstream, social-economy leaders have had to balance the dual, and sometimes conflicting, objectives of partnering with the state, on the one hand, and promoting social change, on the other.[12] Indeed, the sector has always faced a choice between whether the purpose of CED is to reform capitalism or to radically transform it.[13] This tension has generally been resolved through practice, which almost always tends to be messier and less grand than the sector's rhetoric (as is also the case with every other sector in society). In fact, some students of this field argue that the sector is under-theorized, especially, in Canada at least, in terms of *economic* theory.[14]

THE SOCIAL ECONOMY INITIATIVE

Many people lobbied Paul Martin during his tenure as federal Finance Minister and unofficial Prime-Minister-in-waiting, even while the Liberal Party was tearing itself to shreds in fratricidal conflict. Among the organizations that caught his attention were the Montreal-based Chantier de l'économie sociale, an umbrella group created at the 1996 Quebec economic summit chaired by then-Premier Lucien Bouchard. The Chantier represents hundreds of non-profit and cooperative enterprises in day care, affordable housing, disability services, job training and much more, and has become a political force to be reckoned with by both the federal and provincial levels of government.[15] The second organization that educated Mr Martin on the non-profit sector was the Caledon Institute of Social Policy, a socially progressive think tank in Ottawa.[16] Both organizations bent his ear, frequently, on the nature and merits of the social economy. A third organization, the Canadian CED Network (CCEDNET), a professional association, worked with the Chantier and senior government officials on the design of a federal program to support the social economy. So, when the Martin Liberal government announced a set of special measures to promote social enterprises, these three groups were, of course, not surprised.[17]

In early 2004, Mr Martin's Finance Minister, Ralph Goodale, tabled the 2004 federal budget, which contained a major chapter entitled "A New Deal for Communities." Among the measures set out in the chapter were significant funding for the GST-rebate, gas-tax sharing and accelerated infrastructure construction for municipalities, new spending on urban Aboriginals, and updated regulations for registered charities. The government also pledged to explore setting up a new bank for the charitable sector. In the same chapter, the budget proposed four measures to support the social economy, recognizing "the social economy sector's growing contribution to Canada's communities,"[18] including:

- confirming that social enterprises will become eligible for a range of government programs currently offered to small business;
- providing $17 million over two years for a pilot program in capacity building grants for the sector, to be delivered by Industry Canada and the four federal regional development agencies;
- making $100 million available over five years to finance up to four regionally-based, long-term, "patient capital" pools to help social businesses expand and build assets;
- allocating $15 million over five years to the Social Sciences and Humanities Research Council to fund research on the social economy.[19]

Although the total budget commitment to the social economy was modest, by federal standards, at $132 million, the government positioned these measures as a first step that could lead to a larger funding envelope in the future. For the most part, social economy and CED leaders greeted these provisions very positively, proud that their sector had finally been recognized as an official element in federal policy, and anticipating the concrete benefits these measures would yield in their neighbourhoods and villages.

These provisions, collectively, were dubbed the Social Economy Initiative (SEI). Leadership for the file was given to Montreal Member of Parliament Eleni Bakopanos, who was appointed Parliamentary Secretary for the Social Economy.[20] She reported to Social Development Minister Ken Dryden. Industry Minister Lucienne Robillard also played a key role in the SEI. An array of activities were begun through the spring and summer of 2004, with the Parliamentary Secretary convening a series of National Roundtables on the Social Economy to examine key policy issues, obstacles and solutions. Leading practitioners were invited to participate alongside federal officials in these meetings. Under the Parliamentary Secretary's leadership, the Social Development Directorate of Human Resources and Social Development Canada was tasked with creating an inter-departmental, or horizontal, longer-term policy framework for the social economy. The regional development agencies – the Atlantic Canada Opportunities Agency, Canada Economic Development in Quebec, FedNor in Ontario, and the Western Economic Diversification Fund – began to organize consultations with the social-economy sector. Federal bureaucrats began to prepare Treasury Board and Cabinet documents that would give them legal authority to implement the budget measures. A review of small-business programs was undertaken by Industry Canada to determine whether social enterprises were being blocked from accessing these programs; the department's conclusion was that there were few obstacles preventing such access. Capacity building grant-making began in Quebec. Momentum continued to build. The buzz and energy created by the budget announcement, along with the Prime Minister's personal interest in this file, propelled the government and the sector alike forward for nearly 20 months. There was widespread optimism in the sector that SEI funds would begin to flow in late 2005 and early 2006.

As it turned out, though, the sector's high expectations were never fulfilled. By the fall of 2005, the regional development agencies were still finalizing their programs for capacity building and patient capital financing; spending authorities were not yet locked in. As the Gomery Inquiry reported out on the Liberal sponsorship scandal in Quebec, federal-government accountability and due diligence procedures intensified, further slowing SEI approvals. After more than a year and a half, HRSDC had still not yet produced its inter-departmental policy framework. Certainly, there were some skeptics and outright opponents of the SEI within the bureaucracy, particularly in the Department of Finance, who were prepared to wait out this "spasm" of policy energy as they had done in other eras with new governments. However, among the officials within federal departments and agencies who wanted to make the SEI work, there was also frustration. The rapid, externally-driven and top-down design of the program meant that the

Initiative had not built a sufficient foundation *within* the government system. In the view of these officials, the SEI suffered from the lack of a larger vision and framework, lack of clear objectives, and much more. This, in turn, required the agencies involved to build these arguments from scratch, as it were. Being largely unfamiliar with the social economy, these units carried out internal analysis and, unevenly, external consultations. All these extra steps, to be sure, delayed implementation. Yet as one observer put it: "the operation of the machinery of good government explains a lot of what happened here."[21]

Then there was politics. In Parliament, minority-government gridlock and tactical gamesmanship were the order of the day, preoccupying the political leadership and, again, slowing the work of not only the House but of all federal ministries and agencies. In November 2005, a non-confidence motion was triggered by the opposition, led by the New Democratic Party. The government fell. An election was called for January 2006. Benefiting from Liberal woes in Quebec, and running a disciplined campaign, the Conservatives won a minority government, and Stephen Harper became Prime Minister. Several Liberal supporters of the SEI lost their seats, including the Parliamentary Secretary herself. The only spending measures of the Social Economy Initiative that had been fully authorized before the Conservatives assumed power were the $15 million SSHRC research program and a (somewhat reduced) contribution to a patient capital fund in Quebec. The rest of the SEI budget provisions, almost $90 million worth, remained in limbo for six months, and then were officially cut by the Harper government in fall 2006, along with a batch of other social programs. Social-economy and CED leaders outside Quebec reeled, exhausted and bitterly disappointed.

THE ONTARIO EXPERIENCE

The Ontario experience with the SEI illustrates in a more granular way some of the dynamics at work in this policy episode. In late 2004 and early 2005, the lead regional-development agency in Ontario for the federal initiative, FedNor, organized consultations with sector leaders. Although there were (and remain) supporters of the social economy within FedNor, the government side was viewed by the sector in these meetings as stiff, circumspect and cautious.

In response, sector leaders decided to organize themselves to try to shape, and then actually implement, the SEI in their province. In early 2005, the Ontario Social Economy Consortium (OSEC) was formed. The initial core members were the Ontario CED Network (part of the national professional association, CCEDNET), the Ontario Co-operative Association (a lobby group for the cooperative sector, known as OnCo-op), and the Community Economic Development Technical Assistance Program (or CEDTAP, a grant-making program funded by foundations and corporations). These groups had already started working together on a project funded by the provincial government's Ontario Trillium Foundation. Other members of the consortium included the Credit Union Central of Ontario, L'Alliance des caisses populaires de l'Ontario, the francophone Cooperative Council of Ontario, Le Réseau de développement économique et d'employabilité (RDÉE) and the United Way of Greater Toronto. The group employed an external facilitator to chair the founding meeting of organizations with very different mandates, cultures and ways of working.[22] In fact, until that point, OSEC members had more experience in operating separately and competing with each for funds than they had in cooperating with each other.

In mid-2005, FedNor issued a call for proposals to operationalize both the patient capital and capacity building components of the SEI in Ontario. OSEC members mobilized, working hard through July and August, and produced two proposals. The first was led by Credit Union Central and L'Alliance to implement a $30 million financing facility that would make long-term loans and guarantees to social enterprises through the province-wide credit union system, in cooperation with CED organizations. Projections showed that, by attracting additional private financing, this facility could be expanded over a ten-year period to $50 million and could sustain itself at that level in perpetuity. The second proposal, led by OnCo-op, drew on the programming capacities and networks of all OSEC members to provide, over two years, nearly $5 million worth of technical assistance, training and networking in order to build the social economy's capacity at the local, regional and provincial levels. By October 2005, FedNor had evaluated these proposals as the best ones it had received in the competition, and invited OSEC to enter into contract negotiations to do both jobs.

But three factors "above" the SEI combined to terminate these negotiations. First, the general efforts of FedNor managers to make the internal case for their spending programs was constrained by the lack of a larger, clearer and well-documented policy framework for the SEI as a whole. Second, in the wake of the Gomery inquiry into the Liberal sponsorship scandal, contracting authorities and lawyers performed what could be called "hyper due-diligence" on all new federal programs, including the SEI in Ontario. In particular, the internal Treasury Board approval process became more time-consuming. Third, in a gridlocked Parliament, the opposition parties ground House business to a halt. As a result, the two Ontario contracts were never signed. And, when the Conservatives assumed power, the line-items allocated for these programs in the government budget were quickly, and easily, vaporized.

Still, the Ontario story doesn't end there. For the next year, sector leaders grieved this missed policy opportunity as they returned to the ongoing core business of their respective organizations. However, by early 2007, they began to introduce the concept of a patient capital fund for the social economy in Ontario to the *provincial* government, holding talks with ministers and senior officials at Queen's Park. Drawing on the Quebec example, the new proposal called for the establishment of an Ontario Social Enterprise Trust, financed by a major contribution from the Government of Ontario together with additional contributions from the federal government, private financial institutions and social investors. The Trillium project was employed to promote community-level discussions across the province on sustainable financing for CED and the social economy.[23] At the same time, reflecting on the 2004–2005 experience, the Ontario sector leadership asked itself whether it needed a stronger political vehicle, like the Chantier in Quebec, to advocate more forcefully with all levels of government. The Ontario Node of the SSHRC-funded Social Economy Research Networks was used to spark debate and action on this strategic question. By fall 2007, the sector was actively seeking ways to reconstitute itself in both political and programmatic terms. In an October 2007 provincial election, the Liberal Party was returned to power with a solid majority, as well as a reference to a social venture fund in its platform.[24] Yet the leaders also knew that applying both Quebec models – the Trust and the Chantier – in the under-funded, more fragmented and less corporatist context of Ontario, would not be simple. Their journey, they understood, would continue to be challenging and iterative – and probably long.

THE SOCIAL ECONOMY UNDER THE CONSERVATIVES

It took the Conservatives only a few months after assuming office to render the social economy invisible. References to the SEI quickly disappeared from government websites and the federal policy lexicon. This was part of a general "policy-cleansing" effort by "Canada's New Government." The Prime Minister's Office seemed to view social economy leaders as Liberal, NDP and (in Quebec) Bloc sympathizers, which was largely though not entirely accurate. Dumping the SEI was simple partisan politics, but there were some loose ends. First, the SEI didn't disappear from the DEC Quebec website, where capacity building continued and the commitment to a patient capital fund had, in fact, been locked in. Second, in rural and remote parts of Canada, on the ground, plenty of Tories were leading Community Futures Corporations and other CED initiatives to try to diversify and bolster local economies. Global capitalism has never had a plan for rural Canada. In small towns, local leaders of all political stripes must become pragmatists, if they aren't already. Furthermore, in corporate Canada, some business leaders with both Liberal and Conservative ties were integrating CED into their corporate social responsibility efforts. Nevertheless, these realities were not sufficient to compel the new government to re-start work on the SEI.

Yet some hope was kept alive. A small team in the now depleted unit of HRSDC that originally held the SE policy file calculated that the Tories would, in fact, allow some work to proceed on the financing and regulatory dimensions of the non-profit sector. This unit set about organizing the Community Finance Advisory Committee (CFAC), which was convened several times in late 2006 to discuss policy research generated by government analysts. Reporting to a Director-level manager and not to a Parliamentary Secretary, CFAC was a "lower-level" working group of government officials and sector leaders compared to the SE Roundtable. Still, the Committee identified useful policy models on financing the third sector drawn from the United Kingdom and Europe, in particular. Unlike the Roundtable, the committee also included provincial government representatives. Providing a reason (and a venue and money) to enable sector leaders from across the country to continue to meet together was in itself a positive feature of CFAC. In early 2007, at the final meeting of the Committee, at a conference organized by the British Columbia-based Enterprising Non-Profits Program (ENP), sector leaders turned to ENP to carry on network coordination on these issues.

Meanwhile, the social economy sector regrouped. By this time, the SSHRC-funded Social Economy Research hub and its regional nodes were fully active, with over 300 researchers and practitioners mapping, defining, and exploring the capacities of social enterprise and CED.[25] The English-Canadian professional association and sector advocate, the Canadian CED Network, put several federal projects together to stabilize its funding. ENP won a series of small HRSDC contracts, as well. And, after many gruelling months of lobbying politicians and staving off opponents, the Chantier de l'économie sociale finally gained federal, and soon after provincial, approval for substantial public investments in the new social economy trust in Quebec, along with major contributions by two labour-investment funds. At the same time, an energetic initiative on social finance – sparked by the McConnell and Tides Foundations, Plan Canada and Carleton University – also helped to renew momentum outside government. Nonetheless, all these efforts to build new "infrastructure" in the face of a hostile federal government absorbed large amounts of time and energy by sector leaders, further diverting them from their core mission of concrete, on-the-ground work.

WHY THE SEI DISAPPEARED, AND COULD REAPPEAR AGAIN

The Martin Government had worked closely with civil-society actors to formulate a modest policy package to address social and economic problems.[26] A policy evaluation framework had even been developed.[27] However, the combined power of these state and non-state partners proved to be too weak to oblige the government to pass all the policy instruments necessary to implement the Initiative. And, of all the stages of the policy process in which citizens can participate, implementation is, ultimately, the one that matters most. The bottom-line is that, notwithstanding their best efforts, the advocates of this policy change were unable to effectively mobilize significant resources to make change happen.[28]

But why? Three factors help explain why the SEI disappeared so quickly:

1) *Electoral tactics trump policy-making in a minority government:* In late 2005, a badly fractured Parliament, coping with a minority-government situation was captured by the dramatic electoral tactics of all political parties. The NDP felt compelled, in late 2005, to pull the plug on the Liberal government, even though the NDP seemed also to understand that such a tactic would risk losing an array of social programs in which they strongly believed – which is exactly what happened. Many activists have still not forgiven Leader Jack Layton and his party for making the choice it did.

2) *Power asymmetries shape and challenge civil society:* Given the asymmetries of power in the Canadian federation as a whole, organized civil society in Quebec has greater political leverage in Ottawa than do civil society groups from the rest of Canada. Moreover, the corporatist culture and statist tradition in Quebec enable the sector there to organize itself more coherently, on a larger scale than elsewhere in Canada, further reinforcing the "Quebec advantage."The Chantier got its patient capital fund.[29] At the same time, academic researchers from across Canada (boosted by leading Quebec scholars), succeeded in accessing the SSHRC research funds under terms favourable to the academy. Overall, non-governmental, non-academic organizations outside Quebec – already highly fragmented and under-funded – fared worst of all in gaining real benefits.[30]

3) *Good governance requires well-defined and well-substantiated policies:* While there were indeed opponents of the SEI inside government, and the post-Gomery emphasis on hyper-accountability also slowed work on the file, the main factor inside the bureaucracy that delayed implementation was the lack of a clear, comprehensive and well-understood policy framework for the Initiative. In the absence of such a framework and understanding, each of the participating departments and agencies were obliged to return to first principles to try to build a clear policy case and objectives and a common understanding among their own managers and analysts as well as with external actors in the sector. In general, it is a good thing that Canada's public servants take their responsibilities in this regard seriously. Civil society actors must integrate this lesson for their future advocacy work.

To be sure, these proved to be formidable problems. However, at the same time, there is another set of factors that lend support to the possibility of a reappearance of a major social economy policy initiative. These factors include:

1) *Rescaling remains a potent policy driver:* Economic globalization continues to displace Canadian manufacturing jobs in the Ontario heartland, as well as employment in key non-urban sectors (e.g., pulp and paper, agri-food) across the country. In every party, at all levels of government, a constituency has grown for pragmatic community economic development. Municipal and provincial governments, therefore, as well as the federal state, have adopted the discourse of a "communities agenda," and are – slowly and unevenly, but inexorably – putting the policy instruments in place to support local economies and the third sector.[31]
2) *Demographic changes may create new opportunities:* Across Canada, major demographic shifts are underway both inside government and outside. The boomer generation is moving away from mainstream professional roles and toward retirement. Boomers are being replaced by a younger, more diverse group of workers who have grown up in a much more connected and globalized world than their predecessors. It may be that these new-generation public servants and civil society activists will break old patterns and boundaries and find creative new ways of working together and understanding one another.
3) *Civil society has no other choice:* Like most other segments of civil society in Canada, the social-economy sector *must* have a meaningful relationship with the federal government. The corporate sector's support of CED has been tepid and unpredictable. Moreover, notwithstanding pockets of innovation, Canada's philanthropic sector remains small, undercapitalized and conservative in its practices. There is no other choice for civil society in this sparsely populated, cold country but to engage government in a major partnership that supports CED on a significant scale.[32] A new generation of leaders on the sector side could build the skill-set necessary to negotiate such a partnership, including a move away from short-term, project-based funding.

A more ambitious question is whether English-Canada can emulate the United Kingdom's array of policies that promote social enterprise. Part of the answer turns on the question of whether the Conservative Party of Canada, in the process of moving to the political centre in order to secure an electoral majority, could embrace social enterprise along New-Labour lines, or, indeed, along the lines of the UK Conservative Party.[33] Another part of the answer turns on the question of whether Canada's government and nongovernmental actors in the social economy can overcome regionalism and power asymmetries to form a coherent coalition for change.[34] In the current context, answering either of these questions (not to mention both of them) in the affirmative would seem to require a leap of faith that many observers of this policy file may not be prepared to make.

However, the activists might well say yes to both questions. The SEI experience for them provided, at its essence, *political education*. Across Ontario and throughout English-speaking Canada, leaders of the social economy and CED sector continue to strategize, re-organize, share knowledge, lobby, build alliances, unify its various segments, mobilize resources, and prepare for the next federal political aperture, in order to secure the gains they came so close to achieving a few years ago. Some of their Quebec allies continue to accompany them. If they can stay together, their resilience and determination will serve these activists well.

CONCLUSION

The experience of the federal Social Economy Initiative constitutes a case study in how Ottawa *doesn't* spend. While this policy episode involved a relatively modest federal policy effort, the actors and factors in play in the case are likely to parallel those of other policy areas. In particular, the robust interplay of regional power asymmetries, electoral political tactics, the good-government factors, the rescaling of policy discourse and action, political learning by civil society, and in the future, demographic changes inside and outside the state – these are all key dimensions of this case that may resonate across many federal files. On these and other dimensions, it is worth comparing the SEI experience with other policy episodes.

ACKNOWLEDGEMENTS

The author would like to thank Allan Maslove, editor of this volume, and two anonymous reviewers for their insightful comments on an earlier draft of this chapter. I would also like to acknowledge the ongoing support of my research on community economic development and the social economy by the J.W. McConnell Family Foundation.

NOTES

1 I was on this call. In the interest of full disclosure, in my role as co-founder and principal of the Community Economic Development Technical Assistance Program, based at Carleton University, I served on the National and Ontario Roundtables on the Social Economy, the Ontario Social Economy Consortium and, later, the federal Community Finance Advisory Committee. I also helped to design the Ontario Social Enterprise Trust, a patient-capital investment vehicle that was proposed to the

Ontario Government in 2007, and am a member of the foundation-supported Causeway Initiative on social finance.
2 See Cabinet Office, "The Future of the Third Sector in Social and Economic Regeneration: Final Report," (London: Her Majesty's Treasury, 2007). For the British Government, it seemed not to be such a big leap from the "Third Way" to supporting the third sector. Interestingly, in that jurisdiction, a more explicit public debate on the limits (and advantages) of the welfare state and the advantages (and limits) of a more entrepreneurial non-profit, or citizen, sector has ensued. The stability of over a decade of Labour Party governments with solid majorities facilitated continuity in policy planning and implementation with non-state actors.
3 V.F. Henirich, ed., *Civicus: Global Survey of the State of Civil Society: Volume 1-Country Profiles* (Bloomfield: Kumarian Press, 2007), 4. See also H. K. Anheier, *Civil Society: Measurement, Evaluation, Policy* (London: Earthscan, 2004).
4 L.A. Pal, *Beyond Policy Analysis: Public Issue Management in Turbulent Times* (Toronto: Nelson, 2006).
5 Pal, *Beyond Policy Analysis*.
6 S.D. Phillips and M. Orsini, "Mapping the Links: Citizen Involvement in the Policy Process," (Ottawa: Canadian Policy Research Networks, 2002).
7 D.W. Brinkerhoff and B. L. Crosby, *Managing Policy Reform: Concepts and Tools for Decision-Makers in Developing Countries and Transitioning Countries* (Bloomfield: Kumarian Press, 2002).
8 R. Mahon, C. Andrew and R. Johnson, "Policy Analysis in an Era of 'Globalisation:' Capturing Spatial Dimensions and Scalar Strategies," in M. Orsini and M. Smith, eds., *Critical Policy Studies* (Vancouver: UBC Press, 2007), 59.
9 E. Shragge and J-M. Fontan, eds., *Social Economy: International Debates and Perspectives* (Montreal: Black Rose, 2000).
10 E.T. Jackson, "Community Innovation through Entrepreneurship: Grantmaking in Canadian Community Economic Development," *Journal of the Community Development Society* 35, no. 1 (2004): 65–81.
11 M. Toye and N. Chaland, "CED in Canada: Review of Definitions and Profile of Practice," in E. Shragge and M. Toye, eds., *Community Economic Development: Building for Social Change* (Sydney: Cape Breton University Press, 2007), 21–41. Other parts of the non-profit sector work hard to cope with the negative effects and inefficiencies of the "project-funding regime" in an era of hyper-accountability. See, for example, K. Gibson, S. O'Donnell and V. Rideout, "The project-funding regime: Complications for community organizations and their staff," *Canadian Public Administration* 50, no. 3 (2007): 411–35.
12 Shragge and Toye, eds., *Community Economic Development*.
13 J. Loxley, *Transforming or Reforming Capitalism: Towards a Theory of Community Economic Development* (Halifax: Fernwood Publishing, 2007). See also J. Loxley and L. Lamb, "Economics for CED Practitioners," in E. Shragge and M. Toye, eds., *Community Economic Development*, 42–54.

14 J. Loxley, *Transforming or Reforming Capitalism*. Loxley points out that most CED theory has been based on analytic frames mainly related to community development, rather than economics. Drawing on Marxist traditions, he problematizes the concept of community itself, highlighting class, gender and other divisions and critiquing the lack of effective democratic decision-making in many CED initiatives. This is a critique that is shared by critical theorists in social work, sociology and political science, among others. Loxley and his colleagues go on to suggest that a number of dimensions of economic theory should be explored in the case of CED, including: export theory, staple theory, regional economics, gap-filling, convergence strategies, and the role of state subsidies and other policies (see Loxley and Lamb, "Economics for CED Practitioners;" and Loxley, *Transforming or Reforming Capitalism*).

15 For more on the Chantier, see www.chantier.qc.ca

16 The Caledon Institute's work can be accessed at www.caledoninst.org.

17 It is an open question what a broader-based, pre-budget consultation process with the CED and social economy sector might have yielded in terms of a fuller and better-rationalized policy agenda to inform the 2004 budget. It certainly would have helped. But such pre-budget consultations did not happen. And, after the budget was tabled, the consultation process was too narrow-gauge and short in some regions, notably in the Atlantic provinces and parts of the Prairies, to be of much use.

18 Department of Finance, *A New Deal for Communities*, Budget 2004. (Ottawa: Department of Finance, 2004),16.

19 Department of Finance, *A New Deal for Communities*.

20 Mme Bakopanos was an able and energetic champion of the social economy during her tenure, and was particularly effective in external consultations with sector leaders. See the profile of her work in A. Makhoul, "The Honourable Eleni Bakopanos: Social Economy Champion," (Ottawa: Caledon Institute of Social Policy, 2005). However, for a variety of reasons, she did not succeed in developing a larger, cross-departmental policy framework for the social economy before the Martin government fell.

21 This quote must remain anonymous. In fact, the view of some federal officials familiar with the SEI is that the due diligence and good-government factor, not internal opposition or partisan politics, was *primarily* responsible for the delay in implementing the initiative.

22 This facilitator was Dal Brodhead, a respected leader in the CED sector for over three decades.

23 This project was called OncEDco – the Ontario CED Collaborative. As its principals – On Coop, CCEDNET and CEDTAP – tried to cope with a changing policy environment and lack of funding in 2006–2007, they also learned a great deal about the tensions and challenges associated with multi-stakeholder partnerships. In addition to focusing their common efforts on the larger issues of finance and advocacy, they used an evaluation of OncEDco to document their learning on the collaboration process. See D. Howatt, "Ottawa CED Collaborative: Evaluation Report," (Stratford: Solutions Consulting Group, 2008).

24 By early 2008, the Ontario government began steps to design a social venture capital fund for the province, to invest in businesses promoting environmental technologies, green energy, affordable housing and other social-purpose ventures. At the same time, leaders in the CED sector continued to lobby the province for a second, more community-oriented fund along the lines of the social economy trust in Quebec.
25 Now known as the Canadian Social Economy Research Partnerships, this network is coordinated by the University of Victoria and the Canadian CED Network. See www.socialeconomyhub.ca.
26 See, again, Pal, *Beyond Policy Analysis*; and Phillips with Orsini, "Mapping the Links: Citizen Involvement in the Policy Process."
27 The Caledon Institute had prepared the evaluation framework for the SEI, which constitutes a valuable model for future cross-departmental policy initiatives. See E. Leviten-Reid and S. Torjman, "Evaluation Framework for Federal Investment in the Social Economy: A Discussion Paper," (Ottawa: Caledon Institute of Social Policy, 2006). See also E.T. Jackson, "Managing Government – Third Party Tensions in RBM: The Emerging Case of the Social Economy," presented to the Ninth Annual Symposium of the Performance and Planning Exchange, Ottawa, 2005.
28 See Brinkerhoff and Crosby, *Managing Policy Reform*.
29 The Chantier was able to secure, in 2006, a contribution of nearly $23 million from the federal government to the group's patient capital trust. This was about $5 million less than the original Liberal commitment, but it was sufficient for the trust to attract matching contributions from the Government of Quebec ($10 million), the Quebec Solidarity Fund ($12 million) and the CSN Development Fund ($8 million). These investors receive debentures and a seat each on the board of the trust, whose core business is making long-term loans for social-enterprise operations and social real estate investments. The trust began operations in early 2007, a full three years after the tabling of the 2004 federal budget.
30 The Social Economy Research Partnerships are funded under SSHRC's Community-University Research Alliance framework, which is intended to be "practitioner-friendly." However, there are still major barriers in the Council's mandate, legislation and procedures to channeling funds to civil society organizations, especially to cover the very real costs to these groups of managing and conducting research. An irritant to the practitioners, this has meant that an overwhelming percentage of funds from CURAs has been channeled to students, professors and university equipment, and only a very small fraction to community or non-governmental actors, resulting in continuing and often prohibitive opportunity costs to non-academic actors.
31 Also emerging are some new and very helpful analyses for framing this "communities agenda". See, in particular, S. Torjman, *Shared Space: The Communities Agenda* (Ottawa: Caledon Institute of Social Policy, 2007); and, from a social-innovation perspective, F.B. Westley, B. Zimmerman and M.Q. Patton, *Getting to Maybe: How the World's Changed* (Toronto: Random House, 2006).
32 A great deal is known in the social economy sector about how to scale up CED and social enterprise interventions. Such scaling strategies include evaluation of what works

and value-added; replication and dissemination of successful models; innovative social procurement; policy changes within, above and below the nation-state; and large-scale, sustainable financing vehicles for grant-making, loans and guarantees, and equity investing. See T. Jackson, "*All* the Tools, *All* the Time," *Making Waves* 18, no. 2 (2007): 21–5. Former Prime Minister Paul Martin has said that not only did his government not do enough for the social economy, but also that policy, legal and regulatory change, and new social financing vehicles, must be priorities if social enterprise is to make a significant impact in Canada. See Rt. Hon. P. Martin, "Unleashing the Power of Social Enterprise," presented to the Munk Centre, University of Toronto, Toronto, 2007.

33 Among other policies, the Conservative Party in Britain has proposed the establishment of Social Enterprise Zones. Local government authorities would designate neighbourhoods with high-poverty rates and other social problems as Social Enterprise Zones. In turn, the national government would provide special funds to support third-sector delivery of services to promote social enterprises as well as various forms of financing and tax measures to expand these businesses. See Conservative Party, "Social Enterprise Zones," (London: Conservative Party of the UK, 2007). In the United Kingdom, the Social Enterprise Coalition has been active in building support for the sector in both major political parties. While espousing a "Third Way" perspective on social enterprise, and building many links with Blair and Brown Labour governments, the coalition has been careful to also encourage the Conservative Party to make policy commitments to advance the sector even when they are framed within a broader neo-liberal agenda (see www.socialenterprise.org).

34 In this sector, and many others, the fundamental federal power asymmetry remains between Quebec and the rest of Canada. The latter must build a coalition that becomes as unified, focused and influential as the Chantier, though obviously against a very different cultural and political backdrop. And building the strength and unity of the Chantier has not been without pain or price. There also remain competitive dynamics among various sub-networks within the social economy and CED sector, notably between the cooperatives and the non-profit groups, with the former enjoying the advantages of a larger membership base and institutional scale. Outside of Quebec, there is, as well, regional rivalry and economic and political power asymmetries. Finally, "outside" the social economy sector lies the broader universe of third-sector organizations, including the United Way, community foundations, care-giving, health care and social-service non-profits, the arts community, and others. These patterns of segmentation and imbalance must be addressed directly by CED sector leaders and activists in their future advocacy strategies and tactics. At the same time, although the 2004–2007 period was a kind of policy "roller coaster of ups and downs, it also was a time when a wide range of collaborative ventures and coalitions were formed. These experiences, and the relationships they sparked, can serve as valuable touchstones as the sector proceeds with its work in the years ahead.

9 Federal Higher Education Policies and the Vanishing Public University

CLARA MORGAN

In the past two decades, the federal government has redefined its role in higher education. In the 1980s, Ottawa reduced transfers to the provinces under the Established Program Financing Act as it sought ways to reduce its debt. It cut federal transfers to the provinces by $6 billion in 1995. Yet, the federal government has also reinvested more than $11 billion since 1997 in universities. This reinvestment has come in the form of direct intervention in a provincial jurisdiction. In order to steer the higher education agenda, Ottawa has depicted universities as engines of research and innovation in the knowledge economy. Rather than channelling university funding as transfers to the provinces, the federal government has funded a "boutique" of programs aimed at enhancing the international competitiveness of Canadian universities. In their haste to create research powerhouses out of Canadian universities, policymakers did not stop to reflect on some of the negative repercussions these policies may have on eroding the university's public role. Even though federal higher education policies infringed on a provincial jurisdiction, the provinces did not resist this intervention while continuing to demand that transfers be increased to their original pre-95 levels.

My approach is to examine the developments in higher education policy from the "academic capitalism" lens[1] while bearing in mind that federal and provincial politics have been shaped and circumscribed by neoliberal economic policies.[2] I trace how federal policies have facilitated the adoption of market-like activities in higher education and how they have helped integrate universities into the global knowledge economy. The provinces have also devised policies to encourage the implementation of market-like practices among universities. These have included the deregulation of tuition fees, the provision of degree granting status to the private sector by allowing for the establishment of non-for-profit universities, and the encouragement of the adoption of private sector managerial practices.[3] Ottawa and the provinces have largely been allied in favouring higher education policies that contribute to market competitiveness rather than to the public interest. Despite their common objectives, tensions continuously arise between the two levels of government in the areas of jurisdictional boundaries and fiscal imbalance. The federal government has directly interfered in education through various higher education policies it has developed while at the same time reducing post-secondary education transfers to the provinces despite the growth in student enrolment rates.

The chapter begins with an overview of federal involvement in higher education and describes the toolkit that has been instituted by the Liberals in this policy sphere. This toolkit has facilitated and encouraged academic capitalism while simultaneously giving the federal government leeway for pursuing unilateral action in a provincial jurisdiction. As Boismenu and Graefe have argued in their analysis of federal social policy, "[federal] unilateral action is used as a tool for increasing leverage in negotiations, and for legitimizing a claim to leadership."[4] The chapter continues with an analysis of higher education policy under the Harper government and focuses on its science and technology (S&T) strategy. The current government's policies facilitate the transition to academic capitalism by accelerating the commercialization process of research. In the third section, federal-provincial relations and the areas of contention that exist between these two levels of government are explored. A discussion on how provinces have contributed to encouraging the adoption of market behaviour thus reinforcing federal higher education policies is included. The final section explores alternative strategies to academic capitalism which opens up the space for envisioning a different future for universities, academics and students than the one currently put forth by federal and provincial policymakers.

FEDERAL INVOLVEMENT IN HIGHER EDUCATION

Federal involvement in higher education has come in the form of financing arrangements such as direct payments to universities, transfer payments to the provinces, federal research grants, and student loans and scholarship programs.[5] Federal involvement can be described as cyclical. During periods of economic expansion, the federal government has expanded its commitments to higher education funding and during periods of economic slowdown, it has reduced these commitments.[6] After the drastic cuts in the mid-1990s, the federal government has resumed its spending in higher education and has maintained a steady flow of money to directly fund university research.

Given that education is a provincial jurisdiction, federal higher education policies have often led to federal-provincial tensions. The provinces have at various times resisted federal interference in higher education but they have been less willing to "chart courses that would successfully harness universities to serve explicitly defined public purposes."[7] It is partly because of this leadership gap that the federal government has recently become "the more dynamic leader" in higher education, wielding its "spending power of Parliament."[8] However, the federal government did not only wield money as a tool to steer higher education policy, it also tapped into a distinct number of investment structuring strategies.[9]

Up until the late 60s, Ottawa used federal direct grants to fund universities. These were replaced with a federal-provincial shared-cost program. By the mid-1970s, both the federal and the provincial governments were unhappy with the fiscal arrangements they had in place. Ottawa had little control over its budget since it could not determine provincial expenditures and the provinces felt that the fiscal state of affairs distorted their spending choices.[10] The Established Programs Financing (EPF) arrangements were instituted in 1977 to fund post-secondary education and health care. They were redesigned after 1982 to eventually bring their own demise as "provincial tax revenues increased, federal grants would diminish proportionately and eventually disappear altogether."[11] The EPF grants remained in place until 1995 when the Liberal government introduced the Canada Health and Social Transfer (CHST).

Ottawa began to encourage cooperation on university research between the private sector and universities in the 1980s.[12] Established in 1983, the Corporate Higher Education Forum brought together university presidents and senior corporate executives.[13] The Networks of Centres of Excellence (NCE)[14] program was created to foster research partnerships among universities, industry, government and non-profit organizations. The federal government increased business involvement in the policymaking process by creating advisory bodies such as the National Advisory Board on Science and Technology.[15] By the early 1990s, Ottawa's entanglement in higher education was characterized by transfer payments to the provinces, the Canada Student Loan Program, and funding to the granting councils.

The Liberals' election campaign program of 1993 recognized that deficit reduction had to be addressed but this agenda item was not initially a priority for the Liberals. Once in power, the Chrétien government was surprised to find that it had inherited a "bigger than expected deficit."[16] Ottawa was faced with a large government debt that was continuously growing. The primary concerns for the federal government became getting its spending under control and reducing the deficit.[17] As Finance Minister, Paul Martin pursued a retrenchment policy in the areas of government transfers to the provinces and federal program spending.

Instead of scrapping the Established Programs Financing (EPF) arrangements, Ottawa extended it to incorporate the Canada Assistance Plan (CAP) and branded it with a new name, the Canada Health and Social Transfer (CHST).[18] What the CHST effectively did was to cut federal financial transfers by $4.6 billion between 1995–96 and 1997–98.[19] Not only did the federal government curtail its transfer payments to the provinces, it also reduced its funding of other programs such as research funding to the granting councils. These cuts in the federal budget translated into reductions in university and college revenues and in research funding to the granting councils. Moreover, they exacerbated the provincial governments' fiscal pressures and eroded federal-provincial relations.[20]

Even though universities had begun to seek other sources of revenue in the 1980s, this became even more of a priority after the funding cuts of the mid-1990s.[21] To compensate for the shortfall, many universities and colleges increased their tuition fees.[22] Universities sought money in the form of donations from the business community, they fundraised, they developed business-university partnerships, and they signed exclusive rights contracts for selling products to university students.[23] They developed educational programs that were revenue generating such as diplomas and degrees for pursuing professional careers or executive MBA programs. By adopting such market-like behaviour, universities raised funds to finance their operations and infrastructures.

Federal retrenchment was characterized as a crisis in higher education as universities were deeply affected by these cuts. Several interest groups began lobbying for increased funding to universities. The Association of Universities and Colleges of Canada was one such group that was a key actor in helping to formulate new federal policy programs in higher education.[24] Instead of channelling money to core-university funding through the transfers to the provinces, the federal government opted for direct funding through a series of initiatives. The Liberals wanted to ensure that Canadian universities became internationally competitive thereby fulfilling their research and innovation agenda. At the same time, they wanted political recognition for these investments.[25] The potentially negative aspect to this instrumental agenda was that it could marginalize research that was not commercially lucrative and further accelerate the tendency to adopt market behaviour thereby eroding the university's public role.[26]

By 1997, Ottawa was experiencing a federal surplus and the Liberals were keen on pursuing several new higher education initiatives in the areas of student assistance and university research. The government agenda was focused on "investing in innovation",[27] improving Canada's human capital and providing greater access to higher education. The government's strategy was to invest in Canadian research infrastructures to "creat[e] the conditions for long-term job creation and economic growth"[28] and to improve access to lifelong learning so as to "ensure that all Canadians are provided an equal opportunity to participate in the knowledge-based economy of the future."[29]

Introduced in the 1998 Budget, the Canadian Opportunities Strategy was developed to "expand access to the knowledge and skills Canadians need for better job opportunities and a higher standard of living in the 21st century."[30] It included the creation of the Canada Millennium Scholarships and the Canada Millennium Scholarships Foundation, a private, independent organization; the creation of Canada Study Grants; improvements to the Canada Student Loans Program; and tax relief for interest on student loans, extended repayment period and interest relief period and reductions in the loan principal. The Canadian Millennium Scholarship program was criticized for interfering in a provincial jurisdiction since the federal government was directly allocating scholarships to students and for not addressing the problem of student accessibility since it did not resolve the problem of higher tuition fees. Lower tuition rates were viewed as a more effective mechanism for ensuring low and middle income students have access to a post-secondary education.[31] The federal government's student assistance programs did not address the problem of tuition disparities across the country and how such disparities have contributed to inequitable access to higher education.[32]

Research funding became a major component of federal involvement in universities and covered the areas of research infrastructure, human resources, direct research costs, and indirect research costs. The federal government created the Canadian Foundation for Innovation (CFI) to fund research infrastructure and to "strengthen the capacity of Canadian universities, colleges, research hospitals, and non-profit research institutions to carry out world-class research and technology development that benefits Canadians."[33] To fulfil its mandate, the CFI was entrusted with an endowment of $3.65 billion. CFI could only fund up to 40 per cent of a project's infrastructure costs, with the remaining 60 per cent funded by other partners.[34] The structuring of CFI funding contributed to the commercialization of universities and to exacerbating regional and institutional disparities. A business partner that provided 60 per cent financing towards an infrastructure investment could exercise a veto over the choice of the project. This situation may have forced universities to seek projects that were aligned with private needs rather than aimed at the public interest. The co-funding formula favoured richer provinces and urban centres over poor provinces and rural areas.[35] The richer provinces and urban centres received a larger share of funding simply because they had access to greater number of partners.[36] In addition, the Auditor General in 2005 "raised concerns about the governance and the accountability of and accounting for government transfers to foundations" since a significant amount of funds was being transferred to these arms-length entities.[37]

Another set of federal research programs focused on human resources. Ottawa expanded its graduate student support programs, created the

Canada Graduate Scholarship program and put in place the Canada Research Chairs (CRC) program. In 1999, Ottawa set aside $900 million to establish 2,000 CRCs in universities across Canada. The program objectives included strengthening Canada's research capacity by attracting and retaining the best researchers; improving the training of personnel through research; improving universities' capacity to generate and apply new knowledge; promoting the best possible use of research resources.[38] Since universities that submitted nominations to this program could also request infrastructure support from CFI, it was in the interest of university departments to attract and retain Canada Research Chairs that brought the most amount of infrastructure funding. CRCs have contributed to university market activities by pursuing the patenting of their research work and by further integrating universities into the knowledge economy. At the same time, the program has rendered universities dependant on federal funding. Universities that relied on the CRC and CFI as a source of revenue could be at risk once the program has completed its mandate of allocating all 2,000 Chairs.[39]

Concerns have been raised about the CRC program. These have included problems of inequity in the allocation and distribution of research chairs.[40] Recently, the Canadian Human Rights Commission settled a complaint against the CRC's discriminatory structure that was launched in 2003 by eight female university professors. The CRC program has resulted in an unequal distribution of Chairs between men and women. The settlement ensured that the CRC program was structured equitably and was non-discriminatory by targeting disadvantaged groups protected under the *Canadian Charter of Rights and Freedoms*. According to the agreement, the CRC program will work with universities to "set concrete targets for appointments to Canada Research Chairs from the four groups (women, persons with a disability, Aboriginal peoples, and visible minorities), will monitor progress towards those goals, and will take active steps to encourage universities to meet them."[41]

The federal government also encouraged the growth of human resources in research by expanding its scholarship programs through the creation of the Canada Graduate Scholarships. Funding for both these programs is available through the three granting councils. Other programs, such as the Undergraduate Student Research Awards, were aimed at stimulating interest in research and in encouraging undergraduates to pursue graduate studies and research careers in engineering and the natural sciences.[42] Despite this flow of federal funds in human resources, universities continued to face financial constraints and have resorted to behaving as if they are private businesses. They hired contract workers in order to keep up with increased costs associated with higher student enrolments. Rather than employing more tenured professors, universities employed part-time lecturers. Student/teacher ratios and class sizes have risen. A recent study indicates that academics, especially female ones, face high levels of stress. These have been caused by stagnating salaries, the contract status of many instructors, increased workloads, pressures to obtain external research funding, and a greater emphasis on publication.[43] The problem remains that universities are not being appropriately funded.

A third aspect to federal funding was the direct costs of research that came in the form of grants received by university researchers from the research councils – from SSHRC, NSERC and CIHR. The direct costs of research were closely tied with the Canada Research Chairs program since the allocation of Chairs is proportional to the amount of research funding received from the federal granting agencies calculated on a three-year rolling average. Polster has looked at how the growing dependency of universities on research grants as a source of income is transforming university relations. These transformations were significant since they altered the relations between and among various actors in higher education in complex ways.[44] For example, relations among academics were changed as certain professors were rewarded for their ability to obtain research grants; university administrators took a more active role in encouraging academics to apply for research grants and in recruiting team members who could successfully obtain grants; and the federal government indirectly exercised more control over university research directions as university administrators aligned their priorities for research with those of the granting councils. Polster has assessed the negative implications of the current research grants regime including the undermining of the "university's mission, namely teaching, administrative service, and public service."[45] Pocklington & Tupper have also reflected on the university's mission and have criticized the prioritization of research over teaching.[46]

The final area of federal funding of university research involved indirect costs. These costs were closely related to infrastructure costs but they targeted smaller universities that received research grants funds from the three granting councils. Indirect costs of research encompassed various types of overhead costs such as upgrading computer systems and renovating research laboratories. Indirect costs grants were delivered and overseen by the granting councils. Ottawa announced the creation of a one time indirect costs payment by allotting $200 million to 79 degree-granting institutions in its 2001 budget. In its 2003 budget, Ottawa announced new support for the indirect costs program. Funding was increased in both the 2004 and 2005 budgets. Despite federal financing of the indirect costs of research, this money could not replace the deep cuts that universities incurred as a result of the reduction in transfer payments. Since universities continued to be under-funded, they have relied on increased tuition costs and special fees for various student services as sources of revenue.

Universities are a significant contributor to research and development in Canada accounting for between 33 per cent and 68 per cent in all but four provinces.[47] In 2004, total university research and development funding was at $8.4 billion with the federal government contributing 26 per cent, provincial governments 12 per cent and business 8 per cent. The universities contributed 46 per cent to this funding by directing their financial resources to indirect costs of research and faculty research that were not covered by external revenue sources.[48]

Ottawa's approach to university funding has contributed to the disembedding of certain universities from the national context and their integration into the international global marketplace. As Marginson and van der Wende have observed, universities become "disembedded from their national contexts because some driving forces of globalisation exceed the strength of national factors."[49] These universities that were linked to international networks through various research endeavours also actively recruited graduates internationally. In effect, federal funding concentrated research money in a few universities that could successfully compete internationally. Other smaller universities remained nationally embedded but they were not 'star' universities. The transformation of certain university campuses into polytechnic schools, such as the recommendation made in a recent report on post-secondary education in New Brunswick, may be one such fate awaiting nationally embedded universities.[50]

When it comes to data on university sponsored research income,[51] the top ten Canadian universities[52] in 2006 had a total of approximately $3.7 billion in sponsored research income.[53] Several of these Canadian research universities were able to compete globally as demonstrated by international rankings such as the Shanghai Jiao Tong University's Academic Rankings of World Universities. For example, in 2006, the University of Toronto was ranked No. 24, the University of British Columbia was ranked No. 36, McGill University was tied for No. 62 and McMaster University was No. 90.[54]

THE HARPER GOVERNMENT'S APPROACH TOWARDS UNIVERSITIES AND RESEARCH

The Conservative government has continued with the Liberal party's funding commitments to higher education and research funding but it has also modified the objectives of federal entanglement in this policy sphere. The current government has been focused on the commercialization of research while at the same time pushing for a more decentralized form of federalism. Even though the recent Speech from the Throne reiterated the Conservatives' commitment to respecting "constitutional jurisdiction of each order of government,"[55] it also identified the need to "support Canadian researchers and innovators in developing new ideas and bringing them to the marketplace through Canada's Science and Technology Strategy."[56] Student assistance initiatives have come in the form of textbook tax credit and tax exemption from bursaries and grants.

The Harper government increased federal transfers to the provinces. In its 2007 Budget Plan, the federal government proposed to increase Canada Social Transfer (CST) by $800 million per year as of 2008–09 so as "to maintain and strengthen Canada's universities and colleges."[57] Budget 2007 also announced several commercialization initiatives that encouraged universities and colleges to build linkages with the private sector such as the creation of the business-led Networks of Centres of Excellence, the College and Community Innovation Program (CCIP), and the Centres of Excellence in Commercialization and Research which received $105 million in funding with an additional $195 million set aside to the CFI and the granting councils to competitions associated with the Centres of Excellence program.[58] In addition, the government hand picked seven commercialization research centres for 2007 and by doing so, bypassed the granting councils' selection process.[59] While the government did not provide any justification or rationale for selecting these centres, the selection criteria appeared to be politically motivated reflecting a "balanced" geographic distribution.[60]

The Harper government has clearly outlined its approach to higher education and research funding in its science and technology strategy, *Mobilizing Science and Technology to Canada's Advantage*. It is committed to "maintaining Canada's current G-7 leadership in public research"[61] which includes funding university research, infrastructure, and direct and indirect research costs. The government is pursuing two overlapping objectives that reinforce one another. The first is a strategic commitment that targets research priorities in key commercially lucrative fields. The second objective is the commercialization of university research by actively facilitating research transfers from universities to the private sector. These strategies are being implemented through the creation of advisory councils and advisory boards such as the Science, Technology and Innovation Council and the tri-council private sector advisory board for the granting councils.

The government's S&T strategy has been warmly received by university presidents and the private sector and criticized by some scientists and researchers. The Association of Universities and Colleges of Canada (AUCC) has praised the government on its strategy. The president of the AUCC said that "Canada needs to secure its position as a world leader in research – including university research – and this strategy will help our country meet that mark."[62] John Polanyi, a renowned Canadian scientist and a Nobel Laureate in chemistry, has criticized Canada's approach to science policy, describing it as "top down" and "over-managed."[63] There is also concern being voiced by the research community that the peer-review process is being slowly eroded.[64]

When it comes to university students, the government is expanding the scholarship programs and increasing the number of private sector internships that it funds. However, it has not committed to renewing the Canadian

Millennium Scholarship fund that provides $350 million in grants and scholarships to about 100,000 students annually. The fund is up for renewal in 2009.[65] Even though the government is providing students with a textbook tax credit and tax exemption from bursaries and grants, these initiatives do not address the core problems of affordability and accessibility to postsecondary education. Since universities have adopted market-like behaviour, students are conceived as consumers who must pay for a quality education. In this context, higher tuition costs are justified since students make market choices. According to Statistics Canada, average tuition fees have risen 4.3 percent annually over the past decade with students paying on average $4,524. Special universities fees for such things as athletic facilities, health services, technology and computer fees have increased.[66] The universities view these increases as "necessary to cover rising costs and limited improvements to government grants."[67]

Student debt has risen along with the rise of tuition costs. Canadian student students pay the highest debt interest among industrialized countries and have a high debt-service ratio.[68] A student's monthly repayment burden is high because students have a short period of time to repay their debts. In addition, the burden of student indebtedness varies along gender and ethnic lines with women from racialized groups experiencing the highest amount of debt.[69] In its 2007 Budget Plan, the government announced that it will be conducting a program review of the Canada Student Loans Program. Approximately 40 per cent of all full-time students (outside of Quebec) borrowed under the Canada Student Loans Program in 2004–05.[70]

The present government appears to be mainly concerned with the commercialization of research rather than the funding of basic research. However, when countries have pursued a commercialization research strategy, their innovation capacity has fallen. Marginson notes that Australia's research innovation capacity fell when it undertook a strategy of commercialization and of funding research projects rather than investing in its basic research infrastructure.[71] Moreover, the negative repercussions of a commercialization strategy are not been publicly addressed or debated. When university knowledge becomes increasingly privatized, it "introduce[s] more secrecy, competition, and fraud into academic research" and "reduce[s] the public's access to the results of academic research." More significantly, it "deprives us of a reliable and uncompromised source of expertise."[72] The more such a strategy is pursued, the more alienated Canadian universities could become from their public service mission. Instead of facilitating public knowledge production, knowledge is more likely to become privatized.[73]

Commercialization strategies do not address the fundamental problems that universities and students are facing with respect to resource constraints, indebtedness and the quality of teaching. For example, despite an 18 per cent increase in full-time university enrolment between 1994/95 and 2004/05, there has only been a 6 per cent rise in full-time university educators.[74] These types of statistics point to the need for developing a well-thought out strategy toward post-secondary education that considers the quality of the education experience students are receiving across the provinces.

PROVINCIAL-FEDERAL RELATIONS AND PROVINCIAL HIGHER EDUCATION POLICIES

With Canada increasingly integrated into the global economy, both the federal and provincial governments view the role of universities as vital to improving Canada's international competitiveness. In addition, since both levels of government have adopted neoliberal economic policies that favour the operation of the market, building human capital and innovation capacity have become even more politically desirable.[75] They disagree, however, on how funding for post secondary education and research should take place. The provinces prefer to receive more money from the federal government in the form of transfers rather than federal direct involvement in a provincial jurisdiction.

The provinces have pursued their own strategies to further facilitate academic capitalism and the blurring of the boundaries that exist between universities and the private sector. The provinces instituted reviews of their post-secondary education systems. These reviews have produced reports that recommended the restructuring of post-secondary institutions so that they become more responsive to economic and societal needs. Recently, New Brunswick's Commission on Post-Secondary Education recommended that a number of university campuses be turned into polytechnics. As polytechnics, these educational institutions would be equipped to respond to local training and labour market needs. This education delivery model has been described as 'Just In Time Education' whereby the "faculty would be required to tailor their courses to whatever business interest had lately captured the school's attention."[76]

Provinces have increased university funding but they have also demanded in return that universities demonstrate accountability. As part of its *Reaching Higher* plan for post-secondary education, the McGuinty government in its 2005 budget committed $6.2 billion to post secondary education and training while at the same time holding these institutions accountable for improving access and quality. It has signed multi-year accountability agreements with each university and college that set out enrolment and quality improvement targets. In order to monitor the access and quality of Ontario's universities, Ontario has established a council to oversee the quality of higher education. The Higher Education Quality Council of Ontario was created to provide advice on improving the quality, access, and accountability of Ontario's post secondary institutions. To achieve its mandate, the Council would have to put in place performance measures for quality and accessibility outcomes.[77] Such standardized measures may provide the provincial government with a mechanism for regulating institutional behaviour and controlling priorities and activities.[78] Universities, in turn, will institute managerial practices so as to improve their performance on these indicators.

The provinces would like more money in their coffers rather than a federal government meddling in their affairs. The Council of Ministers of Education, Canada (CMEC) has requested that the federal government resume its 1994–1995 level of transfer funding. The Council of the Federation, a body that represents the Premiers, wants the problem of fiscal imbalance resolved. One of the options put forth is to establish a dedicated post-secondary education transfer in addition to the social and health transfers. The Council of the Federation's Advisory Panel on Fiscal Imbalance has pointed to how federal involvement negatively impacts the province's ability to manage and control its finances in this policy area. The Panel observed that the federal government's higher education policies and programs "needlessly complicate policymaking and create a patchwork of programs and initiatives that waste resources and frustrate students, faculty, and public servants."[79]

Tensions between the provinces and the federal government do arise as the federal government directly intervenes and takes a leadership role in a provincial jurisdiction. Yet these tensions do not impede both levels of government from instituting polices that encourage universities to adopt market-like behaviour and to operate more as businesses than as public institutions. In effect, both the federal and provincial governments have supported policies that further distance universities from their public and community role thus contributing to the dwindling of the public university. Federal intervention in this policy sphere will likely continue given that the federal government views universities and research as vital to Canada's economic growth and prosperity. Because neoliberal economic policies constrain and limit government intervention to such areas as post-secondary education and research, it becomes even more important for Ottawa to monitor its investments in higher education as demonstrated by recent calls being made for national post-secondary benchmarks and standards.[80]

ALTERNATIVE STRATEGIES TO ACADEMIC CAPITALISM

Even though universities are increasingly adopting market-like behaviour, they continue to serve as providers of public knowledge and to exist for the public interest. Universities serve several publics but the predominance of catering to the private sector's needs cannot be ignored since it is being encouraged and facilitated by federal and provincial government policies. My claim is that provincial and federal government higher education policies have been overly concerned with encouraging academic capitalism and the international competitiveness of universities. Both levels of government have not put the same level of energy and creativity into pursuing alternative policies that encourage universities to serve the public interest and to address local and community economic development needs.

There is an assumption among policymakers that universities benefit when they address private interests and embrace commercial actors into academia. Yet this assumption is not necessarily true and is, at times, misguided. As Ann Clark points out, often, when researchers pursue industry-sponsored studies, they will come up with conclusions that support the industry viewpoint. Thus researchers are no longer credible or objective. Businesses operate with the intention of selling products, making profits and temporarily fixing a consumer problem. They do not attempt to fix the problem but merely alleviate it. In contrast, academics are critically thinking about problems and are trying to understand their causes and are seeking genuine solutions.[81] Universities share knowledge whereas businesses withhold it for private gains. From this standpoint, it is difficult to see why universities should welcome private interests into a public serving institution when "the goals of pursuing public knowledge and private money profits contradict one another, because the processes of sharing knowledge and accumulating private money are incompatible."[82]

Rather than encouraging the increased commercialization of university research and the penetration of private interests into the public domain, the federal government could take a leadership role and adopt national principles for higher education that embrace the goals of the public university. As recommended by the Canadian Association of University Teachers (CAUT), these principles can include the public administration of universities as non-profit institutions; universal accessibility; governance by academic staff and students; and academic freedom. The federal government can correct regional disparities by providing transfers to the provinces so that funding is allocated on a per capita basis and equalized according to provincial GDP per capita.[83]

In the area of student assistance, there are several venues that the federal government can pursue other than the status quo. The Canadian Federation of Students (CFS) has put together several recommendations in its report, *Strategy for Change*. The CFS recommends that there be federal-provincial cooperation in the area of student assistance. Even though the Canadian Millennium Scholarship fund is up for renewal, the CFS proposes that this money be replaced with a federal needs-based grant program to students. It also recommends that a dedicated transfer for post-secondary education be put in place to reduce tuition fees. The CFS's proposals are sensible policies that need to be considered as part of federal and provincial deliberations on higher education policies.

An alternative strategy that provincial and federal governments can adopt is to cultivate the university's public interest role rather than contributing to its decline. For example, Polster suggests that instead of university knowledge being privatized, it can be placed in a public domain where it cannot be privately appropriated. Such an initiative would bring the cost of research down, instil greater research collaboration among academics, and encourage open communication of research results. Provincial and federal funding can encourage universities to become more involved at the local and community level. They can help foster community economic development initiatives that directly contribute to the well-being of local residents.[84] For example, the Social Sciences and Humanities Research Council of Canada (SSHRC) funds a program that helps to foster alliances between community organizations and postsecondary institutions. The Community-University Research Alliances (CURA) promotes the sharing of knowledge, resources and expertise between universities and community organizations.[85]

Higher education policies instituted at both the federal and provincial levels have contributed to the spread of academic capitalism and to the decline of the university's public role. Such a trend can be reversed. It requires that universities and academics relinquish the enticements and personal benefits of what Harry Arthurs has described as a "production-driven research culture."[86] It necessitates a commitment by politicians and policymakers to be more attentive to and supportive of the university's public role.

CONCLUSION

This chapter has examined recent developments in federal higher education policies and their impact on universities and on federal-provincial relations. It has pointed to tensions that arise among the two levels of government particularly in the areas of jurisdictional boundaries and fiscal imbalance. The chapter has shown that federal and provincial education polices have been allied in favouring higher education polices that contribute to the commercialization of universities rather than to the public interest.

The chapter traced federal involvement in higher education and focused on the toolkit that the Liberals instituted since 1997. This toolkit has encouraged the spread of academic capitalism. The chapter showed how federal spending programs and initiatives in higher education were continued by the Harper government. At the same time, it pointed to the Harper government's emphasis on the commercialization agenda. Even though the provinces were annoyed with federal intervention in their own provincial jurisdiction, the chapter concluded that provinces have contributed to facilitating the adoption of market behaviour thus reinforcing federal higher education policies.

In the final section, the discussion revolved around alternative strategies to academic capitalism. The chapter attempted to open up the space for envisioning a different future for universities, academics and students than the one currently put forth by federal and provincial policymakers. Since policymakers are preoccupied with the goal of achieving internationally competitive economies, they have grown to accept the common-sense belief that the values embodied by knowledge-sharing educational institutions such as universities are the same as those held by market institutions such as businesses. Policymakers and politicians need to be reminded that the university accumulates knowledge that is to be shared in the public domain and critically engages students to question the world they live in. The university is an educational institution that cannot be equated with the private sector's consumption-driven and profit seeking values.[87] Government policies need to turn their attention to nurturing the public university rather than contributing to its demise as the "academe may be one of the few public spheres available, though hardly breathing, where we can provide the educational conditions for students to embrace pedagogy as a sphere of dialogue and unmitigated questioning."[88]

NOTES

1 See Sheila Slaughter and Gary Rhoades, *Academic Capitalism and the New Economy: Markets, State, and Higher Education* (Baltimore and London: The Johns Hopkins University Press, 2004).
2 See for example Garth Stevenson, "Canadian Federalism: The Myth and the Status Quo," in Janine Brodie and Linda Trimble, eds., *Reinventing Canada: Politics of the 21st Century*. (Toronto: Prentice Hall, 2003), 207–8.
3 See Donald Fisher and Kjell Rubenson, "The Political Economy of Post-Secondary Education: A Comparison of British Columbia, Ontario and Quebec," paper presented at the CRUISE conference on Universities and the Powering of Knowledge, Ottawa, Ontario, 19–20 October 2006.
4 Gerard Boismenu and Peter Graefe, "The New Federal Tool Belt: Attempts to Rebuild Social Policy Leadership," *Canadian Public Policy* 30, no. 1 (2004): 76.
5 Neil Tudiver, *Universities for Sale: Resisting Corporate Control over Canadian Higher Education* (Toronto: James Lorimer and Co. Ltd., 1999); David Cameron, "The challenge of change: Canadian universities in the 21st century," *Canadian Public Administration* 45, no. 2 (2002): 145–74.
6 Howard Buchbinder and Janice Newson, "Corporate-University Linkages in Canada: Transforming a Public Institution," *Higher Education* 20, no. 4 (1990), 355–79; Cameron, "The challenge of change."
7 Cameron, "The challenge of change," 155.
8 Cameron, "The challenge of change," 155.
9 See Boismenu and Graefe, "The New Federal Tool Belt," for a discussion on how the government deployed these tools in the social policy areas of health care, child policy and labour market policy.

10 Allan Maslove, "Health and Federal-Provincial Finance Arrangements: Lost Opportunity," in Bruce Doern, ed., *How Ottawa spends 2005–2006: Managing the Minority*. (Montreal & Kingston: McGill-Queen's University Press, 2005), 24.
11 David Cameron, "Shifting the Burden: Liberal Policy for Post-Secondary Education," in Susan Phillips, ed., *How Ottawa Spends 1995–96: Mid-Life Crisis*. (Ottawa: Carleton University Press, 1995), 164.
12 Janice Newson, "The Corporate-Linked University: From Social Project to Market Force," *Canadian Journal of Communications* 23, no. 1 (1998); Buchbinder and Newson, "Corporate-University Linkages in Canada;" Claire Polster, "Canadian University Research Policy at the Turn of the Century: Continuity and Change in the Social Relations of Academic Research," *Studies in Political Economy* 71/72 (2003/04): 177–99.
13 Buchbinder and Newson, "Corporate-University Linkages in Canada;" Cameron, "Post-secondary Education and Research."
14 The NCE became a permanent federal program in February 1997.
15 Polster, "Canadian University Research Policy." This Board is known today as the Advisory Council on Science and Technology (ACST).
16 James Feehan, "The Federal Debt," in S. Phillips, ed., *How Ottawa Spends 1995–96: Mid-Life Crisis*. (Ottawa: Carleton University Press, 1995), 31–58, 33.
17 Allan Maslove, "The Canada Health and Social Transfer: Forcing Issues," in Gene Swimmer, ed., *How Ottawa Spends 1996–97: Life Under the Knife*. (Ottawa: Carleton University Press, 1996), 283–301.
18 In 2004, the CHST was reconfigured into the Canada Health Transfer (CHT) and the Canada Social Transfer (CST).
19 R. Haddow, "How Ottawa Shrivels: Ottawa's Declining Role in Active Labour Market Policy," in Leslie Pal, ed., *How Ottawa Spends 1998–99. Balancing Act: The Post-Deficit Mandate*. (Toronto: Oxford University Press, 1998), 99–126, 114.
20 Maslove, "The Canada Health and Social Transfer", 29.
21 Tudiver, *Universities for Sale*.
22 Tuition was regulated in Québec, British Columbia and Manitoba. Other provinces allowed for tuition increases but imposed ceilings.
23 see Tudiver, *Universities for Sale*.
24 Clara Morgan, "The AUCC and Federal Policies on Universities," in Bruce Doern and Christopher Stoney, eds., *Universities and the Powering of Knowledge: Policy, Regulation and Innovation*. (Toronto: University of Toronto Press, forthcoming).
25 See Maslove. "The Canada Health and Social Transfer."
26 Canadian Association of University Teachers (CAUT), "Canada's Innovation Agenda: CAUT's Response," 2002, available at http://www.caut.ca/en/issues/commercialization/innovationagendaresponse.pdf, accessed 31 October 2007.
27 Department of Finance, *Building the Future for Canadians: Budget 1997* (Ottawa: Department of Finance, 1997). Available at: http://www.fin.gc.ca/budget97/binb/bp/bp97e.pdf, accessed 16 December 2007.
28 Department of Finance, *Building the Future for Canadians: Budget 1997*, 97.

29 Department of Finance, *Budget Speech 1998: Preparing Canadians for the Jobs of the 21st Century: Providing Access to Opportunity* (Ottawa: Department of Finance, 1998). Available at: http://www.fin.gc.ca/budget98/speech/speech2e.html, accessed 16 December 2007.
30 Department of Finance, *The Canadian Opportunities Strategy: Budget 1998* (Ottawa, Department of Finance, 1998).
31 Canadian Federation of Students (CFS), *Canadian Federation of Students' submission to the House of Commons Standing Committee on Finance*, October 2005. Available at http://www.cfs-fcee.ca/html/english/research/submissions/sub-2005-financectteebrief.pdf, accessed 31 October 2007.
32 see CAUT, *Statement to the House of Commons Standing Committee on Finance Regarding the 2005 Federal Budget*, November 2005, available at http://www.caut.ca/en/publications/briefs/2004financebrief.pdf, accessed 31 October 2007.
33 CFI, "CFI Overview," n.d., available at http://www.innovation.ca/about/index.cfm?websiteid=5, accessed 31 October 2007.
34 CFI, "CFI Overview," In several provinces there was a program to match the 40 per cent from CFI with the remaining 20 per cent being raised from the private sector.
35 CAUT, *Statement to the House of Commons Standing Committee on Finance Regarding the 2005 Federal Budget*.
36 Since the Atlantic provinces were at an economic disadvantage in being able to raise money as compared with other Canadian provinces, Ottawa created the Atlantic Innovation Fund in 2001 "to strengthen the economy of Atlantic Canada by accelerating the development of knowledge-based industry." The fund "focuses on R&D projects in the area of natural and applied sciences, as well as in social sciences and humanities, where these are explicitly linked to the development of technology-based products, processes or services, or their commercialization." The program is coordinated by the Atlantic Canada Opportunities Agency (ACOA). See http://www.acoa.ca/e/financial/aif/.
37 Office of the Auditor General of Canada, *A Status Report of the Auditor General of Canada to the House of Commons*, February 2005, 6–7.
38 Canada Research Chairs, "About us," available at http://www.chairs.gc.ca/web/about/index_e.asp, accessed 31 October 2007.
39 Malatest and Associates, *Fifth-Year Evaluation of the Canada Research Chairs Program*, December 2, 2004, available at http://www.chairs.gc.ca/web/about/publications/fifth_year_review_e.pdf, accessed 31 October 2007.
40 CAUT. *Alternative Fifth Year Review of Canada Research Chairs Program* (Ottawa: CAUT, 2005), available at http://www.caut.ca/en/publications/briefs/2005_crc_review.pdf, accessed 31 October 2007.
41 Canada Research Chairs, "Canada Research Chairs Program welcomes equity agreement," November 9, 2006, available at http://www.chairs.gc.ca/web/media/releases/2006/equity_e.asp, accessed 31 October 2007.
42 NSERC, "Undergraduate Student Research Awards," January 2007, available at: http://www.nserc.gc.ca/sf_e.asp?nav=sfnav&lbi=1a, accessed 30 November 2007.

43 See CAUT, *Occupational Stress Among Canadian University Academic Staff*, Summer 2007, 7, available at http://www.caut.ca/uploads/CAUTStressStudy.pdf, accessed 30 December 2007. Also see Pauline Tam, "Pressure takes toll on professors; One in five has health issues tied to stress," *The Ottawa Citizen*, 13 November 2007.
44 Claire Polster, "The Nature and Implications of the Growing Importance of Research Grants to Canadian Universities and Academics," *Higher Education: The International Journal of Higher Education and Educational Planning* 53, no. 5 (2007), 599–622.
45 Polster, "The Nature and Implications of the Growing Importance of Research Grants to Canadian Universities and Academics," 614.
46 Thomas Pocklington and Allan Tupper, *No Place to Learn: Why Universities Aren't Working* (Vancouver: UBC Press, 2002).
47 CMEC & Statistics Canada, *Education Indicators in Canada: Report of the Pan-Canadian Education Indicators Program 2007* (CMEC and Statistics Canada, 2007), 98. Available at: http://www.statcan.ca/english/freepub/81-582-XIE/81-582-XIE2007001.pdf, accessed 16 December 2007.
48 CMEC & Statistics Canada, *Education Indicators in Canada*, 100.
49 Simon Marginson and Marijk van der Wende, "Globalisation and Higher Education," Education Working Paper No. 8 (Paris: OECD, 2007), 29. Available at http://www.oecd.org/dataoecd/33/12/38918635.pdf; accessed 21 October 2007.
50 The Association of New Brunswick University Teachers observes that the recommendations made seek "to make an already-underfunded PSE system cheaper in the long term (after a three-year transition period); and to channel many students away from university education programs into 'just in time' technical training programs to satisfy short-term labour market needs." See "New Brunswick: 'Post-Secondary Education Report Ignites Firestorm of Opposition,'" *CAUT Bulletin*. Available at http://www.cautbulletin.ca/, accessed 21 October 2007.
51 University sponsored research income consists of funds to support research paid either in the form of a grant or a contract.
52 The top ten universities in 2006 were University of Toronto (#1), University of Montreal, University of British Columbia, McGill University, University of Alberta, McMaster University, University of Calgary, Laval University, University of Ottawa, and University of Western Ontario.
53 Research Infosource Inc., *Canada's Top 50 Research Universities 2007* (Research Infosource 2007), available at http://www.researchinfosource.com/media/2007-top50-sup.pdf, accessed 16 December 2007.
54 Ailsa Ferguson, "Shanghai Jiao Tong University rates global universities," *News@UoT*, 18 September 2006, available at http://www.news.utoronto.ca/bin6/060918-2572.asp. The rankings are available at this website: http://ed.sjtu.edu.cn/rank/2006/ARWU2006_Top100.htm.
55 Canada, *Speech from the Throne*, October 16, 2007, 8. Available at http://www.sft-ddt.gc.ca/grfx/docs/sftddt-e.pdf; accessed 26 January 2008.
56 Canada, *Speech from the Throne*, October 16, 2007, 10.

57 Department of Finance, *The Budget Plan 2007* (Ottawa: Department of Finance, 2007), 207.
58 Department of Finance, *The Budget Plan 2007*, 200.
59 Christopher Guly, "What's holding back innovation and productivity in Canada?" *The Hill Times*, 16 April 2007, 37.
60 Christopher Guly, "What's holding back innovation and productivity in Canada?" The centres that the government selected included the Brain Research Centre at the University of British Columbia; the Canada School of Sustainable Energy at the University of Alberta, the University of Calgary and the University of Lethbridge; the Li Ka Shing Knowledge Institute at St. Michael's Hospital affiliated with the University of Toronto; the Heart and Stroke Foundation Centre for Stroke Recovery, affiliated with the University of Toronto and the University of Ottawa; the Montreal Neurological Institute at McGill University; the National Optics Institute in Quebec City; and the Life Science Research Institute in Halifax, affiliated with Dalhousie University. A more formal competition process has been put in place for selecting the 2008 Centres.
61 Industry Canada, *Mobilizing Science and Technology to Canada's Advantage* (Ottawa: Industry Canada, 2007), 29.
62 Brittany Cadence, "New Federal Science and Technology Strategy to Guide University Sector's Research Activities." M2 Presswire, 18 May 2007.
63 John Polanyi, "You want innovation? Liberate Canada's scientists," *The Globe and Mail*, 21 February 2007.
64 For example, the Association of Faculties of Medicine of Canada noted that despite the emphasis on private sector partnerships, the AFMC "remain[s] deeply committed to employing the peer-review system as the proven optimal method to ensure that our valuable, publicly-funded research dollars support excellent research." See AFMC, "Mobilizing Science and Technology to Canada's Advantage," Canadian Press, 22 May 2007.
65 Janice Tibbetts, "Student leaders rally on Hill to save scholarship; Harper Tories mum on fund renewal," Calgary Herald, 28 September 2007, A12.
66 These can be as high as $1,906 – as in the case of Acadia University. Elizabeth Church, "Education: Postsecondary Expenses Rise," *The Globe and Mail*, 10 September 2007, A7.
67 Elizabeth Church, "Education: Postsecondary Expenses Rise."
68 Alex Usher, *Global Debt Patterns: An International Comparison of Student Loan Burdens and Repayment Conditions* (Toronto: Educational Policy Institute), 15–16.
69 Canadian Federation of Students, *Strategy for Change: Money Does Matter* (Ottawa: CFS, October 2007), 39. Available at http://cfsadmin.org/quickftp/Strategy_for_Change_2007.pdf, accessed 31 October 2007.
70 Canadian Federation of Students, *Strategy for Change: Money Does Matter*, 25.
71 Simon Marginson, "Global Position and Position Taking: The Case of Australia," *Journal of Studies in International Education* 11, no. 1 (2007): 21–2.
72 Claire Polster, "Controlling Intellectual Property – The Academic Community and the Future of Knowledge," a conference presented by the Canadian Association of University Teachers (CAUT), October 26–27, 2006.

73 Polster, "Controlling Intellectual Property."
74 CMEC and Statistics Canada, *Education Indicators in Canada*, 93.
75 Stevenson, "Canadian Federalism. The Myth and the Status Quo," 208.
76 Don Desserud, "Unmasking the PSE report," *New Brunswick Telegraph-Journal*, 31 October 2007; available at http://telegraphjournal.canadaeast.com/opinion/article/113601, accessed 6 January 2008.
77 Higher Education Quality Council of Ontario, *Review and Research Plan 2007*, 4; available at http://www.heqco.ca/inside.php?ID=102&, accessed 27 October 2007.
78 See Claire Polster and Janice Newson, "Don't Count Your Blessings: The Social Accomplishments of Performance Indicators," in J. Currie and J. Newson, eds., *Universities and Globalization: Critical perspectives* (London: Sage Publications, 1998), 173–191.
79 Polster and Newson, "Don't Count Your Blessings," 60.
80 See for example the reports published by the Council on Learning in both 2006 (*The State of Post-secondary Education in Canada*) and 2007 (*Post-secondary Education in Canada: Strategies for Success*); available at http://www.ccl-cca.ca/CCL/Reports/PostSecondaryEducation/, accessed 30 December 2007.
81 E. Ann Clark, "Redesigning Academia to Support Organic Farming," presented to the First Annual UBC Farm Research and Education Symposium, Vancouver, B.C., 1 April 2005.
82 Howard Woodhouse, "The Market Model of Education and the Threat to Canadian Universities," *Encounters on Education* 2, Fall (2001): 107.
83 CAUT, "CAUT Policy on Federal/Provincial Funding of Post-Secondary Education," February 2007; available at http://www.caut.ca/en/policies/fedprovfunding.asp, accessed 2 November 2007.
84 Polster, "Controlling Intellectual Property."
85 SSHRC, "Community-University Research Alliances;" available at http://www.sshrc.ca/web/apply/program_descriptions/cura_e.asp, accessed 3 November 2007.
86 Quoted in Pauline Tam, "Publish-or-perish culture at universities harms public good," The Ottawa Citizen, 3 November 2007.
87 See Woodhouse, 2001, for an excellent discussion.
88 Henry A. Giroux, *The University in Chains* (Boulder & London: Paradigm Publishers), 129.

APPENDICES

APPENDIX A

Canadian Political Facts and Trends

2007

1 FEB: The Conservative government announces its plans to purchase 4 Boeing C-17 transport aircraft for the Canadian military in a deal worth $1 billion. A further deal, worth $100 million, is made to buy 18 engines for the planes from the U.S. Air Force.

2 FEB: PM Stephen Harper admits a Conservative plan to address climate change would seek to stabilize Canada's greenhouse gas emissions in the short run, not reduce them. The PM's announcement draws criticism from environmental groups who claim immediate reductions are necessary to avoid long-term consequences.

5 FEB: Opposition MP's pass a non-binding motion 161–115 calling for the Conservative government to reaffirm its commitment to meeting Canada's obligations under the Kyoto protocol.

14 FEB: MP's vote 161–133 in favour of bill C-288 calling for the government to present a plan for complying with targets under the Kyoto protocol within 60 days. The legislation also calls for the government to announce regulations that include fines or jail time for those who do not comply with the plan.

15 FEB: Serge Nadeau, director-general of tax policy analysis at Finance Canada, is charged with criminal breach of trust in relation to an RCMP investigation into whether the former Liberal government's decision not to tax income trusts was leaked to markets in advance in November 2005. It is

widely held that news of the RCMP probe into the matter contributed to a Liberal defeat in the 2006 general election.

19 MAR: Green Party leader Elizabeth May announces she will be seeking the Green Party nomination in the riding of Central Nova held by Conservative Peter MacKay since 1997.

19 MAR: Defense Minister Gordon O'Connor is forced to apologize before the House of Commons over misleading comments regarding treatment of detainees handed over to Afghan authorities by Canadian troops. O'Connor had informed the House that detainees were being monitored by the International Red Cross and that reports of their treatment were being made to Canadian authorities. This was later revealed to be untrue.

19 MAR: Finance Minister Jim Flaherty unveils the 2007–2008 budget in the House of Commons. Highlights include income splitting for seniors, a revamped equalization scheme, increased transfers to provinces, tax incentives for fuel-efficient vehicles, debt relief and tax benefits for families with children. Equalization measures and increased transfers are meant to address long standing provincial concerns over the fiscal imbalance between Ottawa and the provinces. Flaherty also introduces the "tax-back guarantee", whereby he promises that any interest savings from debt relief would be passed on to taxpayers in the form of tax cuts.

23 MAR: A Globe and Mail/CTV news poll conducted by the Strategic Counsel shows support for the Conservatives at 39 per cent nationally. This leads some to speculate that a Conservative majority government could be within reach if an election were called.

26 MAR: Provincial elections are held in Quebec. The Liberals under Jean Charest win a minority with 47 seats out of 125. In an upset, the Action Démocratique du Québec forms the official opposition for the first time with 42 seats. The PQ is reduced to 36 seats.

29 MAR: Federal Ethics Commissioner Bernard Shapiro resigns. The resignation comes a year after PM Stephen Harper had declared that Mr Shapiro no longer had the required qualifications for the job following changes introduced by the Federal Accountability Act. Neither the Conservative government nor Mr Shapiro provide clarification for the reasons of this resignation.

2 APR: Industry Minister Maxime Bernier announces the creation of a subsidy fund for the Canadian aerospace and defense industries. The *Strategic Aerospace and Defence Initiative* sets aside $900 million over five years in order to provide support to Canadian aerospace and defense companies, most of whom are located in Quebec. The move is seen by some as an attempt to build political support for the Conservative party in Quebec.

4 APR: PM Stephen Harper announces the creation of a new $600-million federal health care wait-time reduction trust. In order to gain access to money from the trust, provinces must pledge to create initiatives to reduce wait times for cancer care, hip and knee replacement, cardiac care, diagnostic imaging or cataract surgery within benchmarks set by the federal government. Critics charge provinces may pledge improvement in areas where progress is already being made or that established benchmarks are inadequate. This announcement follows a promise by the Conservatives to create a national health care wait-time guarantee during the 2005 federal election campaign.

8 APR: Six Canadian soldiers are killed in Afghanistan when the explosion from a roadside bomb strikes their armored vehicle. This event marks the worst one-day death toll for the Canadian military since the Korean War.

12 APR: Liberal leader Stéphane Dion announces the Liberal Party will not run a candidate in the riding of Central Nova during the next federal election. The move comes after Green Party leader Elizabeth May announced she would run in this riding against Conservative Peter MacKay. In exchange, the Greens agree not to run a candidate against Mr Dion in his Montreal riding. This is interpreted as an attempt by Liberal and Green Parties to embarrass the Conservative government by knocking off a high profile MP and Cabinet Minister.

12 APR: Defense Minister Gordon O'Connor announces that Ottawa will acquire 100 used Leopard 2 tanks from the Netherlands and lease 20 more from Germany in separate deals worth a total of $1.3 billion.

17 APR: The Charter of Rights and Freedoms marks its 25th anniversary.

26 APR: A poll for the Globe and Mail/CTV news conducted by the Strategic Counsel indicates national support for the Conservatives has slipped back down to 36 per cent, the same level as during the 2006 election.

26 APR: Environment Minister John Baird officially unveils the Conservative government's revamped climate-change plan. Aside from calling for short-term stabilization of emissions and a 20 per cent reduction by 2020, the plan also calls for the creation of a domestic emissions-trading market and of a technology fund for industry. The plan also pledges to impose caps on the emission of air pollutants by 2012 and to impose mandatory fuel-efficiency standards for cars beginning with the 2011 model year. The plan diverges significantly with targets set under the Kyoto protocol.

3 MAY: At a news conference in Toronto, mayors from 22 of Canada's biggest cities call on Ottawa to share 1 cent of the GST with Canadian municipalities. The initiative, spearheaded by Toronto mayor David Miller, would see approximately $5 billion of federal revenue flowing to municipalities per year if implemented.

3 MAY: A Statistics Canada study reports that the gap in family income between those in top and bottom quintiles increased to $105,400 in the decade from 1995 to 2005. The study also indicates that those in the top quintile now pay 60 per cent of all personal income taxes as compared to 50 per cent in 1980.

15 MAY: Following a reorganization of the Information Commissioner's Office under new commissioner Robert Marleau, Deputy Information Commissioner Alan Leadbeater is let go. The move is interpreted by some as an attempt to bring the office under greater control after former commissioner John Reid's criticism of the Conservative government for reneging on promises to strengthen access to information laws. Mr Leadbeater had acted as a major spokesperson under the former commissioner.

22 MAY: The Manitoba NDP wins a third straight majority government. Gary Doer becomes the first Manitoba premier to have won 3 straight majorities in 40 years.

25 MAY: Environment Canada reports that Canadian carbon dioxide emissions remained stable in 2005 from 2004 levels, the first time since 2001 that emissions did not increase. However, the report also indicates that 2005 emissions remained 32.7 per cent above Kyoto targets.

28 MAY: A poll conducted by the Strategic Counsel reveals that 68 per cent of respondents believe Canadians should be concerned about foreign takeovers of large Canadian companies. 54 per cent of respondents also indicated the federal government should act to limit the purchase of Canadian companies by foreign investors. The poll follows a number of high profile takeovers of Canadian companies such as Hudson's Bay Co., Inco Ltd., Dofasco Inc., and a bid for Alcan Inc.

28 MAY: A provincial election is held in Prince Edward Island. The Liberals led by Robert Ghiz oust the governing Conservatives after 11 years in power by winning 23 of the provincial legislature's 27 seats.

28 MAY: Revenue Minister Carol Skelton announces the creation of the position of Taxpayer Ombudsman and of a "taxpayer bill of rights". The ombudsman will be charged with the investigation of service-related complaints against the Canada Revenue Agency after a taxpayer has exhausted mechanisms within this organization. The taxpayer bill of rights establishes a list of 15 rights individuals may claim when dealing with the CRA. In addition to commitments to individuals, the bill of rights also establishes 5 commitments to small companies with an overall goal of reducing the costs of compliance with tax regulations.

29 MAY: An inquiry into spending during 1995 Quebec referendum campaign led by retired judge Bernard Grenier reveals that Option Canada, a federalist

lobby group established by the Canadian Unity Council, broke Quebec law by failing to report approximately $539,000 in spending. The inquiry follows allegations of massive overspending by the federalist camp during the campaign leveled against Option Canada by journalists Norman Lester and Robin Philpot.

11 JUN: PM Stephen Harper responds to criticism from Newfoundland and Nova Scotia Premiers that his government has broken the Atlantic Accords on offshore resource revenues by challenging them to take his government to court. The Premiers' allegations follow the introduction of a revamped equalization formula in the March federal budget, which they claim will result in reduced equalization payments for their provinces. Saskatchewan Premier Lorne Calvert also sides with Atlantic Premiers on this issue.

12 JUN: Mary Dawson, a retired former justice department official, is appointed as Canada's second Ethics Commissioner.

19 JUN: The Senate decides to shelve a bill limiting terms for Senators to 8 years until the Supreme Court can rule on the constitutionality of implementing this change without provincial consent. In response, the Conservative government threatens to mount a Senate reform campaign over Parliament's summer break.

20 JUN: The House of Commons breaks for the summer.

5 JUL: PM Stephen Harper appoints Department of Public Safety bureaucrat William Elliott as RCMP Commissioner. Former Commissioner Giuliano Zaccardelli had resigned in December 2006 in a storm of controversy after having given contradictory testimony to a House of Commons committee concerning his involvement in the Maher Arar case. Mr Elliott is the first non-mountie to head the RCMP.

5 JUL: PM Stephen Harper announces his government will provide $1.5 billion in incentives over 9 years for the production of renewable energy from biofuels. Under this initiative, the government plans to subsidize the production of ethanol by 10 cents per litre and biodiesel by 20 cents per litre. He also announces his government's intention to legislate an average 5 per cent renewable fuel content for gasoline sold in Canada by 2010.

9 JUL: PM Stephen Harper announces his government will spend $3.1 billion on 6 to 8 new arctic patrol ships having the ability to operate in up to one meter of ice. A further $4.3 billion is set aside to repair, refit and supply the ships over their estimated 25-year lifespan. As part of the plan, the Canadian Forces will also get a new deep-water port in the arctic serving as a base for the ships. By this announcement, the Conservatives abandon their election promise to build a fleet of armed icebreakers to patrol the Canadian arctic and defend Canada's sovereignty.

10 JUL: The Bank of Canada increases its target overnight rate by one quarter of a percentage point to 4.5 per cent.

16 JUL: The federal government reaches a $1.4 billion settlement with Quebec Cree over longstanding claims Ottawa had not lived up to its obligations under the 1975 James Bay and Northern Quebec agreements. The agreements had been intended to offer compensation to natives in exchange for allowing the development of hydroelectric electricity generation projects.

18 JUL: A poll conducted for the Globe and Mail/CTV news puts federal Conservatives and Liberals in a dead heat at 31 per cent support each.

31 JUL: A federal court rules that Agriculture Minister Chuck Strahl overstepped his power in introducing regulations that dismantle the Canadian Wheat Board's monopoly on barley sales. The regulation introduced by Strahl was to allow Western Canadian barley farmers to sell their crop independently of the CWB. The ruling states that changes to the CWB's commodity monopolies must be subject to a vote in Parliament.

9 AUG: After a legal battle between the Maher Arar Commission and the federal government, information that had originally been blacked out in the Inquiry's final report is released to the public. Among the points to emerge were that RCMP anti-terrorist units made use of information from countries with poor human-rights records without thorough assessment of reliability, and that the RCMP was aware that information incriminating Mr Arar had been obtained under torture. The information had been held back under national security concerns. A further 500 words of the report remain secret.

9 AUG: Amidst continuing liquidity concerns, the Bank of Canada injects $1.64 billion in additional credit in financial markets. The move is related to fallout from the writing-off of bad debt from the sub-prime mortgage market in the U.S.

14 AUG: PM Stephen Harper shuffles his cabinet. After controversy on his handling of the Afghan mission, Gordon O'Connor is moved from National Defense to National Revenue. Peter MacKay takes over National Defense, while Maxime Bernier is given MacKay's former job as Foreign Affairs Minister. Other high profile moves include the Jim Prentice's appointment as Minister of Industry, Chuck Strahl's move to Indian Affairs and the promotion of junior minister Gerry Ritz to Minister of Agriculture. Minister of National Revenue Carol Skelton is dropped from Cabinet.

3 SEP: Defense Minister Peter MacKay notifies Canada's NATO allies that his government cannot guarantee the extension of the participation of Canadian troops in the Afghanistan mission past February 2009 in its current configuration.

4 SEP: PM Stephen Harper asks Governor General Michaëlle Jean to end the current parliamentary session and begin the next 16 October 2007.

8 SEP: Statistics Canada reports that Canada's unemployment rate has dropped to 6 per cent, a 33 year low.

17 SEP: Three federal by-elections are held in Quebec. The NDP's Thomas Mulcair, a former Quebec Liberal environment minister, wins in the long-time Liberal stronghold of Outremont. In Roberval-Lac-St Jean, Conservative Denis Lebel wins a seat formerly held by the Bloc Québecois. In St-Hyacinthe-Bagot, Ève-Mary Thaï Thi Lac holds the seat for the Bloc. The Liberal's shut-out in all three contests leads to allegations of divisions within the party and questioning of Stéphane Dion's leadership by some.

20 SEP: The Canadian dollar reaches parity with the U.S. dollar, a 30-year high.

24 SEP: New Statistics Canada figures reveal that while the income of the top 5 per cent of earners increased substantially in the period from 1982 to 2004, the income of mid-income earners has remained frozen at the same levels during this time.

24 SEP: PM Stephen Harper announces his government's intention for Canada to become a member of the Asia-Pacific Partnership in October 2007. The partnership, whose founding members include Australia, China, India, Japan, South Korea and the United States, was created as an alternative to the Kyoto protocol in 2006. Environmentalists criticize this move, as the environmental pact does not include mandatory emissions-reduction targets for its members.

27 SEP: The Conservative government announces a budget surplus of $13.8 billion over the last fiscal year, all of which will be applied toward reducing the federal government's debt. PM Stephen Harper pledges to pass on the savings from reduced debt-servicing obligations, an estimated $725 million, to Canadians in the form of tax cuts.

1 OCT: Territorial elections are held in the Northwest Territories.

9 OCT: A provincial election is held in Newfoundland and Labrador. Incumbent Conservative Premier Danny Williams wins an overwhelming majority with 43 out of 48 seats.

10 OCT: Ontario Liberal premier Dalton McGuinty wins a second straight majority, being the first Ontario premier to do so since 1937. The campaign is marked by ongoing public doubts over Progressive Conservative leader John Tory's proposal to fund faith-based schools resulting in what is considered by many to be a poor showing for the Conservatives. Voters also reject a

proposal to adopt the mixed-member proportional system, which receives support from 54 per cent of voters, shy of the 60 per cent support required.

16 OCT: Governor-General Michaëlle Jean reads the Speech from the Throne opening a new session of Parliament. Among the government's priorities outlined in the speech are cutting the GST, strengthening Canada's arctic sovereignty, extending Canada's mission in Afghanistan, tackling crime, apologizing for residential school abuse and measures to cut greenhouse gas emissions.

18 OCT: The Speech from the Throne receives approval of the House of Commons after the Liberals abstain from the vote.

19 OCT: Environment minister John Baird announces Canada will not formally withdraw from the Kyoto protocol. The announcement comes after the government's throne speech declared the climate change pact's targets to be unattainable.

22 OCT: In response to the Supreme Court's decision to strike down portions of Canada's laws on Immigration Security Certificates, the Conservative government introduces legislation that would allow "special advocates" to review secret evidence on behalf of the accused in terror cases. This is meant to address the Supreme Court's ruling that withholding evidence from the accused in such cases violates Charter rights.

30 OCT: Finance minister Jim Flaherty delivers a fiscal update before the House of Commons, announcing tax cuts worth $60 billion over 6 years. These include a 1 per cent cut in the GST as well as other cuts to personal and corporate income taxes. Liberal leader Stéphane Dion announces his party will not oppose the tax cut package.

31 OCT: Opposition parties call for a public inquiry into former PM Brian Mulroney's dealings with German businessman and lobbyist Karlheinz Schreiber. The call comes after revelations that Mulroney received secret cash payments from Schreiber in the amount of $300,000 in 1993 and 1994.

31 OCT: The Conservative government's fall fiscal update passes in the House of Commons after the Liberals abstain from the vote.

6 NOV: The Canadian dollar hits a historic high against the U.S. dollar, closing at $1.08 U.S after peaking at $1.10 during the day's trading.

7 NOV: A provincial election is held in Saskatchewan. The Saskatchewan party led by Brad Wall wins a majority government ending 16 years of NDP rule.

13 NOV: PM Stephen Harper announces a public inquiry into the Mulroney-Schreiber affair. The government's third-party advisor on the matter, David Johnston, is charged with setting the terms of the inquiry.

20 NOV: The Harper government criticizes Ontario Premier Dalton McGuinty as the "small man of Confederation" after McGuinty privately lobbied Liberal leader Stéphane Dion against the adoption of a new seat-distribution formula for the House of Commons. McGuinty claims the legislation would leave Ontario underrepresented in the House of Commons.

21 NOV: The Liberals, NDP and Bloc Québecois strike a deal to open a parliamentary probe into the Mulroney-Schreiber affair. As a result, Karlheinz Schreiber appears before the House of Commons Ethics Committee for the first time on November 29.

22 NOV: A newly released Statistics Canada Study reports that real income in Canada grew 15.6 per cent between 2002 and 2006, nearly two-thirds faster than in the U.S. during the same period.

27 NOV: Statistics Canada reports that national labour productivity grew by only 1 per cent in 2006, down from 2.2 per cent in 2005.

10 DEC: In a Strategic Counsel poll on Canadian foreign policy, 33 per cent of Canadians identify Canada's refusal to join the war in Iraq as the country's greatest achievement in foreign policy, more than any other issue. In the same poll, 25 per cent of Canadians identify Canada's relationship with the U.S. as the major factor influencing Canadian foreign policy today. However, only 5 per cent state they believe this should be the major factor.

13 DEC: Former PM Brian Mulroney appears before the House of Commons Ethics Committee to explain his role in the Mulroney-Schreiber affair.

15 DEC: At an international conference on climate change held in Bali, Environment minister John Baird withdraws his objection to a plan calling for reductions in greenhouse gas emissions of 25 to 40 per cent by the 38 wealthy countries having ratified the Kyoto protocol by 2020. This is subject to a further agreement to be concluded in 2009 that will set specific binding emissions targets for individual countries to be met by 2020. Baird had argued that such targets were unrealistic for Canada.

19 DEC: A Canadian Press Harris-Decima survey places the Conservatives at 30 per cent support nationally, a statistical tie with the Liberals at 32 per cent.

21 DEC: Four by-elections are called for 17 March 2008. Two are to be held in Toronto ridings, one in the riding of Vancouver-Quadra and the other in the Saskatchewan riding of Desnethé-Missinippi-Churchill River.

2008

4 JAN: The Conservative government reneges on its election promise to require ministers to record their contacts with lobbyists. Instead, regulations

surrounding the new Lobbying Act will require lobbyists to file monthly reports on oral communications with federal officials. Written and electronic communications are not subject to these regulations.

16 JAN: The Conservative government announces the signing of a $1.4 billion contract with U.S. defense giant Lockheed Martin for the purchase of the newest version of the Hercules transport plane for the Canadian military.

16 JAN: In a late-night move, Natural Resources minister Gary Lunn fires the head of the Canadian Nuclear Safety Commission Linda Keen. The move comes hours before Ms Keen was due to appear before the House of Commons natural resources committee. The incident stems from controversy surrounding Ms Keen's decision to shut down an AECL nuclear reactor at Chalk River, Ontario due to safety concerns in the fall of 2007. The shut down resulted in a shortage of medical isotopes across North America.

16 JAN: Transport Minister Lawrence Cannon announces tougher new fuel efficiency standards for Canadian vehicles at a Montreal auto show. The new rules bring Canada in line with recent changes in U.S. standards for fuel efficiency.

21 JAN: Amidst fears of a U.S. recession, the S&P/TSX composite index falls by 605 points, the biggest drop since September 11, 2001. This follows a week of stock market decline in which the index dropped by over 1,500 points, representing 11.4 per cent of its value.

22 JAN: John Manley's Panel on Canada's future in Afghanistan delivers its report. The report recommends that the Prime Minister lead diplomatic efforts to persuade NATO members to contribute 1,000 additional troops to assist Canadian forces in the country and that Canada should pull out of the mission if these efforts fail. Further recommendations include purchasing additional drone aircraft and helicopters for the mission.

22 JAN: The Bank of Canada lowers its target overnight rate by a quarter of a percentage point to 4 per cent.

23 JAN: Justice department lawyers acknowledge that Canada halted prisoner transfers to Afghan authorities in November 2007 after compelling evidence of the use of torture was uncovered. The decision was kept under wraps even as human rights groups were preparing to take the government to court in order to stop prisoner transfers.

APPENDIX B

Fiscal Facts and Trends

This appendix presents an overview of the federal government's fiscal position and includes certain major economic policy indicators for the last decade, as well as some international comparisons.

Facts and trends are presented for federal revenue sources, federal expenditures by ministry and by type of payment, the government's share of the economy, interest and inflation rates, Canadian balance of payments in total and with the United States in particular, and other national economic growth indicators. In addition, international comparisons on real growth, unemployment inflation, and productivity are reported for Canada, the United States, Japan, Germany, and the United Kingdom.

Figure B.1
Sources of Federal Revenue as a Percentage of Total, 2006–07

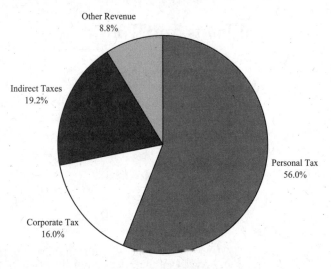

Source: Department of Finance, *Fiscal Reference Tables 2007*, Table 3.

Figure B.2
Federal Expenditures by Ministry 2007–08 Estimates

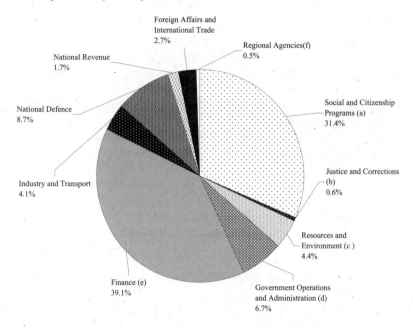

(a) Social Citizenship programs include departmental spending from Canadian Heritage, Citizenship and Immigration, Human Resources and Social Development, Veterans Affairs, Health, and Indian Affairs and
(b) Justice and Corrections includes spending from the Department of Justice
(c) Resources and Environment includes departmental spending from Agriculture and Agri-Food, Environment, Fisheries and Oceans, and Natural Resources
(d) Government Operations and Administration Spending includes that from Public Works and Government Services, the Governor General, Parliament, the Privy Council, and the Treasury Board
(e) Finance expenditures include but are not limited to, spending on public interest charges and major transfers to the provinces.
(f) Regional Agencies includes Western Economic Diversification, the Atlantic Canada Opportunities Agency and the Economic Development Agency of Canada for the Regions of Quebec

Source: Treasury Board Secretariat, *Main Estimates, Budgetary Main Estimates by Standard Object of Expenditure*, Part II, 2007–2008.

Figure B.3
Federal Budgetary Expenses by Type of Payment 1998–1999 to 2006–07

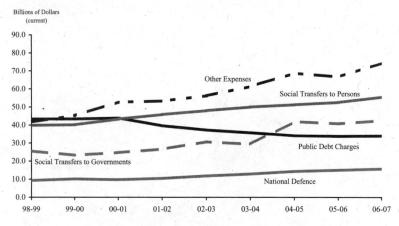

Source: Department of Finance, *Fiscal Reference Tables 2007*, Table 7.

215 Fiscal Facts and Trends

Figure B.4
Federal Revenue, Program Spending, and Deficit as Percentages of GDP 1998–9 to 2008–9

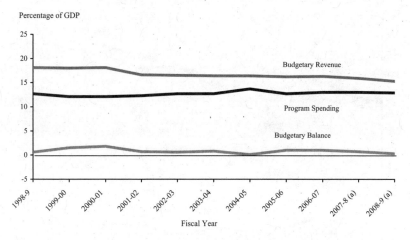

Source: Department of Finance, *Fiscal Reference Tables 2007*, Table 2; Department of Finance, Economic Statement, Table 2.3; Public Accounts of Canada, Statement of Revenues and Expenditures, various years.
Note: Budgetary revenue and program spending are based upon fiscal years, while GDP is based on the calendar year. Revenues, program spending, and the deficit are on a net basis. Program spending does not include public interest charges. GDP is nominal GDP.
(a) estimates

Figure B.5
Federal Revenue, Expenditures and the Deficit 1998–9 to 2008–9

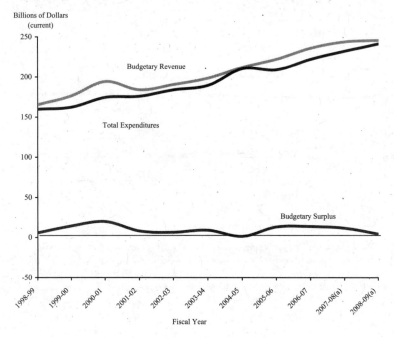

Source: Department of Finance, *Fiscal Reference Tables 2007*, Table 1 and 3; Department of Finance. *Economic Statement*, Table 2.3.
Note: Expenditures include program spending and public interest charges on the debt.
(a) estimates

Figure B.6
Growth in Real GDP 1996–2006

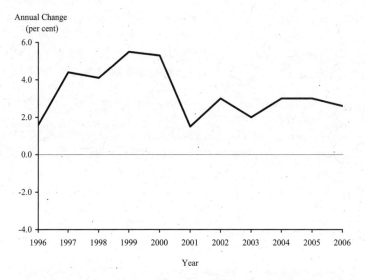

Source: Statistics Canada, CANSIM, Table 380-0017: Gross Domestic Product (GDP), expenditure-based, annual (Constant 2002 Prices).

Figure B.7
Rate of Unemployment and Employment Growth 1997–2007

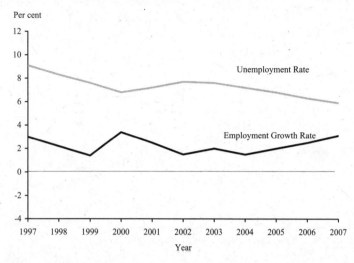

Source: Statistics Canada, CANSIM, Table 109-5004, 109-5304, 281-0023 and *The Economy in Brief*, Department of Finance, January 2008.
Note: Employment growth rate and the unemployment rate apply to both sexes, 15 years and older.

Figure B.8
Interest Rates and the Consumer Price Index (CPI) 1997–2007

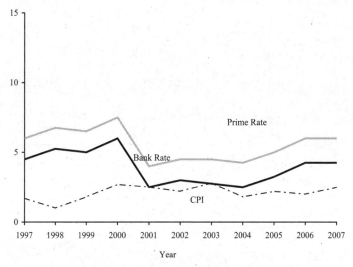

Source: Bank of Canada, *Bank of Canada Review, Banking and Financial Statistics*, Table F1, various years; Statistics Canada, CANSIM, Table 326-0021 and The Economy in Brief, Department of Finance, January 2008
Note: The Prime Rate refers to the prime business interest rate charged by chartered bank, and the Bank Rate refered to the rate charged by the Bank of Canada on any loans to commercial banks.
Note: The Prime Rate and Bank Rate are rates effective at year end.
Note: The Trend line for the CPI shows annual percentage change in the index.

Figure B.9
Productivity and Costs 1996–2006

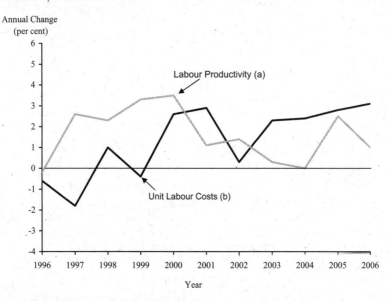

Source: Statistics Canada, CANSIM, Table 383-0008
(a) Labour Productivity is the ratio between real value added and hours worked in the business sector. This trend shows the annual percentage change in the index.
(b) This is a measure of the cost of labour input required to produce one unit of output, and is equal to labour compensation in current dollars divided by real output.

Figure B.10
Balance of Payments (Current Account) 1996–2006

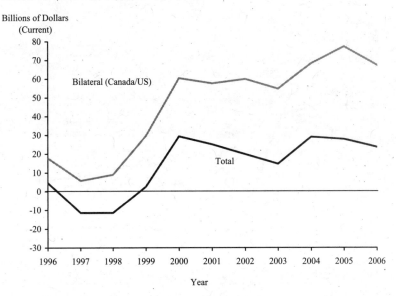

Source: Statistics Canada, cat.# 67-001, various years.

Figure B.11
Growth in Real GDP Canada and Selected Countries 1997–2009

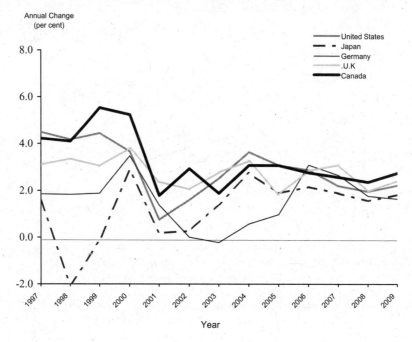

Source: Organization for Economic Cooperation and Development (OECD), Economic Outlook, no. 82, Dec. 2007, Annex Table 1.

Figure B.12
Standardized Unemployment Rates Canada and Selected Countries 1997–2009

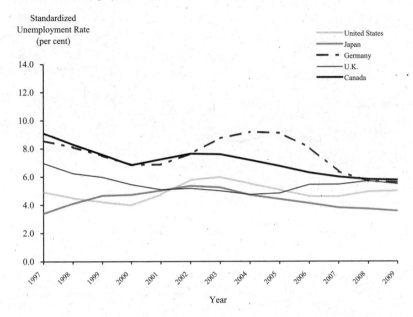

Source: Organization for Economic Cooperation and Development (OECD), Economic Outlook, no. 82, Dec. 2007, Annex Table 13.

Figure B.13
Annual Inflation Rates Canada and Selected Countries 1997–2009

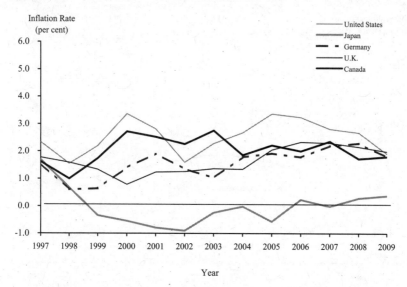

Source: Organization for Economic Cooperation and Development (OECD), Economic Outlook, no. 82, Dec. 2007, Annex Table 18.

Figure B.14
Labour Productivity Canada and Selected Countries 1997–2009

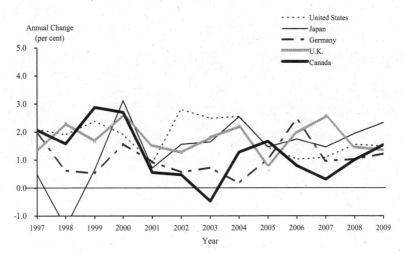

Source: Organization for Economic Cooperation and Development (OECD), Economic Outlook, no. 82, Dec. 2007, Annex Table 12.
Note: Labour productivity is defined as output per unit of labour input. The date is for labour productivity growth in the total economy.

Table B.1
Federal Revenue By Source 1996–97 to 2006–07

	As a Percentage of Totall					
Fiscal Year	Personal Tax[a]	Corporate Tax	Indirect Taxes[b]	Other Revenue[c]	Total Revenue	Annual Change (%)
1996–7	60.3	10.8	19.5	9.4	100.0	6.9
1997–8	59.8	13.2	19.4	7.7	100.0	7.3
1998–9	59.9	12.8	19.2	8.1	100.0	2.9
1999–00	60.3	12.5	18.9	8.3	100.0	6.6
2000–1	58.8	14.6	18.4	8.2	100.0	10.2
2001–2	58.5	13.2	20.2	8.2	100.0	−5.4
2002–3	58.1	11.7	21.7	8.6	100.0	3.6
2003–4	57.2	13.8	20.8	8.1	100.0	4.2
2004–5	56.4	14.1	20.2	9.3	100.0	6.7
2005–6	56.1	14.3	20.8	8.8	100.0	4.8
2006–7	56.0	16.0	19.2	8.8	100.0	6.2

Source: Department of Finance, *Fiscal Reference Tables 2007*, Table 3 and 5.
Revenue by Source is on a net basis.
(a) Employment Insurance and other income taxes are included in the total.
(b) Consists of total excise taxes and duties.
(c) Consists of non-tax and other tax revenue.

Table B.2
Federal Deficit/Surplus 1995–97 to 2008–09 in billions of dollars (current)

Fiscal Year	Budgetary Revenue	Total Expenditures	Budgetary Deficit/Surplus	As % of GDP
1996–7	149.9	158.6	−8.7	−1.0
1997–8	160.9	157.9	3.0	0.3
1998–9	165.5	159.7	5.8	0.6
1999–00	176.4	162.2	14.3	1.5
2000–1	194.3	174.5	19.9	1.8
2001–2	183.9	175.9	8.0	0.7
2002–3	190.6	183.9	6.6	0.6
2003–4	198.6	189.4	9.1	0.8
2004–5	211.9	209.0	13.2	1.0
2005–6	236.0	222.2	13.8	1.0
2006–7	236.0	222.2	13.8	1.0
2007–8[a]	243.9	232.2	11.6	0.7
2007–8[a]	245.8	241.4	4.4	0.3

Source: Department of Finance, *Fiscal Reference Tables 2007*, Tables 1 and 2; Department of Finance, *Budget Plan 2007*, Table 1.1; The Economic and Fiscal Update, Table 2.3.

Note: While revenue, expenditures, and deficit categories refer to fiscal years, nominal GDP is based upon a calendar year. Total expenditures include program spending and public debt charges.

(a) Figures for this year are estimates.

Table B.3
International Comparisons 1997–2009, Percentage Change from Previous Period

	1997	1998	1999	2000	2001	2002	2003	2004	2005	2006	2007	2008	2009
Growth in Real GDP													
Canada	4.2	4.1	5.5	5.2	1.8	2.9	1.9	3.1	3.1	2.8	2.6	2.4	2.7
U.S.	4.5	4.2	4.4	3.7	0.8	1.6	2.5	3.6	3.1	2.9	2.2	2.0	2.2
Japan	1.6	−2.0	−0.1	2.9	0.2	0.3	1.4	2.7	1.9	2.2	1.9	1.6	1.8
Germany	1.9	1.8	1.9	3.5	1.4	0.0	−0.2	0.6	1.0	3.1	2.6	1.8	1.6
U.K.	3.1	3.4	3.0	3.8	2.4	2.1	2.8	3.3	1.8	2.8	3.1	2.0	2.4
Unemployment Rates													
Canada	9.1	8.3	7.6	6.8	7.2	7.6	7.6	7.2	6.8	6.3	6.0	5.8	5.8
U.S.	4.9	4.5	4.2	4.0	4.8	5.8	6.0	5.5	5.1	4.6	4.6	5.0	5.0
Japan	3.4	4.1	4.7	4.7	5.0	5.4	5.3	4.7	4.4	4.1	3.8	3.7	3.6
Germany	8.6	8.1	7.5	6.9	6.9	7.6	8.7	9.2	9.1	8.1	6.4	5.7	5.6
U.K.	7.0	6.2	6.0	5.5	5.1	5.2	5.0	4.8	4.8	5.5	5.5	5.7	5.5
Labour Productivity													
Canada	2.1	1.6	2.9	2.7	0.6	0.5	−0.5	1.3	1.7	0.8	0.3	1.0	1.5
U.S.	2.1	1.9	2.4	1.9	0.9	2.8	2.5	2.5	1.5	1.0	1.1	1.5	1.5
Japan	0.5	−1.4	0.7	3.1	0.7	1.6	1.6	2.5	1.5	1.7	1.5	1.9	2.3
Germany	1.9	0.6	0.5	1.6	0.9	0.6	0.7	0.2	1.1	2.4	1.0	1.0	1.2
U.K.	1.3	2.3	1.7	2.6	1.5	1.3	1.8	2.2	0.8	2.0	2.6	1.5	1.3

Source: Organization for Economic Cooperation and Development (OECD), *Economic Outlook*, no. 82, Dec. 2007, Annex Tables 1, 12, 13.

Contributors

FRANCES ABELE is professor in the School of Public Policy and Administration at Carleton University and research fellow of the Institute for Research on Public Policy. She has been learning about northern Canada for the last three decades.

CHERYL N. COLLIER holds a degree in Journalism from Carleton University and a doctorate in Political Science from the University of Toronto. She is currently an instructor in the Department of Political Science and the School of Public Policy and Administration at Carleton University. Her research interests include Canadian and comparative women and public policy and women's movements.

GEOFFREY HALE is associate professor in the Department of Political Science at the University of Lethbridge.

WALTER HETTICH is professor emeritus of Economics at California State University, Fullerton. His research interests are centered in public economics, public policy and the application of collective choice analysis to governmental decision making and the working of public institutions.

EDWARD T. JACKSON is associate dean (Research and Graduate Affairs) in the Faculty of Public Affairs at Carleton University, where he teaches public policy and international affairs. From 1997 to 2008, he directed the Community Economic Development Technical Assistance Program, a pan-Canadian grant-making program based at Carleton University. Currently chair of the Carleton Centre for Community Innovation, he is also active in the University's Centre for Voluntary Sector Research and Development.

RIANNE MAHON is director of the Institute of Political Economy and a member of the School of Public Policy and Administration and the Department of Sociology and Anthropology at Carleton University. While her earlier work focused on unions and labour market restructuring in Canada and Sweden, over the past decade she has produced numerous articles and book chapters on the politics of childcare. Her new research project looks at the OECD's "reconciliation of work and family" agenda and "policy learning" in Canada, Korea, and Sweden.

ALLAN M. MASLOVE is professor in the School of Public Policy and Administration at Carleton University. He was the founding dean of the University's Faculty of Public Affairs and Management.

CLARA MORGAN holds a Ph.D. from Carleton University's School of Public Policy. Her research interests include provincial, federal and transnational education policies.

MICHAEL J. PRINCE is Lansdowne Professor of Social Policy in the Faculty of Human Social Development at the University of Victoria. A frequent contributor to *How Ottawa Spends*, Prince writes on a range of topics, including Canada-Aboriginal relations, disability issues, fiscal federalism, health care, seniors and social security.

RICHARD SCHULTZ is James McGill Professor and chair of the Department of Political Science at McGill University. In 2005 he was a fellow at the Shorenstein Center on the Press, Politics and Public Policy at the Kennedy School of Government, Harvard University. He is currently writing a book, with Hudson Janisch, entitled *Closed Circuits: The Bureaucratic Transformation of Canadian Telecommunications: 1976–1993*.

ROBERT SLATER is an adjunct professor at Carleton University where he lectures in environment and sustainable development to both undergraduate and graduate students. His teaching is based on over 30 years experience as a senior manager of environmental issues for the Government of Canada. He is a member of the National Roundtable on the Environment and the Economy and is a senior fellow at the International Institute for Sustainable Development. He obtained his degrees from Imperial College.

BARRY STEMSHORN is a senior fellow with the Jarislowsky Chair of Public Service Management and the Graduate School of Public and International

Affairs at the University of Ottawa. His perspectives on regulation reflect 32 years of experience in regulatory science, policy, operations and international negotiations spanning animal health, plant protection, food safety and environmental protection. He retired from the Public Service of Canada as an assistant deputy minister with Environment Canada following senior appointments with the Privy Council Office and the Canadian Food Inspection Agency.

STANLEY L. WINER is the Canada Research Chair Professor in Public Policy at Carleton University. His work combines the traditional analysis of public finance and public economics with the study of collective choice mechanisms and political institutions, and explores the implications of the resulting frameworks for the positive and normative analysis of taxation, public expenditure and public policy generally.

The *How Ottawa Spends* Series

How Ottawa Spends 2008–2009: A More Orderly Federalism?
Edited by Allan M. Maslove

How Ottawa Spends 2006–2007: In From the Cold-The Tory Rise and the Liberal Demise
Edited by G. Bruce Doern

How Ottawa Spends 2005–2006: Managing the Minority
Edited by G. Bruce Doern

How Ottawa Spends 2004–2005: Mandate Change in the Paul Martin Era
Edited by G. Bruce Doern

How Ottawa Spends 2003–2004: Regime Change and Policy Shift
Edited by G. Bruce Doern

How Ottawa Spends 2002–2003: The Security Aftermath and National Priorities
Edited by G. Bruce Doern

How Ottawa Spends 2001–2002: Power in Transition
Edited by Leslie A. Pal

How Ottawa Spends 2000–2001: Past Imperfect, Future Tense
Edited by Leslie A. Pal

How Ottawa Spends 1999–2000: Shape Shifting: Canadian Governance Toward the 21 Century
Edited by Leslie A. Pal

How Ottawa Spends 1998–99: Balancing Act: The Post-Deficit Mandate
Edited by Leslie A. Pal

How Ottawa Spends 1997–98: Seeing Red: A Liberal Report Card
Edited by Gene Swimmer

How Ottawa Spends 1996–97: Life Under the Knife
Edited by Gene Swimmer

Ottawa Spends 1995–96: Mid-Life Crises
Edited by Susan D. Phillips

How Ottawa Spends 1994–95: Making Change
Edited by Susan D. Phillips

How Ottawa Spends 1993–94: A More Democratic Canada …?
Edited by Susan D. Phillips

How Ottawa Spends 1992–93: The Politics of Competitiveness
Edited by Frances Abele

Ottawa Spends 1991–92: The Politics of Fragmentation
Edited by Frances Abele

How Ottawa Spends 1990–91: Tracking the Second Agenda
Edited by Katherine A. Graham

How Ottawa Spends 1989–90: The Buck Stops Where?
Edited by Katherine A. Graham

How Ottawa Spends 1988–89: The Conservatives Heading into the Stretch
Edited by Katherine A. Graham

How Ottawa Spends 1987–88: Restraining The State
Edited by Michael J. Prince

How Ottawa Spends 1986–87: Tracking The Tories
Edited by Michael J. Prince

How Ottawa Spends 1985: Sharing the Pie
Edited by Allan M. Maslove

How Ottawa Spends 1984: The New Agenda
Edited by Allan M. Maslove

How Ottawa Spends 1983: The Liberals, The Opposition & Federal Priorities
Edited by Bruce Doern

How Ottawa Spends Your Tax Dollars: National Policy and Economic Development 1982
Edited by Bruce Doern

How Ottawa Spends Your Tax Dollars: Federal Priorities 1981
Edited by Bruce Doern

Spending Tax Dollars: Federal Expenditures, 1980–81
Edited by Bruce Doern